Theatre History Studies

2006 VOLUME 26

Edited by
RHONA JUSTICE-MALLOY

PUBLISHED BY THE MID-AMERICA THEATRE CONFERENCE
AND THE UNIVERSITY OF ALABAMA PRESS

Copyright © 2006
The University of Alabama Press
Tuscaloosa, Alabama 35487-0380
All rights reserved
Manufactured in the United States of America

Designed by Todd Lape / Lape Designs
Typeface: Minion

∞

The paper on which this book is printed meets the minimum requirements
of American National Standard for Information Sciences-Permanence of
Paper for Printed Library Materials, ANSI Z39.48-1984.

MEMBER
CELJ
Council of Editors of Learned Journals

Cover: Sheet music for "Salvation Nell," by Grant Clarke, Edgar Leslie, and Theodore Morse (New York: Theodore Morse Music Company, 1913). Theatre History Studies

Editor
Rhona Justice-Malloy, University of Mississippi

Book Review Editor
Cheryl Black, University of Missouri-Columbia

Editorial Board
John Poole, President of MATC
Felicia Hardison Londré, University of Missouri–Kansas City
Tice L. Miller, University of Nebraska
Ron Engle, University of North Dakota

Consulting Editors
Rosemarie K. Bank, Kent State University
Suzanne Burgoyne, University of Missouri
Stacey Connelly, Trinity University
Tracy Davis, Northwestern University
Lesley Ferris, Ohio State University
Christopher McCollough, Exeter University
Kim Marra, University of Iowa
Elizabeth Reitz Mullenix, Illinois State University
Heather Nathans, University of Rhode Island
Joseph R. Roach, Yale University
Denis Salter, McGill University
Catherine Schuler, University of Maryland
Delbert Unruh, University of Kansas
Les Wade, Louisiana State University
Daniel J. Watermeier, University of Toledo
Don B. Wilmeth, Brown University

Past editors of *Theatre History Studies*
Ron Engle, 1981–1993
Robert A. Schanke, 1994–2005

Theater History Studies is an official journal of the Mid-America Theatre Conference, Inc. (MATC). The conference encompasses the states of Illinois, Indiana, Iowa, Kansas, Michigan, Minnesota, Missouri, Nebraska, North Dakota, South Dakota, and Wisconsin. Its purposes are to unite people and organizations within this region and elsewhere who have an interest in theatre and to promote the growth and development of all forms of theatre.

President
John Poole, Illinois State University

President-Elect
Bill Jenkins, Ball State University

Vice President
Mary Cutler, University of North Dakota

Secretary
Mark Mallett, Richard Stockton College

Treasurer
DeAnna M. Toten Beard, Baylor University

Associate Conference Planner
Ann Haugo, Illinois State University

Theatre History Studies is devoted to research in all areas of theatre history. Manuscripts should be prepared in conformity with the guidelines established in the *Chicago Manual of Style,* submitted in duplicate, and sent to Rhona Justice-Malloy, Editor, Dept. of Theatre Arts, Isom Hall 110, University of Mississippi, Box 1848, University, MS 38677, or by e-mail to rjmalloy@olemiss.edu. Consulting editors review the manuscripts, a process that takes approximately two months. The journal does not normally accept studies of dramatic literature unless there is a focus on actual production and performance. Authors whose manuscripts are accepted must provide the editor with an electronic file, using Microsoft Word. Illustrations (preferably high-quality originals or black-and-white glossies) are welcomed. Manuscripts will be returned only if accompanied by a stamped, self-addressed envelope bearing sufficient postage.

This publication is issued annually by the Mid-America Theatre Conference and The University of Alabama Press.

Subscription rates for 2006 are $15 for individuals, $30 for institutions, and an additional $8 for foreign delivery. Back issues are $29.95 each. Subscription orders and changes of address should be directed to Allie Harper, The University of Alabama Press, Box 870380, Tuscaloosa, AL 35487 (205-348-1564 phone, 205-348-9201 fax).

Theatre History Studies is indexed in *Humanities Index, Humanities Abstracts, Book Review Index, MLA International Bibliography, International Bibliography of Theatre, Arts & Humanities Citation Index, IBZ International Bibliography of Periodical Literature,* and *IBR International Bibliography of Book Reviews,* the database of *International Index to the Performing Arts.* Full texts of essays appear in the databases of both *Humanities Abstracts Full Text* and *SIRS.* The journal has published its own index, *The Twenty Year Index, 1981–2000.* It is available for $10 for individuals and $15 for libraries from Rhona Justice-Malloy, Editor, Dept. of Theatre Arts, Isom Hall 110, University of Mississippi, Box 1848, University, MS 38677.

CONTENTS

List of Illustrations   {vii}

Remembering Spalding Gray   {1}
—CHARLES R. HELM

Dorothy Parker and the Politics of McCarthyism   {7}
—MILLY S. BARRANGER

A Paradigm for New Play Development:
The Albee-Barr-Wilder Playwrights Unit   {31}
—DAVID A. CRESPY

"The Power of Woman's Influence": Nineteenth-Century Temperance
Theatricality and the Drama of Nellie H. Bradley   {52}
—DEANNA M. TOTEN BEARD

Toward a New Theatre History of Dionysus   {71}
—ELLEN MACKAY

The Salvation Lass, Her Harlot-Friend, and Slum Realism
in Edward Sheldon's *Salvation Nell* (1908)   {88}
—KATIE N. JOHNSON

Irony Lost: Bret Harte's Heathen Chinee and the Popularization
of the Comic Coolie as Trickster in Frontier Melodrama   {108}
—JACQUELINE ROMEO

CONTENTS

BOOK REVIEWS

Ann Hutchinson Guest, *Labanotation: The System of Analyzing and Recording Movement*
REVIEWED BY CHRISTOPHER OLSEN {137}

Penny Farfan, *Women, Modernism, and Performance*
REVIEWED BY REBECCA NESVET {139}

Andrea Most, *Making Americans: Jews and the Broadway Musical*
REVIEWED BY JESSICA HILLMAN {142}

Peter Thomson, ed., *The Cambridge History of British Theatre*, 3 vols.
REVIEWED BY FRANKLIN J. HILDY {144}

Sondra Fraleigh, *Dancing Identity: Metaphysics in Motion*
REVIEWED BY CARRIE GAISER {148}

Simon Palfrey, *Doing Shakespeare*
REVIEWED BY ADRIANNE ADDERLEY {150}

Scott McCrea, *The Case for Shakespeare: The End of the Authorship Question*
REVIEWED BY JULIA SCHMITT {152}

Linda Ben-Zvi, *Susan Glaspell: Her Life and Times*
Patricia L. Bryan and Thomas Wolf, *Midnight Assassin: A Murder in America's Heartland*
REVIEWED BY MARCIA NOE {154}

John Herbert Roper, *Paul Green: Playwright of the Real South*
REVIEWED BY JONATHAN SHANDELL {157}

Christopher Bigsby, *Arthur Miller: A Critical Study*
REVIEWED BY TERRY OTTEN {159}

Books Received {163}
Contributors {165}

ILLUSTRATIONS

CRESPY
Figure 1. On the set of Sam Shepard's *Up to Thursday*. {41}
Figure 2. On the set of John Guare's *To Wally Pantoni We Leave a Credenza*. {44}

BEARD
Figure 1. "Woman's Holy War" (1874). {54}
Figure 2. "The Fruits of Temperance" (1848). {56}
Figure 3. Advertisement for temperance dialogues, dramas, and exercises (1880). {60}

JOHNSON
Figure 1. Sheet music for "Salvation Nell" (1913). {89}
Figure 2. The infamous depiction of Sid's bar in *Salvation Nell* (1908). {91}

ROMEO
Figures 1–10. Illustrations from "The Heathen Chinee" by Bret Harte, illustrated by Joseph Hull (1870). {113}
Figures 11–12. Illustrations from "The Heathen Chinee" by Bret Harte (1872). {119}
Figures 13–20. Illustrations from "The Heathen Chinee" by Bret Harte, illustrated by Sol Eytinge Jr. (1871). {121}
Figure 21. Harry Murdoch's caricature of Charles T. Parsloe as Hop Sing in *Two Men of Sandy Bar* by Bret Harte. {129}
Figure 22. Charles T. Parsloe as Wing Lee in *My Partner* by Bartley Campbell. {129}

Remembering Spalding Gray

—CHARLES R. HELM

As a tribute to the legacy of Spalding Gray, the Department of Theatre at The Ohio State University acknowledged his life's work at a public gathering in Thurber Theatre on November 22, 2004. Charles Helm, Director of Performing Arts at the Wexner Center for the Arts, gave an anecdotal, first-person account of his relationship with Gray. It was transcribed by Beth Josephsen and edited by Lesley Ferris.

When Spalding Gray was scheduled to come to Walker Art Center for the first time, as the multimedia producer for their exhibitions program, I received his technical requirements. In contrast to the other performers I worked with, his technical rider was merely a very short paragraph: he needed a small wooden table, a chair, a microphone, and a glass of water. I instantly thought, "This is it? Could this really be all he needs?" I even called him to confirm this because his requirements were so out of keeping with the expansive, exuberant experimentalism and technology of the other performers I assisted. Too much was never enough for everybody else. But Spalding said, "No, no, that's all I need." And so the day came for Spalding's first performance: we focused a little pool of light around the table, placed the glass of water on the table, and turned on the microphone. Once the show began I had the luxury of not having to manage and organize a battery of technical effects; instead, I could just sit and listen to Spalding's narratives like any other audience member. Any week that Spalding Gray came onto the performance schedule I knew that I was going to have an easy time technically *and* I was going to be vastly entertained by the latest installment of his adventures.

Spalding was always dressed in homey L. L. Bean comfort. He simultaneously exuded bedrock Yankee common sense and a finely tuned, self-absorbed, downtown neuroticism. As a result of this duality he was tagged the WASP

Woody Allen, a fairly apt description. Much of what he wrote and performed I would characterize as dark musings that were self-deprecating in their humor. At the beginning of his shows he spoke very quietly; yet this was a deliberate theatrical device to draw you into his world. He soon revealed his mastery of transforming seemingly small and everyday occurrences into universals with a brilliant economy of means. As an audience member I found myself drawn to him, both physically and emotionally, leaning forward to follow his roundabout narratives that could suddenly and unexpectedly expand into a symphonic epiphany. By the end of the show I realized that what had seemed like ramblings and semi-connected events had actually been well-crafted and thoughtfully designed storytelling. Spalding was simply a master at shaping a narrative.

In the early days when Spalding toured with his monologues, his solo performances started to become critically identified in some quarters as performance art, which I think is a false view of his work. Spalding's solos were not the kind of post-Fluxus work that emphasized the ephemeral performative concepts that developed from what was essentially a gallery scene of vanguard visual artists. Nor was his work an interdisciplinary hybrid, like the work of Laurie Anderson or Meredith Monk. Spalding's monologues easily defied existing categories, and as a result his work was inappropriately tagged with the catch-all phrase "performance art." To me, Spalding was a theatre maker who specialized in monologues. In doing so, he cut straight to theatre's core in his approach to storytelling.

What seemed radical about Gray's work when it was first produced was the way he stripped his performances down to the barest essentials. This is perhaps particularly significant considering Spalding was a founding member of the Wooster Group, a company fueled by its passion for multimedia, experimental stage work. After time with this group, Spalding, for a variety of reasons both personal and artistic, withdrew from active participation as a member of their inspired ensemble creations as a theatre collective. He found solid footing as a solo performer in his fresh approach to narrative, and he found an international audience that eagerly awaited each new installment of his mini-epics.

His autobiographical journeys staged with minimal fuss gave permission to many other performers, who through him saw a way to make work in their own individual way: performers like Eric Bogosian, John Leguizamo, Reno, and Tim Miller. Even storytellers like Garrison Keillor with his popular radio program, *Prairie Home Companion,* which was a very grassroots phenomenon, developed at the same time as Spalding's early solo work. Other solo performers include Danny Hoch, Anna Deveare Smith, Eve Ensler, and many, many more.

They saw a path that was really blazed by Spalding to channel their stories and autobiographical ideas, or the stories of others, into a performance form that was vital contemporary theatre.

It is important not to underestimate the impact of Spalding's minimalist staging. His simple idea of one man at a desk, telling a story, was in many ways a breakthrough idea for theatre performance. His staging made it possible for other theatre makers to think about their own performance in new ways. The one-person show is perhaps now blurred with stand-up comedy, but at the time of Spalding's first performances he demonstrated that it was possible to get work onstage without all the economic and logistical problems associated with creating an ensemble, building sets, getting costumes, finding a director. Many young theatre artists don't have either the time or the means to create larger, complicated pieces when they are trying to survive in New York. Spalding's do-it-yourself aesthetic became a model for people to create theatre without having to rely on expensive and time-consuming infrastructure to do so. You could simply get up on the stage, craft your narrative, and go for it.

Spalding's artfully manicured tales sprang directly from his day-to-day life, a life that was more complex than his minimal staging would suggest. He created a confessional tone, and through this device the audience would feel a close identification with him as both a person and a performer. Yet at the same time, his demons occasionally surfaced to face off with the infinitely lovable persona he cultivated onstage. There was an amazing moment during *It's a Slippery Slope* at the Wexner Center for the Arts where he owns up a bit and slips into his monologue how he was duplicitous and unfaithful to his first wife, Renee, who was also incidentally his producer for many years. He casually mentions that he dumped her and ran away from both her and Kathy, who would be his next wife. It was a particularly callous moment, as Kathy was pregnant with their first child at the time. His escape was predicated on the fact that he couldn't face up to what a train wreck he had made all their lives. Every night during his performance he calmly dropped this underplayed betrayal into the course of his tale. There was an incredible visceral reaction, particularly from the women in the audience. The silent words "Spalding Gray is a cad!" seemed to fill the air. His revelation was practically unthinkable. His performance persona was such a completely sympathetic character that by revealing this unexpected, unsympathetic side it jarred the audience's expectations. It was a hard moment to witness. However, by the time the piece wrapped up he had everyone eating out of the palm of his hand and all was right in the world.

After Spalding met his wife Kathy, who already had a daughter who was approaching being a teenager, they had two children of their own. Through his life with Kathy and the kids, Spalding did grow to embrace a certain domesticity that was a surprise to those who knew him as sort of a coast-to-coast performing arts hellion. Those pleasures that he found in his family life are very much reflected in *Morning, Noon, Night,* one of his last pieces. The sense of self-acceptance that he revealed in this piece was tragically cut short by an accident in Ireland. While Spalding was driving on vacation, a drunk driver crashed into him, crushed his hip, fractured his skull, and left him hospitalized with a head trauma. He went through a very long and difficult recovery process that forced him to become dependent on painkillers. The accident, coupled with the medication, seemed responsible for a writer's block that caused him great difficulties when he was trying to create his last piece, which he was performing as a work in progress at the time of his death.

One of the biggest problems he was having in terms of his writer's block centered on how to continue doing his monologues without turning his family life into a soap opera. His commitment to marriage and to his children changed his relationship to his own autobiographical material.

The car wreck and Spalding's injuries coincided with September 11 in New York City. All the grief, despair, and depression of 9/11 that faced his circle of friends, many of whom lived in downtown New York, engulfed his own personal difficulties. His final monologue attempted to reference both his personal desolation and his sense of civic, national, and international anguish over September 11. Because of the pain and physical problems that he suffered from this accident he could no longer take long walks or ski or enjoy the other kinds of daily sports that he loved. I think walking was a way that Spalding worked out ideas in his head, about his work and where it was going to go. All of these things accelerated his depression; eventually the thoughts of suicide that are often known to haunt the children of suicides started to haunt him. It is well known that Spalding's mother did commit suicide at age fifty-two. He made several suicide attempts while he was creating his final piece, which had the working title *Life Interrupted.* He was presenting this at PS 122 on Sunday nights, and performing this new piece as a work in progress, a process he had used for many years creating, developing, and shaping his monologues.

Coincidentally, I was in New York City the weekend Spalding went missing in January 2004. It happened at the same time as the Association for Performing Arts Presenters Conference in New York. This is a huge annual event where many people in the industry gather to consider performers for their seasons. Spalding's wife, Kathy, is an agent for many performers, including Spalding. Kathy was present, very occupied doing business, going to showcases, organizing things. Looking back on this, I can easily imagine that in Spalding's mind he could see that he would have trouble booking his own performances. He was having difficulty coming up with new material because of his health issues; he knew shows were being booked months in advance. The only life he had known was as a touring performer, and for the first time in decades he wasn't able to commit to bookings. His wife was busy booking other people, he knew that life was going on, but his was not, he was not able to participate.

It was during an extremely cold weekend that Spalding went missing. I remember it being around seventeen degrees. I can recall how harsh that January wind felt in New York. It was on the final day of the conference when the news broke that Spalding Gray was missing. I remember the cold shock that descended on everybody there.

When I returned home I found myself unable to refrain from contemplating Spalding's absence. Perhaps, like anybody who knows somebody fairly well, I wanted to know what had happened, and thoughts of our time together kept coming to me. For example, after every show he always wanted to know what kind of local brews were being made in any place he toured. So I would go out with him to a local bar, have a few beers, talk about the show as well as many kinds of things. Having known Spalding for practically twenty years as I did, I realized that we both learned quite a bit about each other. So I could not help it, I wanted to know, like anyone in my kind of position, "What were the chain of events that led to this final act?" I knew that he had attempted suicide before. On one of these occasions he had left a suicide note for Kathy saying that he was going to jump off the Staten Island ferry. But he had been found on the ferry and taken off. There had been a few other attempts as well. But on this occasion, Spalding was missing for a considerable time.

Shortly after returning to Columbus, I went to see the latest film by the director Tim Burton, called *Big Fish*. It is a delightful, fantastical kind of a tale and I think one of Tim Burton's best movies. After seeing the film I checked the Internet to see if there were any other updates about Spalding. There was a lot of confusing information initially about what Spalding had been doing and who had last seen him. And as we all know now, it would be several months before his body was found. I read a new report on the Web that described his last day with his family. They had gone to see the same film—*Big Fish*—that I had just seen. I imagined a conversation between Spalding and Kathy: "We can take the kids and they can enjoy it on their level and there is something there for us too as parents." I don't think *Sponge Bob* would have been Spalding's kind of film. It really jarred me that this film was possibly the last one he saw. *Big Fish* is about a dysfunctional relationship between a father and a son. The son resents the fact that his father's entire life was spent telling fantastical, embroidered fantasy tales about his existence to try to make himself seem more interesting. On the father's deathbed, there is reconciliation. The son carries his dying father to the river, walks into the water with him, and the father transforms into a large fish and swims away. The son's voice-over says, "That was my father's final joke, I guess. A man tells his stories so many times that he becomes the stories. They live on after him." I couldn't help thinking how that statement must have resonated with Spalding. And maybe in some ways it clarified for him what he felt he had to do at that time. I often think people who commit suicide do so not in a moment of confusion but in a moment of utter clarity.

So it was a cold day, the coldest day of winter. He went to the Staten Island ferry. We know this because they were able to trace a call he made to his son from a pay phone right by the landing for the ferry. It was so cold that nobody would have been on the outer deck of the ferry. No one. Spalding would have known that and known that this time, as opposed to the last time, he didn't leave a note and he could slip over the side unnoticed into the icy water and that would be the end.

Spalding had the uncanny ability to take the stuff of his life and make it into art. I was privileged to have worked with him, to be in a position to present him, and even more, it was a great pleasure to have known him.

Dorothy Parker and the Politics of McCarthyism

—MILLY S. BARRANGER

> I am not a traitor and I will not be involved in this obscene inquisition.
> —DOROTHY PARKER

Known to friends as Dottie and to others as Mrs. Parker, Dorothy Parker was briefly considered a quadruple threat to the nation's security under McCarthyism. Cited in *Red Channels* as a writer and versifier with nineteen pro-Communist credits, she came to the attention of four investigative committees. As a founder of Hollywood's Anti-Nazi League, she gained the attention of Jack Tenney's California Un-American Activities Committee; she was named as a concealed Communist before the House Un-American Activities Committee (HUAC); she was threatened with a subpoena by Joseph R. McCarthy to supplement his investigations into U.S. overseas libraries and information centers; and she was called before the New York State Joint Legislative Committee on Charitable and Philanthropic Agencies and Organizations investigating fund-raising by Communist-front groups. Parker made scornful speeches, sparred, took the Fifth, and walked away with disdain.

Beloved of Robert Benchley, twice married to Alan Campbell, devoted friend of Lillian Hellman, and scorned by Dashiell Hammett, Parker had a love-hate relationship with most people. Hellman described her as a "worn, prettyish woman" and wrote of her originality and wit that "neither age nor illness ever dried up the spring from which it came fresh each day."[1]

As accomplished, acerbic, no-nonsense women, Parker and Hellman shared their left-wing politics and notoriety as alleged Communist Party members.

Their politics in the 1930s brought them a decade of discontent in the 1950s. Parker named one of her pieces for the *New Yorker* "A Terrible Day Tomorrow"— an apt description of her McCarthy years.

A Time of Inquisitions

Parker's second marriage, to actor and future screenwriter Alan Campbell in 1934, coincided with her move to Hollywood, where the couple engaged in lucrative screenwriting careers. Earlier, Parker had worked for Metro-Goldwyn-Mayer for three months writing dialogue for *Madame X*. In Hollywood again in the mid-1930s, she turned to radical politics, which eventually jeopardized her fortunes with the studios.

Parker's attraction to political activism can be traced to two events. In August 1927, Parker and other Algonquinites marched in Boston to protest the execution of Nicola Sacco and Bartolomeo Vanzetti, two Italian Americans who were arrested, convicted, and executed for robbery and murder. Protests during the seven years of litigation focused on their ignorance of American ways and their avowed anarchism, which may have prevented a fair trial. Sacco was accused of the killing, and Vanzetti was tried as his accomplice. Both men had substantial alibis, but some time after their arrest, witnesses altered their reports to police and investigators to fit the prosecution's case.[2]

On the day of the execution, Parker and Edna St. Vincent Millay went to Boston to plead a stay of execution from the governor. Other sympathetic groups marched with placards outside the statehouse where the governor's council was meeting. It is thought that most of the marchers were members of the Communist Party, including Michael Gold, editor of *New Masses,* and Sender Garlin of the *Daily Worker*. It is also assumed that this was Parker's first direct contact with members of the Communist Party.

The police arrived and arrested many of the marchers, including Parker and John Dos Passos. She was fined five dollars for loitering and later told reporters that she had been "treated roughly" by police.[3] After a reprieve, Sacco and Vanzetti were executed on August 3 and Parker declared herself a socialist.

Her second exposure to members of the American Communist Party occurred in 1932 during a transatlantic crossing aboard the luxurious *Europa*. When Parker, who was traveling first class with the Gerald Murphys, learned that the mother of Tom Mooney, the West Coast labor leader convicted of a bombing and serving a twenty-five-year sentence in San Quentin, was aboard in third class, she sought out the eighty-four-year-old woman. Mary Mooney was traveling to Russia with a delegation of American Communists. Parker attended Communist meetings in the ship's third-class dining hall and professed the speeches overly long and muddled.

In 1933, Parker, Hellman, and Hammett became chief organizers of the first trade union of Hollywood screenwriters, the Screen Writers Guild. By April 1936, after several setbacks, the guild called upon the House Patents Committee for legislation to strengthen the rights of authors to decide how their material was to be used. The studios insisted that writers were artists and therefore ineligible to unionize. Then, in June 1938, the National Labor Relations Board ruled that screenwriters qualified as workers under the Wagner Act. An election was held to choose union representation, and the Screen Writers Guild won over the more conservative Screen Playwrights. Parker's organizational efforts were vindicated.

In 1934, Parker, responding to the promise of Communism to feed the hungry and clothe the poor, had declared herself a Communist, although there is no evidence that she was an official member of the Communist Party USA or possessed a membership card.[4] Her friends were astonished by her declaration and baffled by her leftist tendencies. She was now a wealthy Hollywood screenwriter whose radicalism appeared to many observers as playing revolutionary in a proletarian costume. Nevertheless, Parker's attraction to Communism as a means of opposing the growing menace of international fascism was genuine.

In her zeal, Parker joined more than thirty organizations, contributed money to groups later described as Communist fronts, and permitted leftist committees to use her name on their letterheads and in fund-raising appeals. As she said in testimony before a New York state legislative committee in 1955, it never occurred to her to ask questions about the origins of the groups or how the contributed money was actually spent.[5]

During the late 1930s, Parker took up many causes. She railed against poverty and unemployment, the segregation of blacks in the United States, and the growing clamor of anti-Semitism in Germany. Most important, she viewed the situation in Franco's Spain as a threat to the liberty of the free world. "These are not the days for little, selfish, timid things," she said, but few in her Hollywood cocktail-party circuit heard Parker's cri de coeur.[6] Nevertheless, Donald Ogden Stewart, a former Algonquinite and successful screenwriter, did hear his friend. He joined with her as a committed political ally while Alan Campbell begged his wife for moderation and Robert Benchley excused himself as "noncommittally understanding."[7]

With prodigious energy, Parker wrote or worked on eleven screenplays during 1936 and 1937. Likewise an untiring activist, her fund-raising energies were devoted largely to two groups eventually labeled as front organizations. Many believed that Parker's political writings for the pro-Communist *New Masses* marked her as a Communist. Others viewed her political activism as ambivalent if not ridiculous, attributing her seeming ambivalence to ignorance or sentimentalism.[8]

"I Was Blacklisted"

The 1940s were difficult years for Mrs. Parker. On the pleasant side, she was hired to add material to a screenplay written by Peter Viertal and Joan Harrison for Alfred Hitchcock's *Saboteur*, a film about an aircraft factory worker who witnesses the plant's firebombing by a Nazi agent and is wrongfully accused of sabotage. She also shared a cameo role with the director in a brief car scene in which she looks out the window to see Robert Cummings manhandling Priscilla Lane and remarks, "My, they must be terribly in love."[9]

Less pleasant was the fact that in 1942 Alan Campbell, a graduate of Virginia Military Institute, enlisted as a private in the Army Air Force at age forty and proceeded to enroll in Officer Candidate School. Parker talked about enlisting in the Women's Army Corps or attempting to go abroad as a war correspondent. She did neither. Friends concluded that because of her associations with the Anti-Nazi League, the government had branded her a "premature anti-Fascist," an FBI category that included all Communists and outspoken anti-fascists.[10] Others conjectured that the State Department refused to grant her a passport. None remarked on the fact that Dorothy Parker was fifty years old.

Parker was in a quandary. It was rumored in Hollywood that she was blacklisted ("Well, I was told so—how the hell do you know?" she fumed).[11] With military service closed to her, travel abroad prohibited, film work scarce, and her recent writing dismissed as superficial, she took refuge in available work.[12] She wrote the introduction to an illustrated edition of Hellman's *Watch on the Rhine,* published in 1942 by the Joint Anti-Fascist Refugee Committee to raise funds. Parker, Rockwell Kent, and eleven other artists donated their efforts. She wrote: "The woman who wrote this play and the men who made these drawings give this, their book, to those who earliest fought Fascism. Most of those warriors died; on the stiff plains of Spain, behind the jagged wire of French prison camps, in small echoing rooms of German towns. Few of their names are told, and their numbers are not measured. They wear no clean and carven stones in death. But for them there is an eternal light that will burn with a flame far higher than any beside a tomb."[13] In turn, Hellman dedicated *The Searching Wind*, a play about fascism in Europe, to her friend.

Aware that the days of witty epigrams on girls who wear glasses were over and that her polished writing of the past had no connection to the horrors of a world at war, Parker again took refuge in charitable causes, having concluded that her verse was "terribly dated."[14] Her friends tried to alter the situation. Alexander Woollcott included her work in anthologies and Viking Press published *The Portable Dorothy Parker* in 1944, but critics again pointed out that her clever, polished writing "had no very deep roots in human life."[15]

Throughout the late 1940s, Parker continued to speak at rallies and fundraisers. In 1947 she addressed a rally to raise money for the defense of composer Hanns Eisler (brother of Communist Party leader Gerhart Eisler). In her speech she condemned the "shameful persecution" of the German antifascist refugee and vilified HUAC, saying that she was there to "damn the souls" of the committee and its chairman, J. Parnell Thomas. Moreover, she called for the committee's abolition.[16]

Parker was also chairman of the Voice of Freedom, which supported liberal commentators on radio. Right-wingers considered the Voice of Freedom an asset of the Communist Party. As chairman, her name appeared in Dashiell Hammett's FBI file, where she was cited by a confidential informant as a Communist. Hammett's name had been listed in a pamphlet endorsing the Voice of Freedom, and a copy of the publication was turned over to the FBI in July 1947.[17] Although Hammett disliked Parker for her "game of embrace-denounce" toward most people, they shared their support of liberal causes.[18]

In May 1948, the Tenney committee, a smaller version of HUAC, held hearings in Los Angeles on the histories of Communist Party front groups in California. Organizations such as the Hollywood Anti-Nazi League, the Screen Writers Guild, the Hollywood League for Democratic Action, the Actors' Laboratory Theatre, the Civil Rights Congress, and the Congress of American Women were among the 171 groups and publications listed in the Tenney committee's 1948 report under the heading "Communist Front Organizations."[19] Earlier the committee had officially cited the Joint Anti-Fascist Refugee Committee as a "Communist front" organization. Parker's name appeared in public records as a member of many of these groups.

A brief respite from the government inspectors, or so Parker thought, followed the Tenney committee's hearings into the work of the Anti-Nazi League. Nonetheless, in June 1950 Parker's name appeared in *Red Channels: The Report of Communist Influence in Radio and Television* along with the names of 151 other writers, directors, and performers. That year the FBI categorized Parker as one of four hundred concealed Communists based on information provided by informant Louis Budenz, a former Communist and professional witness. Her name also came up during the espionage trial of Judith Coplon, a political analyst for the Justice Department accused of stealing government secrets to aid Russia. (Coplon was arrested, tried, and convicted in 1949, but her conviction was overturned on appeal.) During Coplon's trial, an FBI document that named Parker and actor Edward G. Robinson as traitors was read aloud.[20] Parker's response to the accusation was straightforward: she was acquainted with no Russians—but wished she was—and had no plans to sell them secrets, for the simple reason that she knew none.[21] She was not a traitor. Unlike Robinson, she didn't bother to deny that she had ever been a party member.

In early April 1951, the FBI began investigating Parker as a concealed Communist and thus eligible for a Security Index card as a national security risk with a Security Matter—C classification ("C" for Communist). Informants described her as the "Queen of Communists" and as a leading "character" in the Hollywood Communist movement. Two agents conspicuous in dark hats and suits arrived on her doorstep in West Los Angeles on April 13. They wanted to know about her ties with the Communist Party, whereupon she denied having been affiliated with, having donated to, or having been contacted by representatives of the party. When asked about her associations with Lillian Hellman, Dashiell Hammett, Donald Ogden Stewart, and Ella Winter, she advised that she was personally acquainted with them but denied that she had any knowledge that they had ever been Communist Party members or that she had attended party meetings with them. Following the interview, no recommendation was made to order a Security Index card in Parker's name.[22] Four years later, agents would again visit her in an effort to document the writer's ongoing threat to national security.

Then, in September 1951, screenwriter Martin Berkeley recited a list of Hollywood Communists who attended a meeting in his home in the late 1930s, naming Parker, Campbell, Stewart, Hellman, and Hammett. As Anne Revere and others had learned with some bitterness, to be named by a witness during a HUAC hearing meant certain blacklisting by the studios. Parker was aware that she was now unemployable as a screenwriter in Hollywood. She was never dismissed from a job, but by her own admission she was "blacklisted."[23]

Given the fact that Parker was unemployed in Hollywood, divorced from Alan Campbell, and pressured by the FBI, her thoughts turned to Broadway, where she could potentially restore her failing creative powers (and literary reputation) by writing a successful play. She traveled hopefully eastward to the city she called home.

"A Terrible Day Tomorrow"

Dorothy Parker loved the theatre, although she disliked most of the plays she saw on Broadway. She began a lifelong flirtation with the stage as an avid theatregoer and then as drama reviewer for *Vanity Fair* in 1918, replacing P. G. Wodehouse. Frank Crowninshield explained his unusual choice of reviewer: "Though she was full of prejudices, her perceptions were so sure, her judgment so unerring, that she always seemed certain to hit the center of the mark."[24]

Parker quickly learned the reviewer's craft. Instead of merely summarizing plots and performances, as she did in early reviews, she turned to clever, sardonic quips to poke fun at the shallowness and commercialism of what she saw on Broadway's stages. Of a revival of the French symbolist play *The Betrothal*, by Maurice Maeterlinck, she confessed, "I am always just on the point of going down for the third time in the sea of symbolism." After a week's worth of southern-accented plays, she remarked of John Taintor Foote's *Toby's Bow*: "Somehow, the only thing that one can say of Mr. Foote as a dramatist is that he used to write wholly delightful dog stories for magazines."[25]

In Parker's view, the trivial and the artificial were fair game: William Anthony McGuire's *A Good Bad Woman* was "one of the most serious, not to say fatal, cases of the obstetrical school of drama," and Rachel Crothers's *39 East* was improved by "a property swan in the Central Park Scene who adds a refreshing note of realism." Her serious literary tastes were also trained upon Broadway's silliness. She wrote of the comedy *Tillie*, "To quote the only line of Gertrude Stein's which I have ever been able to understand, 'It is wonderful how I am not interested.'"[26]

In January 1920 she ridiculed two Broadway icons. She compared Florenz Ziegfeld's wife, Billie Burke, who overacted badly in *Caesar's Wife,* to a burlesque star: "She plays her lighter scenes rather as if she were giving an impersonation of Eva Tanguay." She held in contempt *The Son-Daughter,* a Chinese costume drama by George Scarborough and David Belasco, describing the play as a diversion with mandarin coats, black wigs, and pidgin English. As advertisers with the magazine, Belasco and Ziegfeld brought pressure on the publishers to discipline their reviewer.[27] Over tea at the Plaza Hotel, Crowninshield told Parker that her days as drama critic for *Vanity Fair* were over but assured her that the magazine still valued her work in other ways. Suspecting that protests from powerful producers had led to her removal, she and co-worker Robert Benchley resigned in tandem.

Parker's outspoken criticism of Broadway's rich and powerful led to a new monthly column, "In Broadway Playhouses," for the literary magazine *Ainslee's*. With a steady income, Parker assumed a daily routine of going to the theatre and writing reviews for *Ainslee's* and *Life*, freelancing with poems and prose pieces, and holding forth at the Round Table as "the most riveting presence at the table."[28] Between 1920 and 1922 she wrote ninety-one pieces for *Life*: sixty-three poems and twenty-eight prose pieces. Her theatre reviews were snappy, incisive, and sprinkled with caustic puns. She noted gleefully that Avery Hopwood's plays went "from bed to worse."[29]

At twenty-seven, Dorothy Parker was a household name, her portrait was painted by Neysa McMein, and she partied nightly with Algonquin cohorts and associates from the Broadway theatre. She had affairs with Ring Lardner Jr., Elmer Rice, and Charles MacArthur. Her drinking became more and more excessive, leading to quarrels and outrageous behavior. The wild parties and prodigious work established a pattern that would last the remainder of her life. Arthur Kinney remarked that "with mixed success she used the bad times as material for writing during the good times."[30]

In marked contrast to the rich subtexts of her poetry, Parker used her talent for writing clever dialogue to collaborate with members of the Round Table on songs and dramatic skits. She wrote the lyrics of a song called "The Everlastin' Ingenue Blues," sung by Robert Sherwood with a chorus that included Tallaluh Bankhead, Helen Hayes, and Winifred Lenihan, for the musical *No, Sirree!*, staged on a Sunday evening in April 1922 in Broadway's Forty-ninth Street Theatre. She assisted Benchley with his one-act send-up *Nero*, whose characters included Cardinal Richelieu playing solitaire and Generals Lee and Grant and Queen Victoria playing baseball.[31] *Nero* was part of the revue called *The Forty-niners*, with other sketches by Ring Lardner Jr., Heywood Broun, and Howard Dietz and staged by George S. Kaufman and Marc Connelly at the small Punch and Judy Theater for fifteen performances in November. Sometime later she wrote lyrics for Heywood Broun's 1931 revue *Shoot the Works* at the George M. Cohan Theatre.

One evening in 1924, Parker announced to the Round Table that she was set to write a play with Elmer Rice (known for *The Adding Machine*) about two frustrated people who begin an adulterous affair—a subject she knew well. Parker had written the first act and shared it with producer Philip Goodman, an advertising man turned theatrical producer who had produced the recent hit

Poppy with W. C. Fields. Goodman felt that the script had promise but lacked theatrical craftsmanship. He enlisted Rice fresh from his success with the expressionistic play for the Theatre Guild. The playwright had heard tales of Parker's temperament, but he enjoyed the technical side of playwriting and needed the money. Despite misgivings, he accepted the job. When he finally met Mrs. Parker, he said, "It was hard to believe that this tiny creature with the big-appealing eyes and the diffident, self-effacing manner was capable of corrosive cynicism and devastating retorts."[32]

Upon reading Parker's script, Rice was impressed. "The act was as long as an entire play," he observed, "and completely formless. The characters, suburbanites all, just went on talking and talking. But they were sharply realized, and the dialogue was uncannily authentic and very funny." The script's merits lay in Parker's "shrewd observations and pungent writing."[33] Parker was punctual, diligent, and amiable during their sessions. By Rice's account, she did most of the writing while he concentrated on plot development and scene construction. The story, strongly echoing Robert Benchley's unhappy marriage, was "a simple tale of a suburban husband bedeviled by a sweetly dominant wife and an insufferable brat. The husband finds solace in the companionship of a neighbor, a former chorus girl, but habit and convention are too strong and nothing comes of the relationship."[34]

The best part of the play, the ending, was authentic and theatrically effective. In summing up the play as a reviewer for *Life*, Benchley noted: "The delicate writing of this [final] scene ... makes it just about as heartbreaking a thing as we have ever seen on stage." The fact that the play's success relied on this climactic scene did not make for a riveting evening in the theatre. Alexander Woollcott praised the play as Chekhovian in its attempt to make art out of commonplace and dull lives. But, as Stark Young said, the play lacked "the psychological development of Chekhov's plays, even as it employed in the mandolin a Chekhovian symbol."[35]

Copyrighted as *Soft Music* and eventually called *Close Harmony*, the play was staged by Arthur Hopkins at the Gaiety Theatre. It shared its opening night on December 1 with Irving Berlin's *Music Box Revue* and the Gershwins' *Lady Be Good* with Fred and Adele Astaire. Despite good reviews, the material about suburban lives—Stark Young said it was "full of grim gayety, domesticity and dull fates"—held no interest for audiences.[36] By the third week *Close Harmony* was playing to nearly empty houses. Parker wired Benchley: "CLOSE HARMONY DID A COOL NINETY DOLLARS AT THE MATINEE. ASK THE BOYS IN THE BACK ROOM WHAT THEY WILL HAVE."[37] The play closed after twenty-four performances. An embarrassed Parker, who had excoriated many plays as both a reviewer and an Algonquin wit, complained to friends that the play had been "dull." To the smart set, *dullness* was anathema.

Parker's knowledgeable friends reported that *Close Harmony* was a good play that had failed to attract an audience. As an act of defiance, the play reopened with a new producer and a new title (*The Lady Next Door*) in Chicago the following summer and played for fifteen weeks and went on tour to midwestern cities. In contrast to its Broadway reception, the play got good reviews (Parker was called another George Kelly) and played to substantial audiences.[38]

It was said that Mrs. Parker "wrote poetry like an angel and criticism like a fiend."[39] For eight weeks (and twenty-five plays) in the 1930-31 Broadway season she substituted for Robert Benchley as drama critic for the *New Yorker* with fiendish enjoyment. With sensibilities honed by a dozen years of theatregoing and with phraseology that was uniquely her own, she entertained readers with insights into Broadway's tedium, pretentiousness, tastelessness, minor triumphs, and utter boredom. She concluded each column with a personal plea to Benchley: "Personal: Robert Benchley, please come home. Nothing is forgiven." Or, she ended the personal pleas for Benchley's return with such refrains as "Baby taking terrible beating," "Will not be responsible for your debts," "Whimso is back again," "A joke's a joke," "Light burning in the window for you," and "What do you think I am, anyway?"

Parker's feminist leanings emerged in her muted defense of Rachel Crothers's *As Husbands Go*. Aware that the daily reviewers had treated the play with the venomous enthusiasm of those "dancing in the streets" at the fall of the Bastille, she credited Crothers with writing a "mild, agreeable, and roundedly undistinguished" but workmanlike play. In the eight weeks of reviewing twenty-five plays—"a flock of turkeys," Parker called them—Crothers's agreeable story, admirably acted by Catharine Doucet, was a small beacon of light in an otherwise impoverished season that included a revival of George Bernard Shaw's *Getting Married*. Parker dismissed Shaw's play as a "dull and lumbering work of a mighty man."[40]

As drama critic for a weekly magazine, Parker wrote in the first person. Her reviews were personal, deeply felt responses written in language honed by razor-sharp insights into the folly of producers foisting upon audiences the lousy, the dull, and the ludicrous. "You can't make straw without bricks, after all," she pronounced of A. A. Milne's efforts to entertain with *Give Me Yesterday*. Her valedictory as a drama critic came in the second week of her tenure: "I thought that maybe they [the plays] were going to be good. And that sentence, sad reader, can stand as every dramatic critic's epitaph."[41]

During her seven years in Hollywood, Parker seemed to lose interest in the theatre. Meanwhile, Hellman opened *The Little Foxes* on Broadway with a title suggested by Parker.[42] Within two years, Hellman asked Parker, Alan Campbell, and her former husband, Arthur Kober, to write additional dialogue for the Bette Davis film.

Most likely inspired by Hellman's success, Parker and Campbell worked together on a play of their own about a clerk at a plumbing supply house who is about to be fired just as he is to be married. *The Happiest Man,* adapted from a comedy by the Hungarian playwright Miklos Laszlo, provided Parker with an opportunity to inject some Marxist doctrine about capitalistic practices. When the young office worker receives a dismissal slip, he tells a co-worker about the frightening scarcity of jobs: "You've seen them, day after day, the young fellers, standing in line, coming and asking, going away again. . . . I saw a thing yesterday. There was a sign up, 'Porter Wanted.' There must have been two hundred of them, fighting to get a chance at it. And the police clubbing them."[43] Campbell saw the play as his chance to return to Broadway, where he had enjoyed success as an actor. Perhaps Parker envisioned the collaboration as an opportunity to repair their marriage, which had been strained by Campbell's fear of losing employment with the studios because of her activism.

The couple enlisted Otto Preminger to direct and Paul Muni and Burgess Meredith to play the leads in *The Happiest Man.* Max Gordon agreed to produce. Then, without explanation, Gordon dropped his option on the play. One biographer conjectured that Parker's radical politics were most likely the unspoken issue in the loss of Gordon's support.[44] Parker's left-wing activities were evidenced in the deeply felt polemics of the play with its ironic title. As early as 1941, a number of Broadway producers were wary of authors whose left-wing politics surfaced in their plays.

By now Hellman had another hit on her hands with *Watch on the Rhine,* and Parker was eager to prove herself on Broadway. She and Campbell took out a six-month option on *The Happiest Man* but were unable to produce it themselves. In the interim, Hellman dedicated *The Searching Wind* to her troubled friend. Hellman's unwieldy play (called "more windy than searching") examined the interaction between spreading fascism and decent people who might have done more to stop it.[45] It ran for 318 performances.

Parker attempted—with varying success—to write for Broadway three more times. Divorced from Campbell in 1947, she wrote *The Coast of Illyria* with aspiring novelist and current lover Rosser Lynn Evans, who was in his thirties (Parker was fifty-three). The play took its title from the mythical shore in

Twelfth Night where Shakespeare shipwrecked Viola and Sebastian. *The Coast of Illyria* dramatized Parker's familiar themes—loneliness, terror, and despair—and drew mainly on what one critic called Parker's "painful psychological relationship with Alan Campbell."[46]

Loosely based on the life of Charles and Mary Lamb, *The Coast of Illyria* opened on April 4, 1949, at Margo Jones's Theatre 49 in Dallas and ran for three weeks. The predicted Broadway run never materialized. The *Variety* critic reported that the play was "written with intelligence and taste." Brooks Atkinson, on the other hand, journeyed to Dallas and expressed disappointment: "It is an ordinary drama about some extraordinary people. It does not penetrate very deeply into the private agony of brother and sister condemned to a circumscribed life by her tragic insanity."[47]

In 1952, Margo Jones proposed to the William Morris Agency in New York a literary series of thirteen plays for television, among them the Parker-Evans play. The agency rejected *The Coast of Illyria* as unacceptable, saying, "This might have come in like a lamb, but came out a lion." Arthur Kinney took exception to the agency's dismissal of the piece: "Nowhere else would Dorothy Parker ever wrestle with herself in quite this way; nowhere else would she persistently probe the issues of genius and madness, of alcoholism and drugs and art, of women's rights and the plight of the poor, and the cost and anxiety, sweetness and anguish of one person's love for another."[48] In effect, Parker had offered up a cornucopia of Parkerisms.

In 1950, Campbell was working again in Hollywood and he and Parker remarried. A year later, when he walked out on the marriage for a second and final time, Parker returned to New York City and settled into the Hotel Volney, a small residential hotel on East Seventy-fourth Street. Parker was still blacklisted by the studios, but she found a collaborator for a new play. It was Arnaud d'Usseau, a former colleague at *New Masses* who was coauthor of two plays with James Gow: *Tomorrow the World*, the story of Nazi techniques for consolidating power, and *Deep Are the Roots*, about discrimination against blacks in the South. Unlike Evans, d'Usseau was a recognized playwright and held radical views compatible with Parker's. They combined forces to write *The Ladies of the Corridor*, an unflinching portrayal of lonely people living in a residential hotel, with a self-portrait of an older woman who falls in love with a younger man and winds up like all the ladies of the corridor—alone and desolate.

Again enjoying her role as playwright, Parker explained to Ward Morehouse, drama critic for the *New York World Telegram and Sun*, her collaboration with d'Usseau: "I knew him in Hollywood. One day he said to me, 'Let's write a play.' We were going to write a murder play and then later he asked if I ever thought of the great number of women who live alone in hotels. I'd lived in hotels for thirty years and went into that—the unwanted, wasted women who belong to American life. Strong and healthy—and wasted."[49] By the time she gave the interview, Parker viewed the work as a feminist play that warned women to stop sitting around saying, "It's a man's world."[50] "We're trying to show a part of American life—and a very large part of it. There is an enormous population of women alone," she told Morehouse. "It's not so much age as manlessness—and they should be better trained, adjusted, to live a life without a man.... I don't think tragedy is too big a word because the waste is unnecessary."

Taking its title from T. S. Eliot's poem "Sweeney Erect," *The Ladies of the Corridor* opened on October 21, 1953, at the Longacre Theatre, directed by Harold Clurman with a distinguished cast: Betty Field, Edna Best, Shepherd Strudwick, Margaret Barker, June Walker, and Walter Matthau. Reminding readers of the scars that Parker had inflicted as a theatre critic, Brooks Atkinson suggested, "Mrs. Parker has not written for the theatre as vividly as she has written about it." Atkinson had high praise for Clurman's staging and for the "most notable cast of the season," but he withheld praise for the writing. To the spectacle of unattached women living dismal lives in a New York hotel the critic observed, "The authors contribute nothing but a kind of mechanical craftsmanship destitute of ideas."[51] He found the writing platitudinous and journeyman-like, lacking personality or ideas.

The writers and their director had disagreed on the ending. Clurman, who called Parker "an unhappy woman whose tears were mixed with acid," wanted a happy ending, not the Betty Field character's suicide that Parker wrote.[52] To expose the loneliness and despair of the elderly, as Samuel Beckett has shown, is to confront an unrelenting existential condition, and in the early 1950s Broadway was not ready to confront a bitter play about the lives of quiet desperation of lonely divorceés and aging widows. Likewise, fearing that audiences (and critics) would find the play morbid, producer Walter Fried interceded for the director and asked the writers to change the ending. They added a final scene following Mildred Tynan's suicide. Parker thought the story now ended on a false note, and reviewers agreed.[53]

For Parker, the "whole point of the play" was that the central figure, a widow enamored of a younger man, would wind up like all the other ladies of the corridor. She would become a prisoner of herself and a prey to boredom, condemned to live alone. The new ending provided a hollow note of hope for the hotel's inhabitants. In the final line, the character of Lulu, a woman who fails in her last chance at love, says, "I've learned from looking around, there is something worse than loneliness—and that's the fear of it."[54]

Five of the eight New York critics admired the play, and George Jean Nathan named it the Best Play of the Year. Parker rejoiced in her return to the theatre. It was, she said, "the only thing I have ever done in which I had great pride."[55] The play opened the same month as Robert Anderson's *Tea and Sympathy* and Betty Comden and Adolph Green's *Wonderful Town*, followed by Howard Teichmann and George S. Kaufman's *The Solid Gold Cadillac*. After forty-five performances, *The Ladies of the Corridor* closed.

Parker and Hellman converged on Broadway within a period of ten months. In their return to the theatre, both women were looking for a means to improve their finances and literary reputations. Hellman's revival of *The Children's Hour* in 1952 confronted none too subtly the destructiveness of the national political scene that brought her before HUAC that same year and sent Dashiell Hammett to jail. In contrast, Parker uncharacteristically retreated from the national political debate to create a social document about personal fortitude and private desolation. This was Parker's second chance to measure herself against Hellman, and for a second time she was found wanting. *The Happiest Man* and *The Ladies of the Corridor* were not of the same social and theatrical dimensions as *Watch on the Rhine* and *The Children's Hour*.

In order to provide a Broadway credit (and income) for her friend, Hellman enlisted Parker in 1956 to write additional lyrics for *Candide*, the theatrical adaptation of Voltaire's satiric novel, with book by Hellman, music by Leonard Bernstein, and lyrics by Richard Wilbur and John Latouche. When Latouche dropped out due to frictions with Hellman, she replaced him with Parker. Unnerved by Bernstein's "officious energy," Parker dropped out.[56] Later, Parker, who had only one set of lyrics to the song "Gavotte" retained in the musical, opined, "There were too many geniuses involved."[57]

Lacking a thick-skinned, skilled collaborator, Parker was defeated by the exigencies of the theatre. "I am a short-distance writer," she once said.[58] The brevity of the theatre appealed to her for this reason. However, the well-made conventions of the commercial theatre, which demanded a clear through-line of action and character, worked against her talent. She could write lyrics for topical revues and individual scenes for films, but the traditions of the Broadway theatre in the 1950s had not yet been influenced by the absurdists. *Rhinoceros*, *The Homecoming*, and *Who's Afraid of Virginia Woolf?* arrived in the next decade.

The theatre that Dorothy Parker loved and excoriated finally defeated her, and she disengaged from playwriting altogether.

"What Fresh Hell Is This?"

In 1953, Parker read in the *New York Times* that Joseph McCarthy was convening hearings into the purchase of books written by Communists or leftist authors for the State Department's overseas libraries.[59] Although there is no evidence that Parker was a member of the Communist Party, her writings for *New Masses*, her associations with HUAC witnesses, and her activities on behalf of Communist-front organizations led many to conclude that she was a party member. Parker always disputed this charge. In 1937 she wrote that she belonged to no political party. Fourteen years later she denied ever having been a party member.[60] The FBI was eventually persuaded, but not before another adversary appeared on the congressional horizon.

From the time Dashiell Hammett and Arnaud d'Usseau were brought before McCarthy's subcommittee, Parker expected to be subpoenaed as well.[61] She told friends that if McCarthy called her to testify, she would take the Fifth. She admired novelist E. M. Forster, who had written that if he were forced to choose between betraying a friend and betraying his country, he hoped he would have the courage to betray his country.[62] But Parker was not called upon to betray her country or her friends. No subpoena arrived, and McCarthy's censure in 1954 granted her a final reprieve, or so she concluded at the time.

Early in January 1955, the FBI reevaluated its previous recommendation to place Parker on the Security Index as a concealed Communist.[63] Over a period of four years (1951–54), the bureau continued to add information to her file but had little to say other than that she was five feet, four inches tall, weighed 125 pounds, and wore glasses "occasionally." During the early 1950s, Parker was unrelenting in her politics and wholly dismissive of repercussions to herself. Following her April 1951 interview with the FBI agents in Los Angeles, she expressed "only monumental scorn" for the bureau.[64] In 1952 she appeared on the podium with Paul Robeson and I. F. Stone at a dinner honoring the national secretary of the Progressive Party, and in 1953 she spoke against the deportation proceedings of Cedric Belfrage, editor of the *National Guardian*. She appeared at rallies sponsored by the National Committee to Win Amnesty for Smith Act Victims in 1953 and again in 1954. As national chairman of the Spanish Refugee Appeal of the Joint Anti-Fascist Refugee Committee, she solicited funds over four years (1951–54). Unwavering in her support for Paul and Eslanda Robeson, she spoke at a dinner honoring them in October 1954.

Along with the names of screenwriter Lester Cole and actor John Randolph, Parker's name emerged again in 1953 during the HUAC investigation of radio and television actress Jean Muir. FBI informants reported that Parker and Tess Schlessinger invited the actress to a dinner party in Los Angeles where a guest had lectured on Marxism. Muir concluded that the after-dinner speaker was "not just trying to entertain" them.[65]

When agents appeared at the Volney on January 12, 1955, to conduct a second interview with Mrs. Parker, little had changed. Surrounded by her two dogs in an apartment crowded with unread review copies of books, unswept ashtrays, and other detritus of a neglected life, Parker gave the agents the impression of a distracted, nervous woman who was no threat to national security. As she lobbed left-handed a rubber ball from her chair for the poodles to retrieve, she repeated a variation of her earlier defense. When the agents asked about her influence upon the committees that she supported, she replied, "My influence? Look at these two dogs of mine. I can't even influence them."[66]

Despite the many notations detailing her associations with front groups for sixteen years (1939–55), the FBI's special agent in charge of the New York office concluded that there was no reliable evidence of Parker's Communist Party membership. The recommendation to enter her name in the Security Index was withdrawn.[67] Nonetheless, the subpoena that she had eluded for more than a decade finally caught up with her. In late February 1955 the New York state joint legislative committee investigating the alleged diversion of millions of dollars in charitable contributions to the Communist Party by front groups turned its attention to the Joint Anti-Fascist Refugee Committee (JAFRC) and the Civil Rights Congress. The committee had discovered that the JAFRC had spent "less than ten cents on the dollar" of the money collected for refugee aid.[68] As JAFRC's national chairman, Parker was called to testify on February 5 at the courthouse in Lower Manhattan.

Wearing a mink jacket over a brown suit with a smart Tyrolean-style hat and gloves, Mrs. Parker arrived at the hearing. She could not say what happened to the $1.5 million collected by JAFRC, ostensibly to aid refugees from Franco's Spain. She conceded that she made speeches and signed appeals for funds, but she had not composed letters, nor could she recall who asked her to sign the solicitations. As national chairman, she had signed checks that, as far as she knew, "were used to help people who were helpless." Moreover, she politely informed the committee that it had never occurred to her to ask if the Communist Party controlled the group or diverted funds. Management of the committee's finances was not her function, she explained. "My function was to try to help raise money, and that was all it was." Bernard Tompkins, chief counsel for the committee, asked, "Didn't you know, Miss Parker, that the Joint Anti-Fascist Refugee Committee was thoroughly controlled by the Communist Party?"

PARKER: No.
TOMPKINS: You did not know that?
PARKER: No.
TOMPKINS: Did you ever ask?
PARKER: No.
TOMPKINS: It never occurred to you to ask?
PARKER: No.
TOMPKINS: Weren't there people of obvious Communist reputation concerned with the Committee?
PARKER: No.
TOMPKINS: It never occurred to you to ask. The same thing with the Civil Rights Congress?
PARKER: Yes.[69]

When asked about the finances of the Civil Rights Congress (she was on record as a national sponsor), she again denied knowing anything about the group's finances.

TOMPKINS: Did you ever ask in that case whether the money that was raised was actually being used for the purpose that the public was informed it was being raised?
PARKER: No.

Ladylike and demure throughout the hearing, Parker balked at only one question. When asked if she was now or had ever been a member of the Communist Party, she refused to answer on the grounds of possible self-incrimination. She took the Fifth.

Given Parker's cavalier attitude toward money, these were not uncommon responses. As JAFRC's national chairman, she was ultimately responsible for the use and misuse of the group's funds. Nonetheless, she saw herself as a fund-raiser, not a bookkeeper. She had not concerned herself with financial details or with the board's dispersal of funds.[70] This lack of concern for money was characteristic of Parker. Sometimes she had little money; at other times her royalties and screenwriting fees brought her considerable wealth. Most often she claimed, particularly in the later years, to be in a state of penury.

When Hellman published the first of her memoirs, *An Unfinished Woman,* two years after Parker's death, she confused her friend's experience before JAFRC in 1955 with the HUAC hearings in 1952. Although Hellman scrambled the hearings and the years, her pentimentic memory captured a convincing tone for Parker's response to the subpoena that brought her before the state legislative committee. Hellman wrote, "I went to say that I would come with her [to the hearing], she said, in genuine surprise, 'Why Lilly?' . . . I don't think it occurred to her, or to many of her generation, that the ruling classes were anything but people with more money than you had. She acted before the committee as she acted so often with their more literate, upper-class cousins at dinner: as if to say, 'Yes dear, it's true that I'm here to observe you, but I do not like you and will, of course, say and write exactly that.'"[71] Furthermore, Parker was not among those screenwriters subpoenaed by J. Parnell Thomas's committee in 1947, nor was she called before Thomas Wood's committee in the early 1950s. Marion Meade conjectured that the government must have known that it had a weak case against her.[72]

There is another way to consider the almost inexplicable fact that Parker was not called before HUAC in the same sequence of hearings as Larry Parks, José Ferrer, Elia Kazan, Edward G. Robinson, Clifford Odets, Lillian Hellman, and Abe Burrows. By 1952 her excessive drinking was well known, and the blacklist had neutralized her influence in Hollywood. Perhaps of most concern to a public official was her corrosive ability to excoriate—in print and in New York literary circles where her comments found their way into print—those who displeased her or whom she found unworthy. Her verbal pyrotechnics were legion, and such incidents as occurred one evening when a man accosted her in a bar were to be avoided. The man voiced his agreement with the "protectionist campaign of Hollywood bosses against the Reds," and Parker struck back. "With the crown of thorns I wear," she replied, "why should I be bothered with a prick like you?"[73]

Shortly after she took the Fifth during the JAFRC hearing, the FBI closed its case file on Dorothy Rothschild Parker. A four-page memorandum concluded that she was not a security risk.[74] Parker would not have liked this review. The closure of file number 100-56075 implied that her speech-making and fund-raising were just so much sound and fury—signifying nothing to the federal government.

At age fifty-nine, Alan Campbell died of an overdose of Seconal on June 14, 1963. Parker settled his affairs in Hollywood and returned to the Volney, now her permanent residence. Before Campbell's death she had essentially stopped writing, although she was employed by *Esquire* in 1958 to write book reviews. In total she reviewed more than two hundred books for the magazine. She wrote one final short story ("The Bolt behind the Blue") that same year and coedited an anthology of short stories two years before her death. Also, in 1958 the literary world acknowledged her contribution to American letters. She received the Marjorie Peabody Waite Award from the National Institute of Arts and Letters, and the following year the institute made her a member.

Parker's last years were marked by failing eyesight, frail health, heavy drinking, and financial uncertainty. As her staunchest friend, Hellman came to her aid from time to time but stayed only long enough for the crisis to pass. Hellman was retooling her literary interests with *An Unfinished Woman* and found Parker's "heavy drinking and shabby living, as if she were destitute," increasingly difficult to ignore. On one occasion, Hellman in an act of charity sold two gifts from Parker—a Utrillo landscape and later a Picasso gouache—that had been, in Hellman's view, Parker's "charming way of paying off a debt."[75] Hellman sent Parker the money from the sales but received no acknowledgment of the first check (in the amount of ten thousand dollars), for the Picasso. Other checks were found in a bureau drawer after Parker's death.[76]

On June 7, 1967, Dorothy Parker was found dead of a heart attack in her rooms at the Volney. She was seventy-three. The next morning, her obituary on the front page of the *New York Times* described her as "a disillusioned romantic, all the fiercer because the world spun against her sentimental nature."[77] At the memorial service in a funeral chapel on Eighty-first Street, Zero Mostel rose to explain that it had been Parker's wish that there be no formal ceremonies at all. "If she had had her way," he said, "I suspect she would not be here at all."[78] Hellman, whose friendship with Parker had survived for more than three decades, spoke of her friend's individuality: "She was part of nothing and nobody except herself; it was this independence of mind and spirit that was her true distinction, and it stayed with her until the end, young and sparkling." Hellman continued: "She never spoke of the old glories, never repeated old defeats, never rested on times long gone. She was always brave in deprivation, in the chivying she took during the McCarthy days, in the isolation of the last, bad sick years. The remarkable quality of her wit was that it stayed in no place, and was of no time."[79]

Despite the eulogies, Parker had the last word. Her will, dated February 6, 1965, named Hellman as executrix and assigned her entire estate (about twenty thousand dollars after expenses) together with copyrights and royalties to Martin Luther King Jr., to be passed at his death to the National Association for the Advancement of Colored People. She had never met the civil rights leader, but her strong feelings for civil liberties and racial injustice and for those struggling to secure them in the marches of the early 1960s shaped her final gesture.

"It's Not the Tragedies That Kill Us, It's the Messes"

It can be argued that Dorothy Parker had a modest career in the Broadway theatre. However, for the period in which she wrote more than seventy theatre reviews for *Vanity Fair*, *Ainslee's*, the *New Yorker*, and *Esquire*, she was a formidable critic. As a playwright, she was less so.

Although her output for the stage was small, Parker introduced new themes to the Broadway stage: the marginalization of elderly women without families, and the complicated lives of homosexuals living as outsiders in a fiercely heterosexual world. Parker herself had been marginalized by the fury of her politics during the McCarthy years. Like other artists of the time, her politics were shaped by world events abroad and opposed by powerful conservative forces at home. She campaigned ferociously for the poor and victimized of the world. Moreover, she fervently believed that the artistic communities in Hollywood and New York could make a difference.

Nevertheless, Parker's radical politics abbreviated her film career in the 1940s and sidelined a production of her second work for Broadway in 1949. Her screenwriting ended with the studio blacklist in 1949, and her writing for the theatre ended with the unsuccessful *Ladies of the Corridor* in 1953. She lived her last years chafed by memories of her "untidy life." "It's not the tragedies that kill us," she told Marion Capron in an interview for the *Paris Review*, "it's the messes."[80]

Dorothy Parker occupies a distinctive niche in the larger story of Broadway and McCarthyism. Her left-wing advocacy and those conservative forces opposed to it constitute a variation on the theme of McCarthyism at work in the cultural landscape of the 1950s in the United States. Unlike Lillian Hellman's politically engaged writing in plays and memoirs, Parker's crusades on behalf of the poor, the disenfranchised, and the forgotten added a political and historical dimension to her life that is curiously absent from her art. She found pleasure and a sense of purpose in activism. Nevertheless, the decade-long shadow cast over the country's history by McCarthyism, in Marion Meade's view, poisoned Parker's personal and professional life and eventually "undermined her spirit."[81]

Notes

The epigraph to this essay is taken from Leslie Frewin, *The Late Mrs. Dorothy Parker* (New York: Macmillan, 1986), 261.

1. Lillian Hellman, *An Unfinished Woman: A Memoir* (Boston: Little, Brown, 1969), 213, 214–15.
2. Paul Avrich, *Sacco and Vanzetti: The Anarchist Background* (Princeton, N.J.: Princeton University Press, 1991), 3.
3. *New York Times*, August 11, 1927, 1.

4. John Keats, *You Might as Well Live: The Life and Times of Dorothy Parker* (New York: Simon and Schuster, 1970), 192.
5. Testimony of Dorothy Parker, February 25, 1955, *Hearing before the Joint Legislative Committee on Charitable and Philanthropic Agencies and Organizations*, vol. 3 (Albany, N.Y.: Parsons Reporting Service, 1955), 400–414. Parker's testimony can be found in the Archives of the New York State Library, Albany. The hearing took place in the Supreme Court of the State of New York, Room 408, 60 Centre Street, New York City.
6. Dorothy Parker, "Review and Comment," *New Masses*, June 27, 1939, 1.
7. Donald Ogden Stewart, *By a Stroke of Luck!* (London: Paddington Press, 1975), 228.
8. Harold Clurman declared Parker's radicalism not so much "insincere" as "sentimental." See Arthur F. Kinney, *Dorothy Parker*, rev. ed. (New York: Twayne, 1998), 36 n. 104.
9. Marion Meade, *Dorothy Parker: What Fresh Hell Is This?* (New York: Villard Books, 1988), 308.
10. Keats, *You Might as Well Live*, 234. At the time the Communist Party USA was legal, but a "premature anti-Fascist," or PAF, *might* be a Communist.
11. Dorothy Parker, interview, Popular Arts Project, Part 2 (audiotape, 1959), Columbia University Oral History Research Office, New York. See Transcript, page 11, courtesy of Joan Franklin, Cinema Sound Ltd., New York City.
12. J. Donald Adams, "Speaking of Books," *New York Times Book Review*, June 1, 1944, VII:2.
13. Quoted in Richard Moody, *Lillian Hellman, Playwright* (New York: Bobbs-Merrill, 1972), 134–35; also Kinney, *Dorothy Parker*, 43.
14. "Dorothy Parker, 73, Literary Wit Dies," *New York Times*, June 8, 1967, 39.
15. Adams, "Speaking of Books," VII:2.
16. *New York Daily News*, June 13, 1947; *New York Herald Tribune*, November 3, 1947.
17. Richard Layman, *Shadow Man: The Life of Dashiell Hammett* (New York: Harcourt, Brace, Jovanovich, 1981), 208.
18. Hellman, *Unfinished Woman*, 214.
19. Edward L. Barrett, *The Tenney Committee: Legislative Investigation of Subversive Activities in California* (Ithaca, N.Y.: Cornell University Press, 1951), 355–60; also, *Red Channels: The Report of Communist Influence in Radio and Television* (New York: American Business Consultants, 1950), 189–90.
20. *United States of America v. Judith Coplon, Defendant* Washington, D.C., District Court, 1949 (microfilm ed., Fund for the Republic, New York); also see Lauren Kessler, *Clever Girl: Elizabeth Bentley, the Spy Who Ushered in the McCarthy Era* (New York: HarperCollins, 2003).
21. Quoted in Meade, *Dorothy Parker*, 342.
22. Federal Bureau of Investigation memorandum, Los Angeles office, May 8, 1951, Subject: Interview with Dorothy Parker in West Los Angeles, Parker file no. 100-56075.
23. Parker, interview, Popular Arts Project.
24. Frank Crowninshield, "Crowninshield in the Cub's Den," *Vogue*, September 15, 1944, 162–63, 177–201.
25. Reviews of *The Betrothal*, *Vanity Fair*, January 1919, 33; and of *Toby's Bow*, *Vanity Fair*, April 1919, 41.
26. Reviews of *A Good Bad Woman* and *39 East*, *Vanity Fair*, June 1919, 100; and of *Tillie*, *Vanity Fair*, March 1919, 30.

27. Reviews of *Caesar's Wife* and *The Son-Daughter*, *Vanity Fair*, January 1920, 36, 94; "Vanity Fair Editors Out," *New York Times*, January 13, 1920, 10.
28. Dave Smith, "Dorothy Parker and Friends: Reminiscences of the Algonquin," *Los Angeles Times*, May 4, 1976, IV:1.
29. Dorothy Parker, "Life's Valentines: Mr. Avery Hopwood," *Life*, March 16, 1922, 3.
30. Kinney, *Dorothy Parker*, 18.
31. William Rose Benét, "Deep, at That," *Saturday Review*, December 12, 1936, 5; also Kinney, *Dorothy Parker*, 19.
32. Elmer Rice, *Minority Report: An Autobiography* (New York: Simon and Schuster, 1963), 204.
33. Ibid., 203.
34. Ibid.
35. Robert Benchley, *Life*, December 18, 1924; Alexander Woollcott, *New York Telegram and Sun*, December 1, 1924; Stark Young, "*Close Harmony*," *New York Times*, December 2, 1924.
36. Young, "*Close Harmony*."
37. Quoted in Keats, *You Might as Well Live*, 102.
38. Meade, *Dorothy Parker*, 138. *Close Harmony* was first copyrighted as *Soft Music* in 1924 and published by Samuel French as *Close Harmony* in 1929.
39. John Farrar, *The Bookman*, March 1928.
40. Review of *As Husbands Go*, *New Yorker*, March 21, 1931, 34–35; and review of *Getting Married*, *New Yorker*, April 11, 1931, 32, 34.
41. "The Theatre: Just around Pooh Corner," *New Yorker*, February 14, 1931, 33; and "The Theatre: In, or Around, Desperate Straits," *New Yorker*, February 8, 1931, 22.
42. William Wright, *Lillian Hellman: The Image, the Woman* (New York: Simon and Schuster, 1986), 94.
43. Unpublished typescript of *The Happiest Man*, 28. The "First Act of Dorothy Parker's Version" is from the agent's original typescript, in Restricted Material Scripts 637, Billy Rose Theater Collection, New York Public Library for the Performing Arts.
44. Kinney, *Dorothy Parker*, 41.
45. Stark Young, "*The Searching Wind*," *New York Times*, April 1, 1944.
46. Meade, *Dorothy Parker*, 334.
47. *Variety*, April 12, 1949; Brooks Atkinson, *New York Times*, April 13, 1949.
48. Quoted in Arthur F. Kinney, *The Coast of Illyria: A Play in Three Acts by Dorothy Parker and Ross Evans* (Iowa City: University of Iowa Press, 1990), 69; see also Helen Sheehy, *Margo: The Life and Theatre of Margo Jones* (Dallas: Southern Methodist University Press, 1989), 184–86.
49. Ward Morehouse, *New York World Telegram and Sun*, October 18, 1953; see also Keats, *You Might as Well Live*, 262.
50. Meade, *Dorothy Parker*, 350.
51. Brooks Atkinson, "*The Ladies of the Corridor*," *New York Times*, October 22, 1953, 33, and November 1, 1953, II:1.
52. Harold Clurman, *All People Are Famous* (New York: Harcourt Brace, 1974), 219.
53. Quoted in Keats, *You Might as Well Live*, 264–65. Brooks Atkinson, "Hotel Windows: 'The Ladies of the Corridor' Who Have Money, but No Personal Resources," *New York Times*, November 1, 1953, II:1; also Eric Bentley, "How Deep Are the Roots," in *What Is*

Theatre? Incorporating The Dramatic Event and Other Reviews, 1944–1967, 2nd ed. (New York: Hill and Wang, 2000), 110–14.
54. Quoted in Keats, *You Might as Well Live*, 264–65; also Dorothy Parker and Arnaud d'Usseau, *The Ladies of the Corridor* (New York: Viking Press, 1954), 120.
55. Marion Capron, "Interview with Dorothy Parker," *Paris Review* 4, no. 13 (1956): 84.
56. Quoted in Wright, *Lillian Hellman*, 267.
57. Quoted in Meade, *Dorothy Parker*, 360.
58. Quoted in Meade, *Dorothy Parker*, 210; also Keats, *You Might as Well Live*, 253.
59. "McCarthy Calls Three for Book Inquiry," *New York Times*, March 7, 1953, 22. Parker was known to say "What fresh hell is this?" when confronted with a ringing telephone or a doorbell.
60. Federal Bureau of Investigation memorandum, from SAC, New York office, to FBI Director, May 8, 1951, Parker file nos. 100-56075 and 100-32635.
61. Dashiell Hammett testified on March 4, 1953. See State Department Information Service-Information Centers, *Executive Sessions of the Senate Permanent Subcommittee of the Committee on Government Operations*, vol. 1, 83rd Cong., 1st sess. (Washington, D.C.: Government Printing Office, 2003), 945–48.
62. Capron, "Interview with Dorothy Parker," 82–83.
63. Federal Bureau of Investigation memorandum, from SAC, New York office, to FBI Director, January 8, 1955, Parker file no. 100-56075.
64. *Daily Worker*, July 28, 1951.
65. Federal Bureau of Investigation memorandum, New York office, January 5, 1956, Parker file no. 100-98708. See Testimony of Jean Muir, June 15, 1953, *Investigation of Communist Activities New York Area—Part 1*. House of Representatives Subcommittee of the Committee on Un-American Activities, 84th Cong., 2nd sess. (Washington, D.C.: Government Printing Office, 1953), 1–18.
66. *New York Post*, March 29, 1955. Marion Capron also described in 1956 what she called Parker's "Hogarthian" apartment in the Volney Hotel; see "Interview with Dorothy Parker," 73.
67. Federal Bureau of Investigation memorandum, FBI Director to SAC, New York office, February 23, 1955, Parker file no. 100-56075.
68. "Where'd the Money Go?" *Newsweek*, 25–26.
69. Testimony of Dorothy Parker, February 25, 1955, 400–414; also, Parker's testimony is referenced in Federal Bureau of Investigation memorandum, New York Office, March 28, 1955, Parker file no. 100-98708.
70. Charles Grutzner, "Red Fronts Face Fund Appeal Ban," *New York Times*, February 26, 1955, 1, 5. The refusal of the JAFRC's executive secretary and board of directors to comply with a subpoena to hand over the group's records resulted in contempt citations. See Ellen Schrecker, *Many Are the Crimes: McCarthyism in America* (Princeton, N.J.: Princeton University Press, 1998), 128. Also, Donald Ogden Stewart and his second wife, Ella Winter, who had been identified as a Communist agent, avoided subpoenas by moving to England.
71. Hellman, *Unfinished Woman*, 218–19.
72. Federal Bureau of Investigation memorandum, SAC, New York Office, to FBI Director, May 8, 1951, Parker file no. 100-56075. See also Meade, *Dorothy Parker*, 271.
73. Frewin, *The Late Mrs. Dorothy Parker*, 261.

74. Federal Bureau of Investigation memorandum, SAC, New York Office, to FBI Director, April 25, 1955, Parker file no. 100-56075. Even though the Washington bureau initiated no further memoranda of investigations into Parker's activities after 1955, the New York field office maintained its file no. 100-98708 until May 1956. The final entry is dated May 4, 1956.
75. Hellman, *Unfinished Woman*, 223.
76. Moody, *Lillian Hellman*, 339.
77. "Dorothy Parker, 73, Literary Wit Dies," *New York Times*, June 8, 1967, 1, 38–39; "Dorothy Parker Recalled as Wit," *New York Times*, June 10, 1967, 33.
78. "Dorothy Parker Recalled as Wit," *New York Times*, June 10, 1967, 33.
79. Quoted in Moody, *Lillian Hellman*, 340.
80. Capron, "Interview with Dorothy Parker," 87.
81. Meade, *Dorothy Parker*, 341.

A Paradigm for New Play Development

The Albee-Barr-Wilder Playwrights Unit

—DAVID A. CRESPY

Albarwild Inc.'s Playwrights Unit would never have been successful without the unique partnership of its off- and on-Broadway producers Richard Barr and Clinton Wilder and playwright Edward Albee. The Unit was initially financially dependent on income from Albee's *Who's Afraid of Virginia Woolf?*, and the Unit's fortunes were directly tied to Albee's success as a new American playwright and his own explorations of dramaturgical form and content. From 1962 through 1971, Albee had the rare opportunity to serve as a co-producer of his works on Broadway. This fact, coupled with Albee's remarkable early success as a new, young playwright on Broadway, supported and justified to Richard Barr his own central notion regarding the theatre—namely, that the playwright and the play are the unifying element of any theatrical production.[1] Because of the initiatory nature of much of Albee's work, and because Albee did this experimentation in full public view on Broadway with little or no apology, the idea that American playwrights deserved a forum in which to learn and take risks in full (but perhaps controlled) public view was central to the Albee-Barr-Wilder (ABW) producing philosophy. Add to that Barr's interest in the new absurdist work of European authors, including Beckett, Genet, Ionesco, and Arrabal, and it is clear that the ABW producing partnership evolved a remarkably fertile environment for new playwrights and their experimentation in the 1960s. The ABW Playwrights Unit was the jewel in the crown of that producing organization because its work represented the ABW producing philosophy at its most elemental and most important stage—at the point of discovery of new voices for the theatre.[2]

Albee's initial commercial success (in particular with his plays *Zoo Story* and *Who's Afraid of Virginia Woolf?*), the strong critical response to his work, and the free hand Albee experienced as a producing partner to Barr and Wilder captured the imagination of the New York theatre community and stimulated an atmosphere in which new plays and new playwrights were suddenly hot ticket items. The Playwrights Unit was a significant manifestation of Albee's influence, and Albee's success contributed to the much larger not-for-profit business of new play development, which grew out of the off-off-Broadway movement and became fully realized in the creation of the National Playwrights Conference at the Eugene O'Neill Theatre Center. Ironically, Albee has forsworn the business of new play development, but his success as a young playwright and his enthusiasm for supporting new work himself was its springboard.[3] When it comes to the training of playwrights in the theatre, his guiding instruction, now and during the tenure of the Playwrights Unit, is, "Every time you write a play, try to fail . . . do what you don't know you can do."[4] This mantra was the basis for the work at the Playwrights Unit, and Albee's words echoed those spoken by off-off-Broadway impresario Joe Cino to his playwrights at the Caffe Cino: "Do what you have to do."

In the 1960s, the Playwrights Unit provided a meeting place between the professional but somewhat moribund off-Broadway theatre and the freewheeling experimentation of the off-off-Broadway scene. For nearly ten years it provided a professional workshop situation for playwrights. From its ranks came Louis Auchincloss, Mart Crowley, Charles Dizenzo, Gene Feist, Paul Foster, Frank Gagliano, John Guare, A. R. Gurney, LeRoi Jones, Lee Kalcheim, Adrienne Kennedy, Terrence McNally, Leonard Melfi, Howard Moss, James Prideaux, Sam Shepard, Megan Terry, Jean-Claude van Itallie, Lanford Wilson, Doric Wilson, and Paul Zindel. The significance of this group extends far beyond its brief existence as a producing entity. As a playwrights' workshop, the Unit served as an early model for such organizations as Playwrights Horizons and the Center Theatre Group at the Mark Taper Forum (both organizations were founded by Playwrights Unit managers) and, to a certain extent, the playwrights' laboratories of organizations such as Circle Repertory Theatre and the New York Shakespeare Festival.

Albee's point of view regarding new play development was that a new play, if it is going to work, will work, and if it doesn't, it wasn't a very good play in the first place. This is a radical departure from the current model of new play development, which seeks to "fix" plays through incrementally more complex concert and staged readings, workshops, and minimal productions. Albee attacked this model of new play development in a September 1994 interview for *American Theatre:* "It is to de-ball the plays; to castrate them; to smooth down all the rough edges so they can't cut, can't hurt. It's to make them commercially tolerable to a smug audience. It's not to make plays any better. Most playwrights who write a good play write it from the beginning."[5] Working from this perspective, Albee, Barr, and Wilder tested plays at the Playwrights Unit, at the Cherry Lane, and on Broadway by the fire of full production. They were able to do this because their production budgets were tightly managed.[6] If the play worked and the critics were receptive, they kept it open; if it did not work and was losing money, they closed it as quickly as possible and went on to the next play (Albee later complained that Barr was perhaps too eager to close a play because of poor audience response).[7] The scripts were, in the opinion of Albee, Barr, and Wilder, as finished as they needed to be for production, as Barr insisted when he was interviewed for an article in *Theatre Arts* in 1961:

That's the first thing we've learned, or relearned: We are not going into rehearsal until the script we plan to open with, on Broadway, is in our hands. There will be changes made in that script, of course, but they'll be minor changes, not the terrible, frightening business of trying to create a whole new second or third act between New Haven and New York. Which brings us right up to the second point. If you start out with a finished play, there is no need for the week in Wilmington or wherever, and the two weeks in Philadelphia or Boston, where you're bound to lose a substantial amount of money.[8]

Barr and Wilder were certainly interested in the experimentation of the off-off Broadway, but as professionals their focus was always on the development of scripts for the commercial theatre. In that sense, they "invented" play development as it is practiced today, moving scripts from workshop to professional production. Their form of development, however, was focused on full (albeit inexpensive) productions rather than on a series of incrementally more sophisticated readings.

Their reasoning was simple: they were trying to avoid what was then the standard practice of bringing a new play to Broadway—the out-of-town tryout. Plays were tested for critical reception in places like Hartford, New Haven, or Boston to determine what additional changes needed to be made to the script before the all-important New York production. According to Barr and Wilder, the out-of-town tryout was not terribly useful as a means of developing a finished script: "And so you go into production and suffer through the ridiculous agony of having the author—and the director and the actors and various friends, enemies and people you meet in hotel lobbies—rewrite a three-act play in New Haven or Boston or Philadelphia. It's absolutely insane—and it's not really necessary."[9] For Barr, the place to test new plays was off Broadway at his Cherry Lane Theatre and at the Playwrights Unit; he also initiated the preview performance process on Broadway, providing audiences with an opportunity to judge a play on its own merits before a review changed their minds. A successful off-Broadway production provided a far better indication of what New York audiences would accept and support. Barr was convinced that if he liked a script enough to produce it in New York, it was as finished as it needed to be.

On the opposite extreme from the out-of-town tryout is the current model of the play development process with its endless cycle of play readings. The primary difference between how plays were developed in the past and how they are developed now is the difference between the closed professional readings of the past, which led to full production, and the current model of public readings of new work followed by endless discussions and criticism leading to more readings. The open reading or workshop production is not terribly popular among playwrights, as David Kahn and Donna Breed, authors of *Scriptwork: A Director's Guide to New Play Development,* explain:

Any playwright, director, actor, designer, or audience member will prefer a full production to a workshop. Workshops are a means to that end, or at least they should be. Too often, workshops or other development "processes" are excuses to avoid the difficult and risky business of producing new plays. Consequently, there is frequently cited backlash against play development workshops conducted without the prospect of future production, or workshopping a play unnecessarily so that it becomes "developed to death."[10]

Play readings often involve post-reading discussions with the audience, a process many playwrights abhor. Douglas Anderson, in his *Drama Review* article "The American Dream Machine: Thirty Years of New Play Development in America," argues that the new play development process of play readings led to plays that are wordy, untheatrical, and designed primarily to appeal to dramaturgy by committee. Plays that enter into that process as challenging, nonrealistic, nonlinear works that experiment with form and content become realistic, linear works that follow along traditional dramaturgical techniques.[11]

In contrast to this current model of play development, Albarwild's Playwrights Unit was run more as a miniature of its other venue, the Cherry Lane Theatre, than as a workshop per se. Although there were certainly readings at the Unit (they occurred primarily toward the end of its existence), the focus was on production. Each play received a full production on a minimal budget with professional directors and actors. While the production values were certainly not at the level of plays produced in ABW's off-Broadway venue, the plays received very nearly full scenic values, including lighting, sound cues, properties, costuming, and scenic elements. There was little interference from either the producers or the managers of the Unit. As many of the playwrights who were interviewed for this study could attest, the primary relationship was one between playwright and director. While there is evidence of mimeographed handouts for discussion purposes, there were rarely the post-production discussions that have since become a familiar part of the new play development process.

The Unit was the brainchild of Richard Barr, and it was Barr's skill as a producer and his fundamental belief in the playwright that provided the impetus for the Unit's creation. Barr's idealism as a producer grew out of his initial theatrical experiences with Orson Welles's Mercury Theatre. "I used to carry Orson's lunch from Longchamps up to the theatre," he once recalled. Barr took part in Welles's radio broadcast "The War of the Worlds" and went with Welles to Hollywood, where he was executive assistant on the filming of *Citizen Kane*.[12] Barr actually appeared in *Citizen Kane* and caused a continuity problem; in the film he played a reporter but was caught in separate frames with and without his hat (perhaps ending an important career in film).[13] Barr's quixotic quest to produce the absurdists on Broadway and develop risky new work off- and off-off-Broadway were definitely influenced by Welles's mentorship.[14]

During World War II, Barr served as a captain in the Air Force from 1941 to 1946, heading its Motion Picture Unit in California.[15] After the war he served as dialogue director on several films. Thereafter he decided to give up an acting career and went into directing and producing. From 1946 to 1948 he staged various summer stock productions. He directed José Ferrer in *Volpone*, Richard Whorf in *Richard III*, and Francis Lederer in *Arms and the Man*. In the 1950s his Broadway productions, none particularly successful, included *Hotel Paradiso*, starring Bert Lahr; *Fallen Angels*, starring Nancy Walker; and a triple bill titled *All in One* that consisted of Leonard Bernstein's *Trouble in Tahiti*, a Paul Draper dance program, and Tennessee Williams's *Twenty-seven Wagons Full of Cotton*.

Barr left the Broadway theatrical firm of Bowden, Barr, and Bullock in 1959 to found Theatre 1960 off Broadway with H. B. Lutz and Harry Joe Brown Jr.[16] Their first production was an evening of two one-act plays, Beckett's *Krapp's Last Tape* and Albee's first play, *The Zoo Story*, at the Provincetown Playhouse on January 14, 1960. The choice of one-act plays, particularly those of new writers, was calculated. Barr elaborates: "Take men like Williams and Inge . . . they wrote dozens of one-act plays. We want to capture the possibilities of such men while they are still in the one-act stage, to speed the gestation period to Broadway."[17] The decision to premiere Albee's first play was Barr's most inspired. In it he confirmed to himself and the critics that it was indeed possible to use off-Broadway as a springboard for important new playwrights. Several times over the years he stated that his continued support of new plays was part of a search for another Albee.

Clinton Wilder, Barr's partner for much of his producing career, was, according to Albee, "a dilettante, in the very best sense of the word." While certainly the financial heavyweight in the ABW partnership, Wilder was also an experienced Broadway producer. He was born Clinton Eugene Wilder Jr. on July 7, 1920, the son of Clinton Eugene and Frances (Kornreich) Wilder. Wilder's father was a successful engineer and manufacturer. Wilder attended Lawrenceville School in New Jersey and spent three years at Princeton. Serving in the U.S. Army, he manned antiaircraft artillery during 1942 and 1943 and served in the Army Air Force from 1943 to 1945, appearing in its production of *Winged Victory* (1943–44) during World War II. Wilder was a member of the Actor's Equity Association, the League of New York Theatres, the League of Off-Broadway Theatres, and the Theatre Development Fund (he was both a founder and director of the latter).[18]

Wilder began his career in the theatre as the stage manager for the 1947 tour of *Heartsong* and for *A Streetcar Named Desire* at the Ethel Barrymore Theatre on Broadway (December 3, 1947). He then became associated with Cheryl Crawford in the production of *Regina,* Marc Blitzstein's musical adaptation of Lillian Hellman's *Little Foxes,* produced at the Forty-sixth Street Theatre in 1949.[19] He then produced Max Shulman and Robert Paul Smith's *The Tender Trap* at the Longacre Theatre and (with George Axelrod as co-producer) Gore Vidal's *Visit to a Small Planet* at the Booth Theatre. He produced, with Norris Houghton and T. Edward Hambleton, their Phoenix Theatre production of Luigi Pirandello's *Six Characters in Search of an Author* in 1955. In 1957, in concert with Donald Albery, Wilder presented *The World of Suzie Wong* at the Prince of Wales Theatre, London. In 1961 he joined with Richard Barr to found Theatre 1961, and thereafter, until the founding of the Playwrights Unit, he co-produced with Barr until 1968.[20]

The third partner in the producing partnership was, of course, Edward Albee. The inclusion of a playwright in a major producing team was, and remains, very rare. One of Albee's more famous predecessors in this regard was Eugene O'Neill, who contributed greatly to the producing decisions made at the

Provincetown Playhouse in the 1920s.[21] Albee's first play, *The Zoo Story,* was produced in Berlin at the Schiller Theatre Werkstatt on September 28, 1959. Shortly thereafter, Richard Barr produced *The Zoo Story* at the Provincetown Playhouse on January 14, 1960, and in London at the Arts Theatre on August 25, 1960. Albee's *The Death of Bessie Smith* also had its premiere in Berlin, at the Schlosspark Theatre, and was later produced by Barr at the York Playhouse. *The Sandbox* premiered with four one-act plays titled *Four in One* at the Jazz Gallery. Albee's *Fam and Yam* was produced at the White Barn at Westport, Connecticut, that summer. Albee's *The American Dream* was paired with William Flanagan's musical *Bartleby* at the York Playhouse in 1961. Albee's first full-length work was the three-act *Who's Afraid of Virginia Woolf?,* which was produced on Broadway at the Billy Rose Theatre on October 13, 1962, and subsequently on tour in the United States and in London. Albee began his producing career with Barr and Wilder with Ugo Betti's *Corruption in the Palace of Justice* at the Cherry Lane Theatre under the aegis of Barr and Wilder's Theatre 1964. Albee shortly thereafter participated in the organization of the Playwrights Unit.[22]

The Unit was founded on September 29, 1963, the year the Ford Foundation established its funding program for playwrights. Albee, Barr, and Wilder had been producing new works at the Cherry Lane Theatre before this time, but in 1963 the Village South Theatre on Vandam Street became the home of the Playwrights Unit and was leased exclusively for the development of new plays. The initial funding did not come from a foundation but rather from the profits of Albee's Broadway production of *Who's Afraid of Virginia Woolf?* Later Albee and Barr did seek and receive funding from the Rockefeller Foundation,[23] but initially the Unit was funded privately through Albee's generosity. Free of the financial constraints that plague such workshops today, the Unit reflected the idealism and genuine support for writers at the outset of what could be considered a "golden age" of American drama from the early 1960s through the late 1980s.

Of the dramatists mentioned above whose first plays were produced by the Unit, more than fifteen have sustained important careers writing in the theatre and have garnered the highest accolades and critical acclaim the American theatre has to offer. While not every play that came out of the Unit was significant, it certainly provided fertile ground for the stimulation of playwriting talent. If the measure of success for a play development group is the sustained and significant careers of the writers it develops, then the Playwrights Unit was an unmitigated success. If one adds to that achievement the production of two of America's seminal works of alternative theatre, LeRoi Jones's *Dutchman* and Mart Crowley's *The Boys in the Band,* then the Playwrights Unit and the producing philosophy of Albee, Barr, and Wilder remain unparalleled in recent theatrical history. For not only was the Albarwild producing team providing a laboratory for new work; they were also producing that work professionally at the Cherry Lane Theatre and other theatre spaces—work, it must be added, that could only be termed explosively experimental for its time.

The Playwrights Unit had its beginnings well before the initial meeting of playwrights on Sunday, September 29, 1963. The producing organization, Theatre 1960–1971 (the name changed each year), began with Barr's production of Albee's *Zoo Story* in 1959, which was paired with Beckett's *Krapp's Last Tape* at the Provincetown Playhouse. Later, in addition to producing new plays by lesser-known playwrights, Albee, Barr, and Wilder underwrote a series of Monday-evening productions. John Keating describes this enterprise in his 1963 *New York Times* article "Action Speaks Louder . . . ":

> Broadening their search for the avant-garde playwrights they felt the theatre was ignoring, Barr and Wilder also put on occasional, admission-free Monday night performances of works by unknowns whose talents they admired but felt were not yet ready for regular production before a paying audience. Over the last two seasons, they have underwritten four of these "Monday Nights." The Playwrights Unit is a direct outgrowth of this project. Last month, they issued invitations to 35 young playwrights. Twenty-three writers answered the call, bringing a total of 20 scripts with them.[24]

Plays produced in this early period include *A Toy for the Clowns* by Gene Feist (founder of the Roundabout Theatre in New York City), *Chit Chat on a Rat* by C. Skrivanek Atherton, *Prometheus Rebound* by Lawrence Wunderlich, *Ex-Miss Copper Queen on a Set of Pills* by Megan Terry, *This Side of the Door* by Terrence McNally, and *Like Other People* by Jack Owen. However, as Theatre 1964, the triumvirate of Albee, Barr, and Wilder procured the Village South Theatre at 15 Vandam Street, a small, 199-seat off-off-Broadway house that still exists as a working off-Broadway theatre space, and with the managerial skills of director/literary agent Edward Parone they began the first season of the Playwrights Unit. Young playwrights culled from Barr's enormous script collection and from his visits to the off-off-Broadway theatres and cafés were invited to participate. Twenty-four plays were performed in the Unit's initial year. The first successful production, LeRoi Jones's *Dutchman,* directed by Parone, transferred off Broadway to the Cherry Lane Theatre with phenomenal success. The Unit produced Jean-Claude van Itallie's first play, *War,* also with great success, although it did not move immediately to another production. Other plays of the Unit's 1963–64 season that were later produced by Albee, Barr, and Wilder include Lee Kalcheim's *A Party for Divorce* and *Match Play* (produced at the Provincetown Playhouse October 11, 1966), Lawrence Osgood's *Pigeons,* and

THE ALBEE-BARR-WILDER PLAYWRIGHTS UNIT

Frank Gagliano's *Conerico Was Here to Stay* (produced as part of the series Ten New American Plays at the Cherry Lane Theatre on March 3, 1965).

Running underneath the producing decisions made by Albee, Barr, and Wilder was the conviction that the playwright was the single most important artist in the theatre, and its corollary, that the production of plays ought to revolve around the playwright's vision. In her 1968 *New York Times Magazine* article "Triple Threat On, Off, and Off-Off Broadway," Barbara La Fontaine quoted Barr on this subject:

Barr says crisply, "A play needs a firm hand. Sometimes it is in the wrong place."—i.e., when the playwright's is tentative, being new or perhaps spectacularly poor, the hand may be that of a famous director, a star or a backer's wife. But isn't a production a cooperative effort? "Indeed it is," Barr says, "but so is war, and I would like to see the individual in a war speak up and say, 'I'm going to go *this* way.' There is a hierarchy of command, and it should stem from the playwright's intention."[25]

Given this statement, the guidance of the Unit was hands-off, with the playwright in charge of his or her own production. The day-to-day management of the Unit was left to its managing directors: Edward Parone, Charles (Chuck) Gnys, Robert Moss, and Bruce Hoover. All four were energetic theatre practitioners, primarily directors, who shared with the ABW producing team the conviction that the playwright provided the guiding vision in producing the play.

Edward Parone was the first manager of the Unit, guiding its first season from September 1963 to May 1964. An experienced theatre professional, Parone had served as production supervisor of special projects at the Phoenix Theatre and as an assistant to the producers—T. Edward Hambleton and Norris Houghton—for their production of Strindberg's *Miss Julie* and *The Stronger*. Parone then joined the staff of William Liebling and Audrey Wood as a play reader, and later he became an agent at the William Morris Agency. While at William Morris he brought Albee's *Zoo Story* to the attention of Richard Barr and started Barr off on his cycle of Albee productions.

Parone then moved to California, where he directed all of Albee's short plays. Following this he was invited by Barr and Albee to serve as managing director for the Playwrights Unit. Parone was the original director of Jones's *Dutchman* at the Playwrights Unit and at the Cherry Lane.[26] He also directed Lawrence Osgood's *Pigeons* at the Playwrights Unit. After Parone left the Unit, he founded the playwrights workshop of Mark Taper Forum, initially producing an evening of plays from the Playwrights Unit titled *Collision Course*, which he later published as an anthology of plays under that same title.

Chuck Gnys, the manager of the Playwrights Unit from September 1964 through May 1970, was its longest-term and most important influence outside Albee, Barr, and Wilder. A native of Central Falls, Rhode Island, Gnys served as the company manager of the Broadway productions of *Camelot* and *Kwamina* and was a production assistant for *The Perfect Setup, Viva Madison Avenue,* and *The Poker Game.* He directed Ann Jellicoe's *The Knack* at Dinner Theatres of America and served as the administrative producer of Jerome Robbins's American Theatre Laboratory. Gnys directed more productions at the Playwrights Unit than any other director involved in its productions, including *Up to Thursday* and *4-H Club* by Sam Shepard, *Hunting the Jingo Bird* by Kenneth Pressman, *The Rape of Bunny Stuntz* by A. R. Gurney Jr., *A Great Career* by Charles Dizenzo, *The Club Bedroom* by Louis Auchincloss, *The Palace at 4 AM* by Howard Moss, and *Watercolor* and *Criss-Crossing* by Philip Magdalany. Gnys also staged both *Up to Thursday* and *Hunting the Jingo Bird* at the Cherry Lane Theatre for Theatre 1965's New Playwrights Series. He produced Emanuel Peluso's *Good Day* and *The Exhaustion of Our Son's Love* in a double bill at the Cherry Lane. In 1970 Gnys directed Philip Magdalany's *Watercolor* and *Criss-Crossing* on Broadway at the American National Theatre and Academy (ANTA) as a production of the Playwright's Unit.

Following Gnys in 1970 was Robert Moss, the indefatigable director and producer who ran the Unit with Bruce Hoover, a director and professional stage manager, until its end in 1971. Moss spent four years as the production manager of the Association of Producing Artists Repertory Company. In 1966 he directed Cliff Arquette in a summer tour of *You Can't Take It with You*. In 1967 he staged *Two Gentlemen of Verona* for the Los Angeles Theatre in the Parks program. He directed Stephen Jacobsen's *Needs* and Kenneth Pressman's *For Breakfast, Mr. Sachs* at the Playwrights Unit. Moss directed Louis Auchincloss's *The Club Bedroom* for the ANTA Matinee Series, *Summertime* for the American Academy of Dramatic Art, *Room Service* for the Comedy Club, *The Marriage of Figaro* for the McCarter Repertory Company, *Tunnel of Love* for Dinner Theatres of America, and *As You Like It* for Equity Library Theatre.

With a mailing list borrowed from the Playwrights Unit, Moss then founded Playwrights Horizons at the Clark Center for the Performing Arts. In a very real sense, Playwrights Horizons sprang forth directly from the Unit's mailing list, which Moss took as his final payment as the Unit's last manager. According to Edward Cohen, the former associate artistic director of Jewish Repertory Theatre and a playwright at the Playwrights Unit, Moss carried with him from the Unit the conviction that "if a new play had a page of talent, he would produce it."[27] It was perhaps this guiding principle that later led one reporter to

Figure 1. *Left to right:* Mimi Levine (Sherry), Stephanie Gordon (Terry), Sam Shepard (playwright), Harvey Keitel (1st Man), Lee Kissman (Young Man), Richard Mansfield (2nd Man), Robert F. Lyons (Larry), and Kevin O'Connor (Harry) on the set of Sam Shepard's *Up to Thursday.* Photo by Alix Jeffrey, courtesy Harvard Theatre Collection, Houghton Library, © Harvard University.

call the Unit "surely the most generous and effective theatre workshop in the country."[28]

Speaking of Gnys's management, Richard Lipsett, a production assistant and script reader at the Unit, reinforced the notion that Albee, Barr, and Wilder left Gnys and his playwrights to their own devices.[29] While the "carte blanche" attitude of the producers with regard to both the playwright's work and Gnys's management provided a certain degree of freedom, the producers were not entirely absent from the Unit's activities. Barr directed several productions at the Unit, all three producers attended many of its performances, and Albee, noticing a lack of member playwrights at performances at the Unit, wrote a general letter to the Unit playwrights exhorting them to read each other's scripts and attend performances. In an interview, Albee offered the reasoning behind his letter:

A very important thing was the fact that I wanted each of the playwrights to involve themselves in the work of the other playwrights. On the understanding that you learn not only from what happens to your work but from following through what happens to another playwright's work—you might learn something constructive and useful about revision or lack of revision or digging your heels in. I wanted them to be helpful to one another, not only to themselves.[30]

Despite Albee's best hopes that the writers at his Unit would grow into a genuine community of writers, this was not happening. And Albee had growing concerns about internal operations of the Unit, the quality of the work, and the decisions regarding which plays were being produced. This led him to submit his own short play *Box* to the Unit under the assumed name of Rayne Endars. Gnys's subsequent rejection of this script, while later dismissed as unimportant in a *New York Times* article about the Unit's activities, was the primary reason for Albee's decision to remove Gnys from his position.[31] In 1970 Gnys left to direct a rock musical, *The Survival of Saint Joan,* which had its beginnings at the Playwrights Unit, and went on to a successful career managing actors, musicians, and other performers under the aegis of Curtis Brown Management.

Despite the decision to fire Gnys, interference from the ABW producing management was minimal over the course of the Unit's existence. In fact, the producers' decision to keep a low profile was a conscious one. Albee stresses this in Keating's article for the *New York Times:*

"We hope the playwrights themselves will dictate the operation," he [Albee] said. "What we're going to do is to provide a theatre to work in, a stage, actors, a director, whatever we can do to be helpful. We are not going to say anything about the kind of work that should be done. If a man wants to do something that seems completely incomprehensible to us, fine." Mr. Albee stressed the fact that the unit will not be a course in playwriting—"You can't teach that," he said—but he will be on hand to discuss, analyze and advise any writer who wants his help. "It will be a workshop operation," he said.[32]

The absence of Albee, Barr, or Wilder was of course a double-edged sword, for on the one hand there were none of the pressures associated with producing under the aegis of a famous producing group, while on the other hand there was little of the hoped-for advice, good or otherwise, that was expected or desired from the playwrights.

Of the three producing partners, Albee was perhaps the least available for consultation. Playwright and screenwriter James Prideaux offers this remembrance, caught at a moment after a successful production of his play *Postcards* at the Playwrights Unit, a moment when Prideaux was particularly hungry for a response from Albee himself:

THE ALBEE-BARR-WILDER PLAYWRIGHTS UNIT

    On the way home, walking through Greenwich Village, I glanced into the window of a dusty old bookstore and there he [Albee] was, sitting in the back, bent over a book. For a moment he looked up and our eyes met. I was dying to go in, to tell him how much I admired his work, but he gave no sign of recognition and looked right down again. I walked on, a little saddened. Surely he must have thought something of me and my play or I wouldn't be a part of his Playwrights Unit. Later Richard told me he hadn't read *Postcards*. It was unusual that he had stopped into the Cherry Lane at all. In the years to come, I was never to forget that it was through Edward's Playwrights Unit that my career as a playwright was made possible. How could I not be grateful to him for that?[33]

It must be added that while other writers at the Unit had similar stories of only seeing Albee in the back of darkened theatres or catching a rare glimpse of him as he entered or left with brief business, others, such as Kenneth Pressman, remember Albee as a motivating force in playwriting at that time.[34] Playwright John Guare, whose *To Wally Pantoni We Leave a Credenza* was produced at the Unit, considered Albee a sort of playwright-hero who had battled the forces of Broadway and won.[35] Guare went so far as to state that Albee figured even more importantly than Barr as the motivating force behind the Unit, for even though his was a fleeting presence, it gave the Unit its notoriety and importance in the milieu of the off-off-Broadway movement.

    In 1970, after Gnys's departure, the Unit's management was handed to Robert Moss, who had previously directed several productions at the Unit, and to his partner, Bruce Hoover, a director and Broadway stage manager. Moss managed the Unit until May 1971, producing the plays of Michael Carton, Edward M. Cohen, David Trainer, Steven Jacobsen, Doric Wilson, Michael Wilkes, and Kenneth Pressman. The Unit closed shortly after the critical and financial failure of Albee's *All Over*, which was directed by John Gielgud on Broadway. The critical failure of *All Over* was an immediate financial cause for the Unit's closure, but the very nature of producing in New York City had changed since the heady days of the early 1960s. By 1966 the three producers had already made a major outlay of over $120,000 to run the Unit in its three years of existence. The budget of the Unit grew from its initial outlay of $23,232.88 in 1964 to $29,045.33 in 1967, with a 25 percent increase in the cost of its operation in three years. In the summer of 1968, Albarwild Theatre Arts, Inc. received $197,000 in funding from the Rockefeller Foundation, $65,000 of which was to be matched. Of those funds, $32,000 was used to maintain the Playwrights Unit, while $165,000 was to be used to cover operations at the Cherry Lane Theatre.[36] Thus by 1968 the cost of running the Unit had increased by at least 38 percent. By 1971, the year the Unit closed, the costs of operation had reached $1,000 a week, or $52,000 a year, by Albee's own estimates.[37]

{ 43 }

Figure 2. *Left to right:* Edwin Patrick Aldridge (director), Mary Farrell (Her), John Guare (playwright), Eugene R. Wood (Him), Jeffrey Siggins (Wally Pantoni), and Igors Gavon in John Guare's *To Wally Pantoni We Leave a Credenza.* Photo by Alix Jeffrey, courtesy Harvard Theatre Collection, Houghton Library, © Harvard University.

In another sense, the very success the Unit achieved may have sown the seeds of its own demise. In the interviews conducted for this study, the playwrights frequently commented that no reviews were written of the productions of the Unit—in general the critical eye of the New York theatre was not upon off-off Broadway. However, with the phenomenal success of *The Boys in the Band* in 1968, off-off Broadway was suddenly seen in a different light. John Guare, in a discussion about the Unit's production of his play *To Wally Pantoni We Leave a Credenza*, suggested that the success of *The Boys in the Band* somehow ended experimentation of off-off Broadway:

One of the great things about it was that they [the off-off-Broadway productions] weren't reviewed . . . and then bit by bit, they got to be reviewed. One of the other things that was great was that they were sort of just done, I mean you just felt very safe and free. . . . There wasn't anyone there to move it or buy it. And then they suddenly got to be reviewed, brutally or extravagantly . . . off-off Broadway had become something that fed commercial theatre rather than being experimental.[38]

THE ALBEE-BARR-WILDER PLAYWRIGHTS UNIT

In addition to the burgeoning critical consideration of off-off Broadway, another reason for the closing of the Playwrights Unit and the demise of the importance of the off-off-Broadway scene was the growth of competing not-for-profit theatres such as Circle Repertory and the New York Shakespeare Festival, which rendered the Unit somewhat redundant in its mission to develop new playwrights.

The milieu of the off-off-Broadway theatre of the 1960s and its coffeehouse theatres—Caffe Cino, Cafe La Mama, the Judson Poets Theatre—provided a fertile ground for the sort of experimental theatre that Albee, Barr, and Wilder were trying to develop. There is a sense, however, that Barr in particular felt that these playwrights were not being served in the cafés, that their talents were being dissipated in less-than-professional surroundings.[39] In addition, the ABW Playwrights Unit was specifically geared toward the playwright's work, unlike the Playwrights Unit of the Actors Studio, which at that time was controlled by actors and directors. James Prideaux offered this brief statement about the work at the Actors Studio:

We met on Mondays at 5:00 PM, about 200 of us, all budding playwrights. Generally we would see a one-act or a scene from a play one of us had written, followed by an open discussion. These were savage. They all hacked away at what they had seen with a kind of vengeance. It was as if were one to succeed, others must be made to fail. I had entered the group in the hope of presenting some of my work there, but I soon saw that my self-confidence, tough as it was, couldn't withstand the kind of attacks they made on each other's work. I could never show them anything of mine. And many times, at the end of these discussions, I would swear to leave and never return.[40]

To this memory of the Playwrights Unit of the Actors Studio, Edward Parone, manager of the ABW Playwrights Unit, in his preface to his collection of plays from the Unit, *New Theatre in America,* adds this description:

The Actor's Studio formed its Playwrights Unit a few years ago. Plays or scenes from plays by the members are performed usually, though not always, by Studio actors. The unit is run by a committee; meetings are held. Discussions take place after the performances. The unit is supported by the Studio, with foundation money for a specific number of projects. But the Studio, it seems from my observation, is in theory and practice an *actor's* studio, not a playwright's or even director's. And perhaps the following true story may be pertinent, though it may not be typical. A young actress, a member of the Studio, came to read for the part of the girl in LeRoi Jones's *Dutchman.* She mounted the stage and riffling the script in her hands and looking somewhere between the playwright and the director, said, "Uh, you don't care if I don't bother to use the lines, do you?"[41]

Terrence McNally had a similar complaint about the Actors Studio: "The Actors Studio, for all the good work that was done there, was always Lee's building somehow. Even though there was a playwrights unit there, you felt that you were talking about acting as much as the play. It was so hard to escape Lee's presence."[42] Given the growing fascination with the performer and director, the ABW Playwrights Unit seemed a safe haven for playwrights learning their craft.

The ABW Playwrights Unit also offered a somewhat more upscale venue—staffed as it was by theatre professionals. Experienced directors and well-known actors such as Frank Langella, Viveca Lindfors, James Coco, Margaret Hamilton, and Nancy Marchand were available for performances at the Unit because of the short runs and because of the influence and connections of Albee and Barr. What the Unit offered, then, was a professional production in a theatre with talented actors, an experienced director, and a mailing list of patrons who could be expected to support the work and perhaps provide the connections to move the plays or the playwright to another level of production.

The Playwrights Unit came to be a stepping stone, in that sense, from the experimentation and freedom of the cafés and coffeehouse theatres to a new level of professionalism. If a play was successful in the Playwrights Unit, the eyes of Albarwild were certainly upon it, although the plays were produced without options or obligations.[43] In the spring of 1965 a New Playwrights Series was produced by Theatre 1965 at the Cherry Lane Theatre; it consisted of ten plays, including *Giant's Dance* by Otis Bigelow, *Up to Thursday* by Sam Shepard, *Home Free* by Lanford Wilson, *Balls* by Paul Foster, *Conerico Was Here to Stay* by Frank Gagliano, *Pigeons* by Lawrence Osgood, *Lovey* by Joseph Morgenstern, *Hunting the Jingo Bird* by Kenneth Pressman, *A Lesson in a Dead Language* by Adrienne Kennedy, and *Do Not Pass Go* by Charles Nolte.

In addition, Lanford Wilson's full-length *The Rimers of Eldrich* was first professionally produced by Theatre 1968 at the Cherry Lane. Wilson speaks of the experience of having an earlier work, *Home Free,* produced professionally:

Home Free [at the Cherry Lane] was the first professional thing I had ever had done . . . had been done at La Mama earlier but [at the Cherry Lane] it was for money! I got a percentage of the house, it was fabulous! Who had ever heard of such a thing—what a concept! . . . It certainly made you feel professional . . . it was your first professional recognition also. I mean we were reviewed for crying out loud . . . at the Cherry Lane. Most of them had never been reviewed before. At the Cherry Lane it was for real—it was for a limited run—but it was for real.[44]

As Wilson explains, the Playwrights Unit and the productions given at the Cherry Lane were a validation of the artistic experimentation these playwrights were attempting. It is hard to imagine any major Broadway producers today—let alone any single American playwright—who would invest, for example, in an off-Broadway production of Adrienne Kennedy's *Funnyhouse of a Negro*. There was a certain heroism tied to this kind of producing and sponsorship of playwrights.

The positive reaction from most of the playwrights interviewed in the course of my research was somewhat deflated by one note of discord. Lawrence Wunderlich, whose plays *Nine-to-Five-to-Zero,* parts one and two, and *Prometheus Rebound* were performed at the Unit in 1964 and 1965, respectively, wrote of this experience:

> I don't want to belabor the whole first year's operation of the Playwrights Unit. But if Albee's "guess" is "that the theatre in the United States will always hew more closely to the post-Ibsen/Chekhov tradition" because "it is our nature as a country, a society," he was quite right when it came to *this* group; a good majority of the playwrights were hewing very closely indeed, so closely, in fact, that a quaint, nostalgic air of the past hung over most of their work; so closely that I could see very little in their work that had much if anything to do with *us, here,* and *now,* in the final third of the twentieth century.[45]

Wunderlich's primary criticism of the Unit concerns its lack of consistent support for work that was experimental. And from the above excerpt it is clear that he did not feel the Unit was producing scripts that represented the most avant-garde or most challenging work available (with the exception of several plays, including his own).

What is fascinating about Wunderlich's article is the discussion of several details. Wunderlich was not only a playreader for the ABW workshop but also the manager of the Village South Theatre, where the Unit was located in its first seven years. He chronologizes the first four years of the Unit through September 1967, discussing the initial meetings, the correspondence between the producers and the Unit playwrights, the various management techniques that Parone and Gnys used to organize and inform the playwrights, and the sources of funding for the Unit. He ends his article with an excellent chronology of productions through spring of 1967.

At several points Wunderlich seems to question the very nature of a playwrights workshop, wondering if a workshop as such can actually produce fine playwrights:

> We find ourselves face to face with a hodgepodge of romantics, cynics, realists, stoics, naturalists, nihilists, absurdists, Philistines, and incompetents. And while we dimly

suspect that such a "group" may contain the raw materials for the making of a democracy, we know that it contains little of the select material for the makings of a playwrights workshop. It is, and it remains, a pastiche. And to paraphrase a statement attributed to Voltaire, I disapprove of a pastiche but I will defend to the death the right of the individual parts of the pastiche to operate autonomously.[46]

What Wunderlich offers, then, is a contrarian's view of the achievements of the Unit, which, even if it is not terribly successful in its criticism, at least provides a fairly detailed and well-supported argument for the Unit's eclecticism.

Certainly Wunderlich's reaction is a minority opinion. Almost all the playwrights interviewed had positive responses to their productions at the Unit, with James Prideaux articulating what seemed to be the "prototypical" experience:

When finally Richard forced me into the theatre, there were no seats left and so we had to sit on the steps next to the exit. The lights came down. The curtain went up. And the audience began to laugh. And clap. And laugh. And clap some more. *Postcards* is hardly more than thirty minutes long, but they were the greatest thirty minutes of my life. My heart soared, literally soared as I listened to the audience. At the end they wouldn't stop applauding and Richard pushed me to my feet, saying, "Jimmy, you'd better go up." So I ran up on stage and took a bow with my beaming actors. I suppose I went someplace after that. I assume I got home. But I have no recollection of it. I was in another world.[47]

Prideaux, in his interview for this study, confessed that in his career as a playwright and screenwriter no other moment was quite as stupendous or as memorable as this successful evening at the Unit.[48]

Mart Crowley, author of *The Boys in the Band* (produced at the Playwrights Unit in January 1968), spoke of the Unit's audience in quite dramatic terms. Looking out at the huge line of people waiting to get into the theatre on a rainy January evening, he imagined it was "like the third act of Wilder's *Our Town*—there were all these umbrellas."[49] Crowley later discussed the experience in an article in San Francisco's *Bay Area Reporter*: "*Boys* might have ended in that five-day workshop, except for one small miracle—audiences were wild about the play. 'The first night,' Crowley says, 'I don't think anybody was there. But the second night, there was a line around the block. The New York intelligentsia [began to] descend on the play. And suddenly it was famous.'"[50] The audience at the Playwrights Unit was invited and attended the performances free of charge. They were the product of a very carefully prepared mailing list that had been nurtured over many years by Gnys and the other managers. Jean-Claude Van Itallie speaks about the houses being "packed, simply packed to the rafters," and other playwrights also refer to the responsive audiences.[51] Parone spoke of the way the audience talked directly to actors in Jones's *Dutchman*, in particular remembering Leontyne Price, "who lived in the neighborhood, suddenly bursting out with 'Right on!' and 'Say it!' several times."[52]

The Unit's success was directly tied to the Broadway professionals who sponsored its activities. Ironically, even though Barr and Wilder rejected the worst of the commercial tastes of the Great White Way, they retained all the rigorous demands of professional production standards in the off-Broadway and off-off-Broadway milieu at their Playwrights Unit. It was also the connection with Broadway theatre professionals—actors, directors, designers, stage managers, and administrative staff—that allowed Barr and Wilder to provide an extraordinary nurturing experience to each new play they chose to produce. However, the Playwrights Unit existed within the milieu of the off-off-Broadway theatre of the 1960s, which provided a fertile environment for the Unit's success. Most of the playwrights who came to the Unit, though not all, had been produced earlier at venues such as Cafe La Mama or Caffe Cino, and most continued to produce work at other off-off-Broadway venues during and after their productions at the Unit. However, the Unit and the Cherry Lane Theatre gave most of these playwrights their first experience working within the world of New York's professional theatre, an experience, for better or worse, that was very different from the cafés and storefront theatres of off-off Broadway, and one that brought them into the critical focus of the New York theatre community.

Notes

1. Stuart Little, *Off-Broadway: The Prophetic Theater* (New York: Coward, McCann & Geoghegan, 1972), 216.
2. Since 1995, I have done extensive interviews with participants in the ABW Playwrights Unit, including its playwrights Edward Albee, John Guare, Lanford Wilson, A. R. Gurney, Jean-Claude van Itallie, Ursule Molinaro, Terrence McNally, Doric Wilson, Mart Crowley, Robert Heide, James Prideau, Frank Gagliano, Stephen Jacobsen, and Lee Kalcheim, among many others. In addition, I interviewed many of the ABW staff, including Unit managers Edward Parone (the first manager) and Bob Moss (the last manager), as well as Barry Plaxen, Lynn Prather, Joseph Cali, and Richard Lipsett, all of whom worked in ABW productions at the Cherry Lane Theatre and the Unit. I spent a great deal of time examining Playwrights Unit scripts, production notes, and financial papers, all of which are preserved in the Billy Rose Theatre Collection of the New York Public Library. I have also spent a great deal of time examining the extensive Richard Barr–Clinton Wilder Papers, which include a substantial amount of material on the Playwrights Unit (grant applications, correspondence, programs), as well as Barr's

unpublished biography, "You Have to Hock Your House." I also explored other theatre collections, including the privately held papers of Chuck Gnys, the primary manager of the Playwrights Unit, at Curtis Brown, Ltd.; the Michael Kasdan Collection at the Lawrence and Lee Theatre Institute at Ohio State University; and the La MaMa Theatre Collection at La MaMa, E.T.C. in Lower Manhattan.

3. For a discussion of play development and its discontents see Michael Bloom, "The Post-Play Discussion Fallacy," *American Theatre* 5, no. 9 (1988): 31; Edward Clinton, "The Literary Manager: Vanguard of a Frustrating System," *Dramatists Guild Quarterly* 25, no. 1 (1988): 17–19; Amy Davis, "Development of New Play Often a Rocky Road," *Variety*, March 16, 1988, 105; Shelly Frome, "Fault-finding Can Be Fun for All Except the Paranoid Playwright," *Dramatists Guild Quarterly* 24, no. 3 (1987): 27–28; Marsha Norman and Jeffrey Sweet, "The Plight of the Playwright in Regional Theater, 1986–87," *Dramatists Guild Quarterly* 23, no. 4 (1987): 18–33; Louis Phillips, "Why Shakespeare Might Not Succeed in Today's Theater," *Dramatists Guild Quarterly* 29, no. 4 (1993): 31–33; Dale Ramsey and Thomas G. Dunn, "Speaking of Dramaturgs and Literary Managers," *Dramatists Guild Quarterly* 24, no. 1 (1987): 12–17; Peregrine Whittlessey, "Developed to Death? Here's a Possible Antidote," *Dramatists Guild Quarterly* 25, no. 3 (1988): 21–22; Peregrine Whittlessey, "Is There Life after Literary Management?" *Dramatists Guild Quarterly* 25, no. 3 (1988): 18–19.

4. Edward Albee, interview by author, tape recording, New York City, June 19, 1996.

5. Stephen Samuels, "Yes Is Better Than No: An Interview with Edward Albee," *American Theatre* 11, no. 7 (1994): 38.

6. John Keating, "A Producer Should 'Produce,'" *Theatre Arts*, September 1961, 76.

7. Albee, interview.

8. Keating, "A Producer Should 'Produce,'" 75.

9. Ibid.

10. David Kahn and Donna Breed, *Scriptwork: A Director's Approach to New Play Development* (Carbondale: Southern Illinois University Press, 1995), 79.

11. Douglas Anderson, "The Dream Machine: Thirty Years of New Play Development in America," *Drama Review* 32, no. 3 (1988): 55–84.

12. Mervyn Rothstein, "Richard Barr, 71, Stage Producer and Theater League Head, Dies," *New York Times*, January 10, 1989.

13. Barry Plaxen, interview by author, tape recording, Bloomingsburg, N.Y., May 4, 1996.

14. Richard Barr, "You Have to Hock Your House," pp. 69–111, unpublished MS, Richard Barr–Clinton Wilder Papers, Billy Rose Theater Collection, New York Public Library for the Performing Arts at Lincoln Center.

15. Walter Rigdon, ed., *Notable Names in the American Theatre* (Clifton, N.J.: J. T. White, 1976), 542–43.

16. Little, *Off-Broadway*, 219.

17. Faye Hammel, "Three for the Play: Theatre '64 says the Writer Must Be King," *New York Times*, March 3, 1966, 10.

18. Rigdon, *Notable Names*, 1226.

19. Thomas Morgan, "Clinton Wilder Is Dead at 65; Helped Develop Playwrights," *New York Times*, February 15, 1986, 33.

20. Rigdon, *Notable Names*, 1226.

21. Barnard Hewitt, *Theatre U.S.A. 1665 to 1957* (New York: McGraw-Hill, 1959), 360–65.

22. Rigdon, *Notable Names*, 500.
23. Sam Zolotow, "Playwrights Unit Receives Subsidy for Staging," *New York Times*, June 1, 1968.
24. John Keating, "Action Speaks Louder . . . ," *New York Times*, October 20, 1963, X3.
25. Barbara La Fontaine, "Triple Threat On, Off and Off-Off Broadway," *New York Times Magazine*, February 25, 1968, 36–46.
26. Edward Parone, interview by author, New York City, March 14, 1995; contact sheet from Merle Debuskey from the Edward Parone Clippings Folder, Billy Rose Theater Collection.
27. Edward M. Cohen, interview by author, New York City, May 3, 1995.
28. La Fontaine, "Triple Threat," 37.
29. Richard Lipsett, interview by author, Bloomfield, N.J., February 27, 1995.
30. Albee, interview.
31. Ibid.
32. Keating, "Action Speaks Louder . . . ," X3.
33. James Prideaux, "Memoirs," unpublished, May 1995, 212–13.
34. Kenneth Pressman, interview by author, tape recording, New York City, November 19, 1994.
35. John Guare, interview by author, tape recording, New York City, March 28, 1995.
36. Zolotow, "Playwrights Unit Receives Subsidy."
37. Patricia Bosworth, "Will They All Be Albees?" *New York Times*, July 18, 1971, D1, 3.
38. Guare, interview.
39. Barr, "You Have to Hock Your House," 263–70.
40. Prideaux, "Memoirs," 232–33.
41. Edward Parone, ed., *New Theatre in America* (New York: Dell, 1965), 11.
42. Terrence McNally, "In Conversation with Terrence McNally: Edward Albee," *Dramatists Guild Quarterly* 22, no. 2 (1985): 17.
43. Albee, interview.
44. Lanford Wilson, interview by author, tape recording, New York City, March 27, 1995.
45. Lawrence Wunderlich, "Playwrights at Cross Purposes," *Works* 1, no. 2 (1968): 23.
46. Ibid., 35.
47. Prideaux, "Memoirs," 214.
48. James Prideaux, interview by author, tape recording, New York City, March 27, 1995.
49. Mart Crowley, interview by author, tape recording, New York City, February 19, 1995.
50. Wendell Ricketts, "Talking Truth: *Boys in the Band* Author Mart Crowley on His 'Gorgeous Little Monster,'" *Bay Area Reporter*, February 8, 1990, 35.
51. Jean-Claude Van Itallie, interview by author, New York City, February 16, 1995.
52. Parone, interview.

"The Power of Woman's Influence"

Nineteenth-Century Temperance Theatricality
and the Drama of Nellie H. Bradley

—DEANNA M. TOTEN BEARD

> "Woman's influence, wrongly exerted in a thoughtless moment, first led me astray, yet to her influence, properly directed, I attribute, to a great extent, my love for all that is good and true. I am impressed with the belief that the fairer portion of creation are not fully aware of the power they yield for good or evil over the destinies of men.
> —NELLIE H. BRADLEY, *The First Glass; or, the Power of Woman's Influence* (1868)

A glimpse through the history of nineteenth-century American theatre and drama quickly reveals the temperance movement's impact on the commercial entertainment of the day. William H. Smith's *The Drunkard; or the Fallen Saved* (1844) was the first American play to have a run of one hundred consecutive performances, and William W. Pratt's 1858 adaptation of Timothy S. Arthur's novel *Ten Nights in a Bar Room and What I Saw There* was, as Walter J. Meserve observes, "second in popularity only to *Uncle Tom's Cabin* in the theatre of the late nineteenth century."[1] These popular plays of sin and redemption reveal much about the pervasiveness of temperance culture in the United States and are excellent examples of morality issues in the melodramatic form. Yet as useful and interesting as they are, the dominance of *The Drunkard* and *Ten Nights in a Bar Room* as exemplars of temperance drama has unfortunately overshadowed the legions of small, noncommercial dramas and "dialogues" that flooded the country in the last quarter of the nineteenth century. These little plays, printed cheaply and performed in communities large and small around the country, have much more to teach us about the relationship between performance and the temperance movement than do the more recognizable dramas. What is more, the minor American temperance dramas—many written by women—more fully illuminate the complex role women played in nineteenth-century temperance culture.

When the temperance cause became a political push for legal prohibition in the early twentieth century, men dominated the movement's leadership; to appreciate temperance culture, however, one must recall that the movement began as a remarkably aggressive campaign organized by women. In years following the Civil War, petticoated Christian soldiers armed only with Scripture began routinely storming saloons around the country. There they would lay their Bibles on the bar and pray aloud for the spirit of God to fill the barkeeper and patrons, opening their eyes to salvation and closing forever the tavern doors. After one such attack in Fredonia, New York, on December 14, 1873, the rejoicing female demonstrators spontaneously christened themselves the Woman's Christian Temperance Union (WCTU).[2] This Progressive Era phenomenon, which would become the single largest women's organization in the United States during the nineteenth century, consciously chose the singular "woman" in its title to suggest the presence of an ideal American "Woman" rather than a group of miscellaneous, everyday "women."

Needless to say, public participation by women in social activism was viewed suspiciously, seeming to bring members of the fairer sex too far from their appropriate domestic duties. The WCTU succeeded because its leadership effectively articulated the need for female public activism, as unusual as the measure seemed, as a reasonable response to the extraordinary dangers of alcohol intemperance. Women must intervene, said the WCTU, because of their duty to protect the family. Women are especially able to solve the problem, the WCTU further argued, because through emotional persuasion women are naturally civilizing in the lives of men. Such rhetoric was highly successful, encouraging improved tolerance for female activism and bolstering the morale of those women serving as foot soldiers in the cause. Popular print images such as "Woman's Holy War" from 1874 (fig. 1) visually reinforced the exciting, and often militant, message. Women were told they had powerful weapons that could be used to save drinkers, and they then worked hard to make that assertion true. The culture of the temperance movement offers numerous examples of women, both in the WCTU and in other organizations, employing highly emotional and theatrical devices to persuade their audiences toward alcohol abstinence. Among these devices are demonstrations, song, and theatrical performance.

At its height of fame and influence in the 1880s and 1890s, the WCTU was

Figure 1. "Woman's Holy War," Currier and Ives color print (1874).

led by Frances Willard, the former president of Evanston College for Ladies, who resigned as dean of women at Northwestern University to become involved in the temperance movement full-time. Willard was the WCTU's official spokesperson, and her numerous pamphlets, essays, and speeches help characterize the general personality of women's temperance work in the late nineteenth century. Under her leadership, the WCTU created a campaign of "social housekeeping," predicting a future American society made more peaceful and "home-like" by the power of women's involvement. Indeed, Willard's decision to adopt "Home Protection" as the central WCTU platform was an act of public relations genius. The concept invoked traditional feminine values of domesticity and yet could be used to justify women's public involvement in any number of social issues: alcohol temperance, domestic violence, labor justice, and women's suffrage.[3] Willard was very conscious of social activism as performance and gave her followers guidance on presentation, appearance, and public speaking. The WCTU sponsored essay- and speech-writing contests on the topic of alcohol abuse, designed to teach winning techniques of public persuasion. Throughout all WCTU activities, conventional femininity was reinforced by conservative dress and gentle manners. In her guidebook *Do Everything: A Handbook for the World's White Ribboners,* Willard instructs WCTU groups to choose leaders of the highest moral standard, "women who can and do command the respect of the community for their devoted and religious lives and whose influence is without doubt on the side of Christianity and pure living."[4] Thus the ability of women to persuade was linked to their believable portrayal of the good Christian woman. The characteristics of such a good Christian woman were expressed not only in Willard's instructions about behavior but also in popular iconography. See, for example, the 1848 Currier and Ives print "The Fruits of Temperance" (fig. 2). Its caption reads, "Behold the son of Temperance, with buoyant heart and step, returning to his home; the partner of his bosom looks up and smiles his welcome;—his children fly to meet him, their little arms embrace him, and with lip and heart they bless him." The ideal of a peaceful Christian household, ruled over by a nondrinking husband and blessed by his righteous helpmate, was continually held up by temperance women to remind audiences of the inevitable outcome of alcohol reform. This image was especially popular in temperance ballads.

Like other nineteenth-century temperance women, Willard picked up excellent lessons about conversion strategies from evangelical Protestantism. She was especially mindful of the power of music in the process of inspiration and conversion. As with Christian hymns, popular temperance songs were at once entertainment and a call to fight; singing them could be both a social activity and a personal act of prayer. Every WCTU chapter had at least one choir, and singing was important to the organization as a means of creating group unity within the chapter as well as sharing the temperance message with audiences at rallies or school presentations. "Teach them how to sing with the spirit and the understanding," Willard wrote to local WCTU youth choir organizers; "above

Figure 2. "The Fruits of Temperance," Currier and Ives color print (1848).

all impress upon their young hearts that a song is a sentiment maker, and that every chorus rendered at a public entertainment ought to add new converts to the cause of Temperance and Purity."[5]

Temperance music was, however, hardly the invention of Frances Willard and the WCTU. Hymns, ditties, and ballads on the theme of alcohol temperance were widely popular in nineteenth-century America and were prevalent until well past the repeal of Prohibition in 1933. George W. Ewing, author of *The Well-Tempered Lyre*, an extensive study of temperance songs and verse, presents this material as one part of a much larger public temperance culture: "The parades and songs, the poems and pageantry, the fraternities and revival-type meetings, and the interpersonal relationships [were] calculated to change the very mores of society."[6] Temperance songs were spread in the United States through temperance society rallies, church choirs, Sunday-school hymnals, school pageants, and popular songbooks. The highly dramatic content of many temperance ballads certainly contributed to their success in the broader culture; indeed, this was the key to their effectiveness as propaganda. And this is why temperance music blended so easily with the emotional rhetorical style of temperance women.

Colored by intense sentimentality, temperance ballads dramatized the very domestic dangers that the WCTU addressed in its public work. As James W. Frick notes in *Theatre, Culture, and Temperance Reform in Nineteenth-Century America,* "Next to melodramas, few temperance vehicles were more effective than the vast array of songs advising women to use their innate moral influence to save their families from the ravages of intemperance."[7] The comparison to melodrama is quite appropriate; musical accounts abound of children starving to death because father—and indeed, the drunkard who ruined home life was usually male—spends all his meager wages on rum. Songs also depicted long-suffering wives killed by the intemperance of their husbands, creating a subgroup of domestic tragic ballads, which George Ewing calls "father's-a-drunkard-and-mother-is-dead" songs.[8] In *The Well-Tempered Lyre,* Ewing reprints the music and lyrics of the most famous version of this kind of ballad. The song, by an author identified only as "Stella of Washington," with music by Mrs. E. A. Parkhurst, is simply titled "Father's a Drunkard, and Mother Is Dead." It is sung to a mournful waltz:

> Out in the gloomy night, sadly I roam,
> I have no Mother dear, no pleasant home;
> Nobody cares for me—no one would cry
> Even if poor little Bessie should die.
> Barefoot and tired, I've wander'd all day
> Asking for work—but I'm too small they say;
> On the damp ground I must now lay my head—
> "Father's a Drunkard and Mother is dead!"
>
> *Chorus:* Mother, oh! why did you leave me alone,
> With no one to love me, no friends and no home?
> Dark is the night, and the storm rages wild,
> God pity Bessie, the Drunkard's lone child!
>
> We were so happy till father drank rum,
> Then all our sorrow and trouble begun;
> Mother grew paler, and wept every day,
> Baby and I were too hungry to play.
> Slowly they faded, and one Summer's night
> Found their dear faces all silent and white;
> Then with big tears slowly dropping, I said:
> "Father's a Drunkard, and Mother is dead!" (Chorus)
>
> Oh! if the "Temp'rance men" only could find
> Poor, wretched Father and talk very kind—
> If they could stop him from drinking—why, then
> I should be so very happy again!

> Is it too late? "men of Temp'rance," please try,
> Or poor little Bessie may soon starve and die.
> All the day long I've been begging for bread—
> "Father's a Drunkard, and Mother is dead!" (Chorus)

The printed text of the ballad almost always included a preface about the origins of the song. One cold winter night in Washington, D.C., so the story goes, a poorly clad little girl was seen under a tree near the White House. When asked why she was out in such foul weather, the child "raised her pale face, and with tears dimming her sweet blue eyes, answered mournfully: 'I have no home, Father's a Drunkard, and Mother is dead.'"[9] This mournful, if apocryphal, tale was part of the song's charm. Its popularity was, therefore, based not only on the pitiful lyrics and high emotionalism but on the "real" tragic scene that audiences were taught to associate with it.

The tactic of highly emotional presentation within the temperance movement did not end with temperance ballads, however. Willard and the WCTU applied theatricalism to all public aspects of their work—demonstrations, rallies, meetings, and conventions. As Carol Mattingly details in *Well-Tempered Women: Nineteenth-Century Temperance Rhetoric*, WCTU meetings drew upon biblical allusion, domestic imagery, and patriotic sentiment to effectively "meld a progressive message with a rhetorical presentation and image comfortable to a large number of women and men."[10] Like a church service, WCTU meetings and rallies always began with group prayer and hymn singing; banners or needlework featuring Scripture helped reinforce the sense of Christian mission in the meeting. The program of a temperance rally was structured to remind the audience of revival meetings, with sermons punctuated by songs and testimonials culminating in a call to conversion. The WCTU paid careful attention as well to the visual rhetoric of temperance meetings. Willard encouraged workers "to decorate with flowers and banners of their own work and design, as well as with national flags and state escutcheons so as to add a conducive atmosphere based on patriotic authority."[11] Indeed, the WCTU meeting hall platform was a carefully designed theatrical set. Willard's own description of a WCTU conference meeting confirms the importance she placed on setting:

> The platform was beautified by plants and vines; an ice-pitcher stood upon a handsome table at one side . . . while easy chairs and warm rugs gave the place a homelike look, clearly showing that it had been arranged by women. On a table in the center, which was draped with the flag, were Bible and hymn book, and in ornamental letters over our heads were the words "For God and Home and Native Land." . . . These women evidently thought that if Henry Irving, the greatest of English actors, had

built up not a little of his reputation by the unrivaled, artistic skill with which his plays were put upon the stage, they could well afford, for the splendid real drama of the "Home Protection" Cause, to arrange such a picture as should remind each person present of home itself![12]

The stage picture Willard describes here is a near-perfect physical manifestation of the rhetoric she and other temperance women created. The set is well balanced, with conservative symbols such as the flag and the Bible placed side by side with a temperance hymnal and the WCTU slogan. Moreover, the easy chairs, plants, and "warm rugs" illustrate the power women have to domesticate and thereby reform any environment. As Willard's description of a temperance stage reveals, women had successfully crafted a female public space from which to speak.

It was within this highly emotional atmosphere of rich oral and visual rhetoric that some temperance women chose to create plays dramatizing their ideals and, even more interestingly, their issues. Extant plays are rare and records of performances are slim, found occasionally in the minutes of temperance society meetings.[13] A large number of titles have survived, however, through the numerous advertisements for printed "dialogues" distributed by companies such as the National Temperance Society and Publishing House. The advertisement shown in figure 3, for example, was printed in an 1880 publication called *Talks on Temperance*.[14] Among the items for sale are ten previously published short plays, most listed without author attribution. While the advertisement does not offer the playwright's name, five of the "Excellent Dialogues previously published" are by the same playwright: an American temperance worker named Nellie H. Bradley. While Bradley appears to have not cared much for self-promotion, her authorship of these titles is confirmed by seven extant published texts.[15] Bradley's surviving plays are fascinating documents of the late-nineteenth-century temperance movement, as evidenced by their evocative titles: *The Young Teetotaler; or, Saved at Last* (1867); *The First Glass; or, The Power of Woman's Influence* (1868); *Marry No Man If He Drinks; or, Laura's Plan and How It Succeeded* (1868); *Reclaimed; or, The Danger of Moderate Drinking* (1868); *The Stumbling Block; or, Why a Deacon Gave Up His Wine* (1871); *Wine as Medicine; or, Abbie's Experience* (1873); and *A Temperance Picnic with the Old Woman Who Lived in a Shoe* (1888).[16]

Nellie Bradley was an active temperance reform worker in Washington, D.C., as well as a poet and amateur dramatist. She was a signer of the original WCTU charter papers and served as superintendent of the organization's Washington, D.C., chapter.[17] Her plays were clearly available to her fellow temperance workers, and judging by their prominence in advertising, the pieces ap-

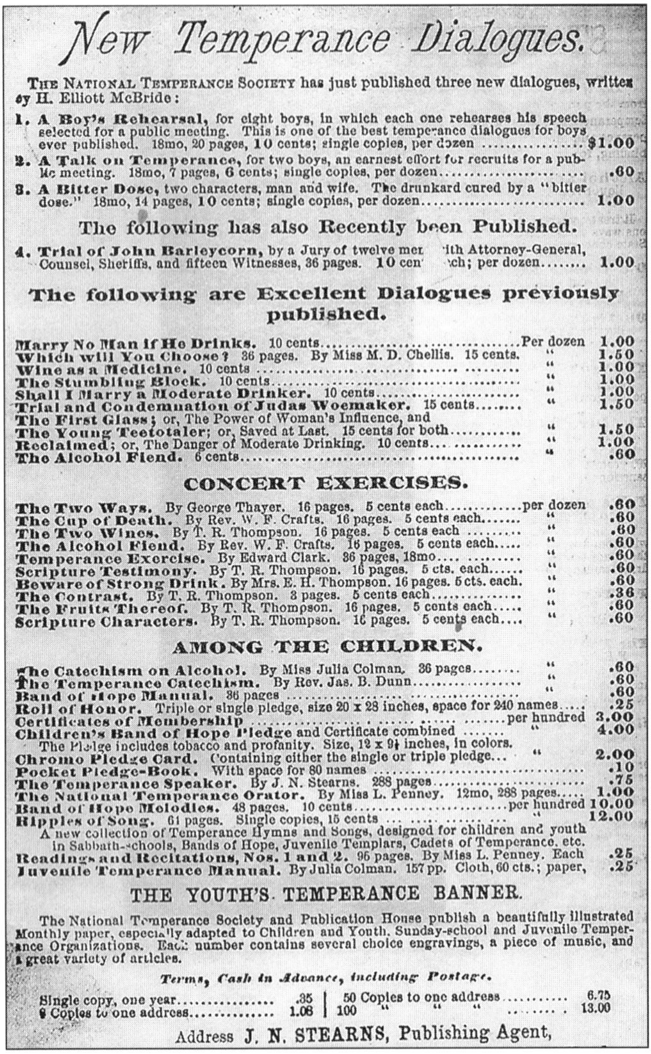

Figure 3. Advertisement for temperance dialogues, dramas, and exercises published by the J. N. Stearns Company of New York (1880).

pear to have been popular within the ranks. It is highly unlikely that the plays, mostly small-cast one-acts, were ever produced professionally. No records of any kind—announcements of productions, descriptions of shows, or cast lists, for example—have surfaced to suggest that the plays had a professional life in the manner of *The Drunkard* or *Ten Nights in a Bar Room*.

Yet Bradley's plays did find a live audience in the throngs of temperance workers gathered at their local meetings. It was very common to offer a dramatic presentation, frequently performed by the youth of the chapter, as part of the regular proceedings of a temperance meeting, and the short length and relative simplicity of Bradley's little plays seem quite suitable to amateur theatrics. We know that her scripts were available at the affordable cost of a dollar a dozen. What is more, based on textual notes from Bradley's published scripts, it appears that the playwright herself assumed that the plays would be performed, or at least read aloud, by temperance organizations. For example, in the opening pages of *The First Glass,* Bradley comments, "Divisions, Lodges, Temples, etc., performing this Drama, may use the names of their respective organizations instead of 'Society'; and the titles of Officers peculiar to themselves, instead of 'presiding officer,' and 'secretary.'"[18] Thus, not only did she imagine temperance groups performing her plays at their meetings, but she expected the performers to personalize the details in order to increase their impact.

The question is, then, what purpose did Bradley imagine her plays would serve within the temperance meeting? The most obvious goal for a temperance playwright would be conversion; indeed, most of the energy of a temperance group was supposed to be directed outward to the unsaved. At face value, Bradley's plays satisfy this great commission by showing drinkers who experience a dramatic change of opinion onstage and decide to reject alcohol. Yet while one cannot doubt Bradley's devotion to the cause, conversion of unsaved drunkards does not seem to be the real intention of her dramatic work. Instead of dramatic proselytizing to the inebriate, Bradley's plays appear to be a theatrical means of strengthening convictions within the temperance ranks through high emotional appeal. What is more, in many of her plays we can see Bradley using the stage as a medium for teaching the temperance catechism to people already involved in the cause. Through dramatic dialogue she highlights key arguments within the temperance movement and clarifies right doctrine for her audience. To use an analogy from the nineteenth-century evangelical Christian culture that surrounded her, Bradley's drama's were not an altar call so much as Sunday school.

For example, Bradley's 1868 play titled *Reclaimed; or, The Danger of Moderate Drinking* dramatizes the debate over moderation versus abstinence. This was a contentious point of discussion in the United States, for while the movement operated under the banner of alcohol "temperance"—that is, moderation— it was clear that the ambition for most workers was total alcohol abstinence. Eventually, the goal would even become legal prohibition. Groups like the WCTU claimed that abstinence was the only solution to America's alcohol problem because temperate drinking was in fact impossible. Moderation was a trap that would inevitably lead a person to full-blown alcohol abuse. Catholic groups, among others, supported reduced alcohol consumption in order to improve family health and harmony, but they did not stand with groups like the WCTU in the cause for complete abstinence. The debate over moderation and abstinence would continue to divide temperance ranks until the movement's final days.

Bradley's play on the subject begins with a discussion between Willis Hamilton, a total abstainer, and his moderate-drinking friend Charles Tracey. As they sit in a bar together, Tracy explains that his self-control will keep him from becoming a complete drunkard. The righteous Hamilton responds to his friend,

> Tracey, I implore you not to drink to-night. I have observed with sorrow that this appetite for liquor is daily increasing, and although you are now what is termed a "moderate drinker," you will ere long, unless you abandon this destructive habit, become that most wretched and repulsive being—a confirmed drunkard.[19]

To which Tracey declares, while filling his glass,

> Oh! fudge, Will. If you were not my friend I should believe you wanted to insult me by such language. . . . I only take a glass occasionally without injuring myself or anyone else. You total abstinence men are too radical on this subject. It's all well enough for you to preach to the drunkards, for they need it sadly; but we who have pride and self-control are entirely beyond your sphere of action—we don't require any temperance talk because we are already temperate.[20]

Of course, Tracey's use of the word "temperate" is entirely accurate, and what is more, the play makes it clear that he really does drink moderately and never gets drunk. Yet Bradley's orthodox WCTU position on the issue of moderation versus abstinence is quickly made clear to the audience. Also at the bar is a filthy drunkard, and soon his wife and daughter enter the scene and plead for him to come home. The man cruelly refuses his family, and they leave brokenhearted. Hamilton then tells Tracey that this drunkard was once a moderate drinker, but eventually he became utterly lost to alcohol. Tracey, clearly shaken by the horror he has witnessed, immediately declares that he will give up drink altogether. The play ends with Tracey converted to abstinence without ever having to suffer the full effects of alcohol abuse in his own life. The audience of temperance men and women gathered to see this play would be encouraged in their work by such a clear example of the power of a persistent friend to convert through words and illustrative examples. They would also be dramatically reminded that although moderate alcohol use can appear harmless and sound reasonable, it is nonetheless a mistake. Most important, they would be emotionally motivated to share the official WCTU position against moderate drinking, armed in the debate with clearly articulated reasons for total abstinence.

Bradley's 1871 play *The Stumbling Block; or, Why a Deacon Gave Up His Wine* stages the temperance argument against Christians drinking. This issue often drove a wedge between groups of temperance workers, especially in the first half of the nineteenth century. Evangelicals in the United States and England debated for years about the biblical support—or lack thereof—for total abstinence. As believers in a literal reading of the Bible it was imperative that the evangelicals find a plausible way to make scriptural sources comply with a policy of total abstinence. This was accomplished through the publication of several dubious scholarly studies that meticulously documented every biblical reference to wine and explained when Scripture referred to an alcoholic drink and when it really meant nonfermented grape juice. Bible exegeses such as Frederic Richard Lees's 1870 book *The Temperance Bible-commentary* helped justify the substitution of grape juice for wine at communion.[21] The push to distance Christian practice from alcohol consumption was given even more practical support, however, by Thomas Bramwell Welch, who in 1869 developed the first pasteurized grape juice specifically to satisfy the needs of his fellow teetotaler Christians.

In *The Stumbling Block,* Bradley dramatizes the conflict some Bible believers felt when faced with the contradiction of a Lord who drinks wine at weddings and a contemporary religious culture that condemns all alcohol. She heightened the conflict by writing a clergyman into the center of the debate. Bradley gives her audience a fascinating onstage scriptural volley between a moderate-drinking deacon and his abstaining parishioner, during which the deacon comes to understand that he must give up drinking to help weaker Christians. The parishioner's argument, taken straight out of the Bible, was a popular anti-alcohol maxim for WCTU members: "Take heed lest by any means this liberty of yours become a stumbling block to the weak" (1 Cor. 8:9, ASV). The deacon's last speech of the play is given in direct address to the audience:

Before me are many Christian friends, who use wine as conscientiously, but, alas!, as blindly as I have done. I adjure you to stop, for already some struggling, tempted soul may have been externally wrecked by the force of your example. I would commend to you the example of Paul who would neither eat meat nor drink wine, if by doing so a weaker brother might be caused to offend or stumble. You cannot serve God faithfully while you are a stumbling block to the least of his children.[22]

The biblically literate members of the local temperance society would have known that this reference to Paul's first letter to the Corinthians was coming simply by the play's title. And they also would have likely recalled another stirring use of "stumbling block" in the New Testament, when Jesus says dramatically to the disciple Peter, "Get thee behind me, Satan: thou art a stumbling block unto me: for thou mindest not the things of God, but the things of men" (Matt. 16:23, ASV). Clearly, Bradley knew her audience well; she effectively crafted dramatic situations that could stir a room of committed temperance workers to redouble their efforts, even when that labor might include standing up for righteousness' sake against a fellow Christian.

The particular issue being played out in Bradley's 1873 play *Wine as Medicine; or, Abbie's Experience* is the medical practice of prescribing alcohol as a "strengthener." Temperance workers were just beginning to understand physical dependency on alcohol, and Bradley makes the danger of addiction very real in her play. *Wine as Medicine* is also interesting because it is the only extant example of an American temperance drama featuring a female alcoholic. In real life, temperance women were vocal about the problem of female drinking, which they considered a less common but nonetheless significant social problem. In the play, Abbie has become addicted to her glass of wine a day, as prescribed by her personal physician following an extended illness. Her friends advise Abbie that the prescription is dangerous and old-fashioned, encouraging her to visit the young, new doctor in town who is "totally opposed to the use of stimulants as a medicine."[23] Abbie is saved by this knowledge and is able to give up her alcohol. The play therefore not only illustrates the fearful possibility of female drunkenness but also proves that alcohol is addictive and that the practice of using wine as medicine is quite unsafe even though it is prescribed by well-established doctors. By choosing a female protagonist in this story of medicinal alcohol, Bradley succeeds in raising the sense of danger caused by old-fashioned doctors. What is more, she emotionally engages the audience's need to protect Abbie from misinformation about alcohol.

Bradley's interest in women characters was broader than just Abbie, however. Indeed, together with her effort to clarify issues of doctrine within the temperance movement, Bradley tends to focus on another reoccurring theme, what she calls in one of her subtitles "The Power of Woman's Influence." She repeatedly creates situations in which the force of female morality is able to generate social change and personal renewal. This concept was at the very foundation of the WCTU, and it was a precious belief for many women who worked in the cause. Bradley usually expressed her understanding of the power of woman's influence by dramatizing conversions led by female temperance workers. Her 1868 play *Marry No Man If He Drinks; or, Laura's Plan and How It Succeeded,* for example, features a female protagonist self-described as a reformer. In the first scene of the play, Laura articulates the philosophy that had motivated Frances Willard's "social housekeeping" campaign for the WCTU. "It is part of woman's mission," Laura tells her friends, "to refine the minds and morals of men."[24]

In a *Lysistrata*-esque gesture, the activist Laura vows that she will "accept neither the general nor special attentions of any gentlemen, who, after having this subject fully presented for his consideration continues to smoke, chew, or drink."[25] This idea of women withholding themselves from intemperate men was popular in the rhetoric of the movement, though it is hard to know just how often it occurred in real life. A popular temperance ballad from the time mirrors Laura's plan:

Your lips, on my own when they printed "Farewell,"
Had never been soiled by "The beverage of hell";
But they come to me now with the bacchanal sign,
And the lips that touch liquor must never touch mine.[26]

The power of woman's influence to improve men's behavior, it seems, is not just in woman's civilizing spirit but also in the strength of her sexual appeal.

In Bradley's play, Laura rejects her lover, Morris, until he pledges to abstain from alcohol. The plan works, of course, and Morris thanks Laura for loving him enough to give such a stern ultimatum. "If all young ladies would pursue the same course," he declares, "there would be fewer drunkards, and consequently less unhappiness and misery."[27] Although Bradley's character is grateful, popular songs record some less positive—and much more humorous—musical responses to the demands made by fictional characters like Laura: "The lips that touch liquor don't hanker to touch / The lips of a maiden like you—not much."[28] Nonetheless, in Bradley's drama the message of woman's influence on the lives of men is made clear to the audience, which at most local temperance meetings would be composed overwhelmingly of women. Yet, according to the temperance rhetoric of the day, the positive ability to redeem men from alcohol was not the only power of woman's influence.

The movement celebrated women's proven ability to marshal moral forces and fight against alcohol traffic in the name of God and "Home Protection," but nevertheless, the archetypal female temptress was never allowed to disappear. Bradley's play *The First Glass* (1868) best exemplifies the problematic position women were told they held in the cause of temperance. In the play, Bradley displays both species of womanly influence, creating a female character, Mollie, who unintentionally leads a good man to drink and then works to shepherd him back to temperance. On her birthday, Mollie demands that her friend Frank West toast her with a glass of wine. When Frank declines the offer, with the encouragement of his teetotaler sister, Alice, Mollie teases him, saying, "Who ever heard of any one becoming a drunkard by drinking one little glass of wine? Now do please me this time, Mr. West."[29] What Mollie doesn't realize is that Frank and Alice's father died a drunkard, and the siblings have promised never to touch a drop of spirit. Indeed, the "first glass" to which Frank is tempted by Mollie leads him almost immediately to complete ruin by drunkenness and gambling. In the end, it is the power of Alice's and, moreover, Mollie's love for Frank that helps him put down the bottle. Having just been elected president of the local temperance society, Frank is radiant at the end of the play:

Woman's influence, wrongly exerted in a thoughtless moment, first led me astray, yet to her influence, properly directed, I attribute, to a great extent, my love for all that is good and true. I am impressed with the belief that the fairer portion of creation are not fully aware of the power they yield for good or evil over the destinies of men. I think if they could realize this, they would oftener utter a solemn warning to those who are going downward, and endeavor to turn their footsteps from the path of evil. They would speak kindly words against temptation; and many, reclaimed and happy, would bless them for the noble deed.[30]

The First Glass also illustrates the strong link temperance rhetoric suggested between female influence and the emotional power of children. Feminized by virtue of their power position relative to the male drunkard at center stage, children are frequently made to be agents of salvation. In temperance culture, young daughters represent the most emotionally powerful force for reform. In the second scene of *The First Glass* we are shown the depths to which Frank has fallen due to alcohol. He is drinking and gambling with a rotten, greedy drunkard named Howard. Howard's two small daughters, little Bessie and her older sister Maggie, arrive "with bare feet and torn clothes" to beg their father to come home. Maggie touches her father's shoulder, saying, "Father, come home! Bessie and I have had nothing to eat all day and we're so hungry!" Howard rejects them roughly in his drunken rage. Here, Bradley gives the stage direction that "After a brief pause, both advance to the front of the stage with their arms around each other, and sing or recite the following":

> Oh! if the Temperance men could only find
> Poor, wretched father, and talk very kind;
> If they could stop him from drinking—why, then,
> We should be so very happy again.
> Is it too late? "Men of Temperance," please try!
> Or two little sisters may soon starve and die;
> All the long day we've been begging for bread;
> "Father's a drunkard, and mother is dead!"[31]

The lyrics would have been very familiar to the original audience an interpolation of the popular temperance ballad by "Stella of Washington" and Mrs. E. A. Parkhurst. The presentational quality of the scene intentionally brings us out of the world of the play and connects the stage action with the larger American culture. The cry for "Men of Temperance" to save the poor family, coming as it does in a play intended to be produced by temperance societies as a part of their meetings, is a fascinating use of the stage, suggesting that the play's intention is to inspire society members to go out in search of little Bessies and Maggies. At the same time, the play urges female temperance workers to be responsible with their power to influence men toward good or evil. The purpose of Bradley's play is, therefore, not conversion of drunkards but morale bolstering for temperance soldiers. Within the world of the play, however, the song does have the power to convert the drunkard father. As his daughters sing, Howard begins to stir; by the end of the song, he is sitting upright holding his face in his hands. Bradley describes how the children turn upstage and approach their father, each taking one of his hands. They command him "Come, father!" and lead him slowly from the room. In the last scene of the play, the former drunkard Howard is elected secretary of the temperance society and proposes successfully to Frank's teetotaler sister, Alice, who will make an honorable stepmother to Bessie and Maggie.

The inclusion of an interpolated ballad in a temperance drama is not particularly surprising. In fact, the scene of a child entering the tavern to beg her father to come home is the subject of another very famous temperance song, "Father, Dear Father, Come Home" by Emmet G. Coleman.[32] Yet there is a special reason why Bradley includes "Father's a Drunkard and Mother Is Dead" in the play instead of "Father, Dear Father, Come Home." Indeed, as the frontispiece of the published text of *The First Glass* indicates, Nellie Bradley in fact is

"Stella of Washington." The real identity of "Stella" is further confirmed in the 1885 collection *Woman in Sacred Song,* which credits Bradley as "Stella" for the lyrics to "Father's a Drunkard and Mother Is Dead." Under her own name, Bradley is also the lyricist for one published version of the ubiquitous temperance ditty "Don't Sell My Father Rum." It appears that the talent for emotional manipulation that Bradley employed as the lyricist of some of the most popular temperance ballads of the era was also a skill she discovered could be used for making plays. Yet the style of Bradley's plays does not entirely share the tone of her songwriting. Rather than simply offering emotional connection to the suffering alcohol creates, Bradley used the stage also to inspire temperance workers, teach them WCTU orthodoxy, and clarify issues that faced the movement.

Thus, the temperance dramas of Nellie H. Bradley, though not as popular or as well documented as *Ten Nights in a Barroom* or *The Drunkard,* are useful for understanding doctrinal issues within the movement as well as the perceived role of women in the cause. Bradley's plays deserve to be studied as one of several highly theatrical tactics employed by American temperance women in the years after the Civil War and before the great male-dominated political push for national Prohibition. As inheritors of the tradition of evangelical Protestantism with its revival meetings and testimonials, and as members of a greater culture of temperance in the United States that enjoyed sentimental ballads, temperance women in the late nineteenth century discovered their own emotional and theatrical methods for accomplishing the great task of "social housekeeping," a job that the country in general agreed was possible only through the power of woman's influence.

Notes

The epigraph to this essay is taken from Nellie H. Bradley, *The First Glass; or, The Power of Woman's Influence,* and *The Young Teetotaler; or, Saved at Last* (Rockland, Maine: Z. Pope Vose & Co., 1868; 1873), 1.3.

1. Walter J. Meserve, *An Outline History of American Drama* (New York: Feedback Theatrebooks and Prospero Press, 1994), 98.
2. According to the last official WCTU history, similar attacks were staged on taverns in Jamestown, New York, on December 17, 1873, and in Hillsboro, Ohio, on December 22, 1873. See Helen E. Tyler, *Where Prayer and Purpose Meet* (Evanston: Signal Press, 1949), 13.
3. In 1881 the WCTU adopted the policy "Do Everything" and added to its alcohol temperance agenda the much more controversial call for women's suffrage. Susan B. Anthony was in attendance at the WCTU convention that set this new official course. See Ruth

Bordin, *Woman and Temperance: The Quest for Power and Liberty, 1873–1900* (Philadelphia: Temple University Press, 1981), 119.
4. Frances E. Willard, *Do Everything: A Handbook for the World's White Ribboners* (Chicago: Woman's Temperance Publishing Association, 1895), 187.
5. Ibid., 66.
6. George W. Ewing, *The Well-Tempered Lyre: Song and Verse of the Temperance Movement* (Dallas: Southern Methodist University Press, 1977), 5.
7. James W. Frick, *Theatre, Culture, and Temperance Reform in Nineteenth-Century America* (Cambridge: Cambridge University Press, 2003), 156.
8. Ewing, *Well-Tempered Lyre*, 72.
9. Ibid., 75. The story is also printed in Eva Munsou Smith's *Woman in Sacred Song: A Library of Hymns, Religious Poems, and Sacred Music by Woman* (Boston: D. Lothrup, 1885).
10. Carol Mattingly, *Well-Tempered Women: Nineteenth-Century Temperance Rhetoric* (Carbondale: Southern Illinois University Press, 1998), 1.
11. Ibid., 67.
12. Willard, *Do Everything*, 80.
13. Many incidents of play performances are recorded in WCTU meeting minutes. Here is one example from the records of the Windfall, Pennsylvania, chapter: "A regular meeting in the home of Mrs. H.R. English Friday Evening May 23 1902. Opened by song 'Stand up for Jesus'. Recitation of 27th Psalms by Miss Lewis. Lord's Prayer by all standing. Song 'A Dark Cloud'. The young people (17) then rendered *The Bridal Wine Cup* as a drama. Many compliments were bestowed on the principal character, Miss Grace Packard. Song, 'Blest be the Tie'. . . . Refreshments consisting of lemonade and cake were served to the large number of guests, and a good social time enjoyed. Mayme B Lewis Recording Sec'y." See "The Organization of the Woman's Christian Temperance Union, Windfall, Penna.," http://www.rootsweb.com/~srgp/articles/wctu1898.htm. John W. Frick attributes the piece performed at this meeting, *The Bridal Wine Cup*, to Nellie H. Bradley (*Theatre, Culture, and Temperance Reform*, 163), although I have not been able to verify this attribution. *The Bridal Wine Cup* is also the name of a temperance dialogue by Sidney Herbert that was frequently anthologized in oral interpretation collections.
14. Rev. Canon Farrar, *Talks on Temperance* (New York: National Temperance Society and Publication House, 1880).
15. Bradley's plays can be found in the microform collection "English and American Drama of the Nineteenth Century."
16. In her unpublished dissertation, "Beyond *The Drunkard*: American Temperance Drama Reexamined" (Indiana University, 1991), theatre scholar Ann Ferguson provides an expansive study of the 110 extant American temperance plays. Of these, twenty-three are known to have been written by women; and of those by women, seven—nearly a third—are by Nellie Bradley.
17. Key pieces of Nellie Bradley's biographical information are unknown at this time, including her birth and death dates. However, her husband's *Washington Post* obituary from March 8, 1915, shows that she survived him.
18. Nellie H. Bradley, *The First Glass; or, The Power of Woman's Influence and The Young Teetotaler; or, Saved at Last* (Rockland, Maine: Z. Pope Vose and Co., 1873), 1.1.

19. Nellie H. Bradley, *Reclaimed; or, The Danger of Moderate Drinking* (Rockland, Maine: Z. Pope Vose and Co., 1868), 1.1.
20. Ibid.
21. Frederic Richard Lees, *The Temperance Bible-commentary: giving at one view, version, criticism, and exposition, in regard to all passages of Holy Writ bearing on 'wine' and 'strong drink', or illustrating the principles of the temperance reformation* (New York: Sheldon & Co., 1870).
22. Nellie H. Bradley, *The Stumbling Block; or, Why a Deacon Gave Up His Wine* (Rockland, Maine: Z. Pope Vose and Co., 1871), 1.1.
23. Nellie H. Bradley, *Wine as Medicine; or, Abbie's Experience* (Rockland, Maine: Z. Pope Vose and Co., 1873), 1.1.
24. Nellie H. Bradley, *Marry No Man If He Drinks; or, Laura's Plan and How It Succeeded* (Rockland, Maine: Z. Pope Vose and Co., 1868), 1.1.
25. Ibid.
26. Ewing, *Well-Tempered Lyre*, 48.
27. Bradley, *Marry No Man If He Drinks*, 1.1.
28. Ewing, *Well-Tempered Lyre*, 49.
29. Bradley, *The First Glass*, 1.1.
30. Ibid., 1.3.
31. Ibid., 1.2.
32. Emmet G. Coleman, ed., *The Temperance Songbook* (1907; New York: American Heritage Press, 1971), 68–69.

Toward a New Theatre History of Dionysus

—ELLEN MACKAY

For historians of the Western theatre, *The Bacchae* tells a peculiarly fecund tale. Compressed into its 1,394 lines is the origin story of our object of study—or, to put a finer point on it, in its short traffic of the stage the vexed conditions of theatre's civic foundation are played out. It follows that this tragedy cries out for the affixation of prefixes: *The Bacchae* has been canonized as ur-drama and metatheatre;[1] it comes down to us as the masterwork whose master narrative shapes the drama into an art form that is not just culturally meaningful but socially constitutive. Not incidentally for one so influential, this is a narrative that is notoriously grisly; Dionysus, god of the theatre, patron divinity of the Athenian stage on which Euripides' penultimate play was produced, arrives in Thebes to scourge those complicit in his cult's repression. Before *The Bacchae*'s devastatingly inconclusive ending—in Arrowsmith's translation, "what was most expected / has not been accomplished. . . . / So ends the play" (1390–91; 1394)[2]— the blasphemy of Thebes' secular government is repaid with sexual humiliation, slaughter, and incestuous cannibalism. The lesson is clear enough: those who profane dramatic rites will find their disbelief permanently suspended—like King Pentheus's head from his mother's thyrsus.[3] Which is to say that blatantly, by the frank doings of the god of our idolatry, scholars and practitioners of the theatre are implicated in this bloody coup. As Martin Puchner writes, "Without a doubt, *The Bacchae* is a play about the theatre, a play about the impossibility of escaping the theatre, and also a revenge of the theatre against its enemies."[4] Given the terms of this redaction, our allegiances are ordained.

The givenness of these terms is Nietzsche's bequest to dramatic theory. Since their elaboration in *The Birth of Tragedy*, the battle lines drawn by Dionysus have inspired a mythologized theatre history in which the stage plays the insurgent to a host of repressive regimes, psychic and political, formal and civilizing. For though Nietzsche's romance of tragedy's archaic past is famously an account of the conjoining of Apollonian and Dionysian forces, his is not a pairing of equals; unabashedly, Nietzsche worships at the altar of Dionysus, the god of intoxication who presides over a sublime nexus of music, excess, "sexual indiscipline,"[5] and "self-forgetting"[6]—in brief, the god of atavistic urges, the god of a people that has yet to suffer its subjection to a pantheon of gods. To safeguard the populace from Dionysus's totalizing theatre experience, the Apollonian serves as aesthetic anesthetic. Armed with harp and hymnal, Apollo reconciles tragedy to a society threatened by the prospect of "orgiastic self-destruction"[7] by constraining the genre within what Nietzsche calls his "artificially dammed-up world of semblance and measure."[8] Given the infelicity of this description, it is not surprising to find that however necessary Apollo's mediating influence, Nietzsche is remarkably keen to shrug it off, to "dismantle," as he says, "the artful edifice of Apolline culture" and "catch sight" of its Dionysian "foundations."[9] So when he calls for "the rebirth of tragedy" as the means to cultural liberation, he does so as the charismatic priest of a singular deity: "Now you must only dare to be tragic human beings, for you will be released and redeemed. You will accompany the festive procession of Dionysus from India to Greece! Put on your armor for a hard fight, but believe in the miracles of your god!"[10] And according to the work's final and fervent prophecies, it is under the spell of Dionysus, albeit dressed up in the garb of Siegfried, that the "German spirit" will seize its destiny: "One day it will find itself awake, with all the morning freshness that comes from a vast sleep; then it will slay dragons, destroy treacherous dwarfs, and awaken Brünhilde—and not even Wotan's spear itself will be able to bar its path!"[11] By the time we turn from tragedy's birth to its hotly anticipated resurrection, Dionysus has become the crusading hero in a Wagnerian saga, and the promised slayings of dwarfs, dragons, and divinities, rendered here with all the twee grandiosity characteristic of this strain of Germanic nationalism, represent the casualties of his revolutionary art.[12] According to Nietzsche, and his is an opinion not easily neglected, the purpose of tragedy is to topple its Valhalla, or, less operatically put, to bring down its cultural superstructure by the giddy violence of its Bacchic refrains.

None of this would resonate quite so much had not Nietzsche's vision of tragedy's once and future history turned out to be astonishingly predictive of the theatre of the American avant-garde. By some alchemy of unconfessed influence and historical accident,[13] *The Birth of Tragedy*—particularly its rousing finale—reads like the dramaturgical treatment of Richard Schechner's landmark production, *Dionysus in 69*. It is a tired but useful critical overstatement to say that The Performance Group's inaugural and much-acclaimed mise-en-scène chalks out the great divide between established theatrical practice, epitomized by the insulating conventions of fourth-wall realism, and radical performance, as set forth in the bold schematics of *TDR*. As it happens, Schechner charts the operation of a liberated theatre that is markedly familiar. Like Nietzsche, Schechner advances a project of cultural reclamation; like Nietzsche, he calls for a ritualized and participatory event; like Nietzsche, he describes the profit of this undertaking as social transformation; and like Nietzsche, he maps the coming revolution onto the figure of Dionysus, by choosing *The Bacchae* as his palimpsest.

The result is a production that ineradicably marks both Euripides' tragedy and the theatrical landscape of the twentieth century. Premiering the day after Robert Kennedy's assassination, on June 9, 1968, *Dionysus in 69* was plainly styled to channel the rage of the disenfranchised; Froma Zeitlin writes that the title was chosen to herald "a revolution that would elect Dionysus president" by the following November.[14] To mobilize the audience to that end, the production famously disposed of all traces of what Nietzsche calls Apollonian "semblance." The conventional divisions of stage from audience, spectacle from spectator, and performance from real event were aggressively breached, such that playgoers were not just inhabitants of the scene but participants in the ritual slaughter of Pentheus, refashioned as the scapegoat for America's widespread malaise. While Schechner was hardly alone in choosing this moment to rescind the theatrical contract, the instant celebrity of *Dionysus in 69* reflects the confluence of the Group's experimental philosophies, the tumultuous state of the union, and *The Bacchae*'s tragic plot. William Shephard, who performed the role of Dionysus, recalls, "the basic themes of the play—violence, madness, ecstasy, challenge of authority, moral choice—were all issues of great concern in American society at the time. And they seemed particularly suited to the Group's extremely physical, impulse-oriented way of working."[15] Yet what goes unsaid in the records of the production is Schechner's self-reflexive deployment of tragedy's founding myth. A tacit but crucial factor in the play's reception by no less a cultural arbiter than the *New York Times* as a work that "anyone who wants to know where the modern theatre is going will have to see" is the fact that *Dionysus in 69* wields the story of the theatre god's revenge as the manifesto for a new theatre.[16]

Recall that Schechner opens *Performance Theory*—his declaration of independence from the mainstream stage—by describing *The Bacchae* as the drama widely known to offer "the clearest example" of the "form" of "Primal Ritual," that source from which all meaningful performance descends.[17] Recall too that by positioning himself *Between Theater and Anthropology*, Schechner advances the cause of art that "reduplicate[s] its origins" in the holistic rites of the community (he lists "dances, cruel and joyful celebrations, orgies, cures, trials") for the liberation it offers from the stultifying tyranny of aesthetics.[18] Necessarily, then, the politics of his production operate in two registers at once: certainly, they attack the American status quo in the drop out/freak out idiom of 1968's summer of discontent, but they also promote an unmistakable theatrical revolt. Squaring off before an institution that Schechner (among others) dismisses as bourgeois and ineffectual, *Dionysus in 69* undertakes a transfiguration of the stage from a site of imitated actions into a site of real rites.[19] And the agent of this uprising is Euripides' foundational text, a work already haunted by Nietzsche's messianic vision of tragedy's second coming, and a work that always cries out for the liberation of the stage by taking as its centripetal crisis the repression of Dionysus and the resulting "revenge of the theatre against its enemies."

In light of the disciplinary debates sparked by the show's reformist agenda, the dictum proves surprisingly apposite. As though in fulfillment of Nietzsche's fervid desires, *Dionysus in 69* might be said to eventuate in precisely the apocalyptic pattern the philosopher outlines by staging the birth of an object of study made up of "trances, dances, [and] ecstasies"[20]—or, to recur to the terms of the production's slogan, of "feeling, loving, wanting, killing, hearing, tasting, touching, living." In other words, as a consequence of the essential consequence of Euripides' original drama, the revolution of *Dionysus in 69* might be said to deliver unto us the discipline of Performance Studies, over which Schechner has subsequently presided as charismatic priest.[21]

I raise this history for the sake of remembering how hard it is to forget. Before 1968, *The Bacchae* was a blank slate; notwithstanding its academic significance, it had received no professional production in America's memorial past.[22] Since the éclat of *Dionysus in 69*, Euripides' play slips into the role of our discipline's alpha and omega: at once the origin story of the theatre we have lost and the truth, way, and light of the theatre to come. The manner of this transfiguration is the reason for its influence: embraced as a shining model of drama's past and future greatness, Schechner's show produces a theatre history founded upon three essential facts: first, that the stage is a liberating force; second, that the profit and purpose of performance are found in its ecstatic impulse; and third, that ecstasy is the unfettered expression of sex and violence. The effect of rendering these precepts performatively obvious, so memorably self-evident as to go without saying, is the elevation of Nietzsche's speculations into demonstrable certainties. In fine, the recovered history of this recovered history works something like this: once Schechner stages *The Bacchae* in the image of Nietzsche's foretold crusade, the spirit of Dionysus is subsequently bound up in a hermeneutics that idealizes the orgiastic and the destructive (or the "orgiastic-destructive," as Schechner puts it)[23] as the means of theatrical liberation. For *The Bacchae*, and for the practice of theatre more largely, the implications are profound.

As revenant as Peter Brook's trapeze-and-slinky take on *A Midsummer Night's Dream*, *Dionysus in 69* needs little elaboration; it is by now a matter of theatre lore that Schechner's directorial coup was to defrock Dionysus's mysteries by staging them as naked revels served up in the form of participatory rituals—or, as J. L. Styan more clinically writes, "the Bacchantes required people to take off their clothes and mimic [their] sexual behavior."[24] To Schechner, scenarios of this sort supplied an exhilarating "opportunity for authentic interaction,"[25] while to Styan the result was "sexual by-play" of dubious "legitima[cy]."[26] To be sure, the work's enchantment, or lack thereof, was a subjective and volatile matter. Less arguable is the fact that these naked rites inspired the production's acclaim as a work on the cutting edge of the avant-garde. There could be no finer proof of its subversive credentials than The Performance Group's arrest at the University of Michigan on obscenity charges in January 1969, a fracas that also generated the production's national media coverage.

Given the happy paronomastic associations called to mind by *Dionysus in 69*'s form of total disclosure—among these, "naked truth," "stripped-down theatre," "bared soul"—it is easy to see why the explicit body became a hallmark of the Group's authenticity, and even of its generativity; in the words of Shephard, for instance, the opening birth ritual "served to canalize the libidinal energy of the Group and transform it into symbolic procreation."[27] While Shephard shows himself eager to assign "symbolic" purpose to what some condemned as gratuitous exhibitionism, explicit in his unfortunate metaphor is the reflexiveness with which the Group's performance absorbed the teleology of heterosexual sex. This drive is repeatedly written into the recorded history of the production, though sometimes with a lighter touch: even as Shephard remembers the upshot of the Group's naked labor in terms of figurative parturition, Schechner relegates to the footnotes of *TDR* the fact that the "erotic contact between performers and audience" which took place particularly in a short-lived scene entitled "the Total Caress" produced "several cases where male spectators had orgasms."[28] To Schechner, those "sorts of spectators" who sought out *Dionysus in 69* with the hope of getting some "action" misunderstood the "intrinsic logic" of the work.[29] But as Stephen Bottoms has so influentially written, Schechner's advocacy for "efficacious" performance as the scourge of America's "decadent," "lying," and "homosexual" theatre routinely organizes the avant-garde under the sign of straight, virile masculinity.[30] In "Speculations on Radicalism, Sexuality, and Performance," an essay that defends the sexual politics of *Dionysus in 69*, Schechner goes so far as to configure the gratification of male desire as the goal of his liberatory agenda when he offers as a cure for political disillusionment a "revolution that eradicates privileges of pleasure ... [such that] each man would be entitled to pleasure whenever he wished."[31] In the spirit of Nietzsche's Dionysian rapture of "exuberant fertility" and "procreative lust" that "release[s] and redeem[s]" its beholder,[32] the Bacchantes's "authentic interaction" thus seems to have staked its claim to revolutionary truthfulness in the all-too-real form of release it was widely rumored to incite, a fact that a more cynical critic might argue was made plain in the come-on of the show's title.

The other strand of the production's radicality, its sacralized violence, is no less politically fraught. In Schechner's chronicle of the production, the climactic scene of Pentheus's murder prompted an eruption of "participation and belief"; according to analogies of his own choosing, the event unfolded like "a kind of new Mass" or "a revival meeting."[33] Still in the flush of this heady (and naked) rite, the audience was then greeted with a harangue, delivered by Dionysus from atop the shoulders of the cast, in a style that Ruby Cohn recalls as "a medley of Mussolini and Billy Graham":[34] "I love the smell of riots, the orgasms of death and blood! We will tolerate no more false revolutions, no more false rituals and phony bloodbaths! We want the real thing!"[35] Although the Group's intention was to exhibit the god's quick slide from victim to tyrant, in practice spectators rallied to Dionysus's cause. The conflation of Pentheus with authoritarian hypocrisy rendered the king's homicide an exhilarating slaughter that Zeitlin remembers as unsettling for the thoughtless frenzy it generated. Borrowing a phrase from Schechner's own reflections on the "politics" of the work's "ecstasy," she recalls the god's final triumph as a kind of "fascist liberation," uncannily evocative of the mass spectacles of the Third Reich.[36]

Now, all evidence to the contrary, my point in offering this grim summary of the production's highlights is not to recapitulate the hand-wringing response of those self-appointed community leaders who bewailed the indecency of The Performance Group and lobbied, with some success, for the arrest of its members. I do not believe that *Dionysus in 69* is reducible to the politics I have just outlined, nor do I contend that those politics have been neglected—either by critics (particularly in the wake of Bottoms's excellent article) or by the Group's own membership, including Schechner.[37] I have recollected the production in these stark terms because what interests me is the legacy of *Dionysus in 69*, by which I mean the way its diffuse and elusive memorial impression has slipped by theatre's critical apparatus rather too surreptitiously. In his elegant survey of the manner in which performance leaves its mark, Marvin Carlson writes that all plays are haunted by the ghosts of past productions, surely never more so than when this ghost proves to be a zeitgeist, or spirit of the age.[38] But this does not yet say enough of the peculiar fantasmatic power of *Dionysus in 69*, for among the shadows cast by the remembrance of plays past, the specter of its ur-tragedy is uniquely persistent: by serving up what is for all intents and purposes the inaugural performance of the story of the theatre's bloody origins, Schechner's production of *The Bacchae* represents an especially restless ghost, a universal ancestor to the Western repertoire whose crime dooms it to possess all stages, and all spectators, in perpetuity.

This spectral influence is hardly accidental. One of Schechner's lasting insights is that performance is "twice-behaved behavior";[39] in other words, it derives its force from a genealogy of proximation that points back to an original but lost "truth." It is likewise his speculation that this pedigree must be exceptionally charged when it comes to a staging of *The Bacchae*, in which catching sight of foundations promises nothing less than a disciplinary epiphany—the revelation of "Primal Ritual" in its "clearest" form. Schechner's production does more than rise to meet this promise—it is designed to excite the desire for just such a conversionary encounter by pledging release and redemption for any spectator who makes himself (or, less signally, herself) complicit in its tragic interactions. It is therefore a measure of the show's astonishing success that *Dionysus in 69* was embraced as an immaculate resurrection of the theatre's primal past; again, the *New York Times* proves indexical, and doubtless generative, of this reaction for attaching to the show the following accolade: "[It is] as faithful a production as *The Bacchae* can have received since its original performance."[40] The consequence of this much-heralded fidelity, this apparent return to the gritty and ecstatic matter repressed by the false consciousness of a disenchanted age, is a revision of the script of tragic performance. That is, in place of the more anodyne dyad of pity and fear, *Dionysus in 69* offers straight sex (verified by the requisite expression of gratification that Schechner cannot quite keep from disclosing) and mass violence.

Let me draw out these terms in turn. First, by designating the state of male arousal as the unfakable sign of liberation, Schechner proselytizes the dictum that what Nietzsche calls "the ecstasy of the Dionysiac state" is the same tumescence so manifest in the iconography of the theatre's satyr-god.[41] In so doing, he takes titillation for truth without recognizing that, as Linda Williams writes, arousal is a "reflex" that is always "culturally mediated"—hidebound by the

{ 77 }

same repressive politics (in this case sexist and homophobic) from which it promises emancipation.[42] But what is more crucial, once fomented by Schechner's Bacchae as the requisite condition of Dionysian rites, this reflex is left to lurk in the murky substratum of a more politic historiography as an index of theatrical authenticity. Again, the issue is not that *Dionysus in 69* interprets Euripides' tragedy in a style that Schechner has conceded was sometimes too eagerly embraced by the "drool circuit" of "off-off Broadway,"[43] but instead that this interpretation is now deeply embedded in the imaginary of our discipline as the theatre's Primal Ritual—the essential matter that we practice and preach.

Second, by marshaling the spirit of fascist liberation to set the tone of the theatre's avenging triumph, *Dionysus in 69* lets that spirit loose, as it were, to fly beneath the radar of the rising avant-garde. Considered within the shadowy networks that Diana Taylor (via Derrida) calls the "hauntologies" of dramatic performance,[44] this stealth flight is something of a crypto-theatrical inevitability: as an agent not-so-secretly in the service of Nietzsche's theatrical revolution, which is in turn possessed by the crusading nationalism of Wagner's *Sigfried,* Schechner cannot keep from casting something like a totalitarian spell. Yet by captivating audiences with the sort of sound and fury made famous at Bayreuth and made infamous at Nuremberg, Schechner's triumph of the Dionysian will assigns to the dramatic impulse a fascist militancy; in effect, the celebrants of tragic liberation are shown to draw their legitimacy from the barrel of a gun. Particularly because *Dionysus in 69* so effortlessly allegorizes the founding of performance studies, a disciplinary rebirth that recodifies theatre as a set of rites and rituals unencumbered by any narrative purpose or edifying payoff, Schechner's production thus insinuates a rationale for "pure" theatre that is at once bloodily enforced and philosophically hollow. Put in the terms of the production's partisan address, the revolution that would install Dionysus as president and entitle "each man" to "pleasure whenever he wished" raises a coalition of the roiled and the aroused who are invited to read the excitations of the flesh for theatrical transcendence.

It is important to remember that audiences of *Dionysus in 69* were never so easily unified under the banner of that deity's campaign (Cohn, for one, narrates her experience of the show's final moments with reproving dispassion: once the "still naked" "Performance Group women [start] wash[ing] the stage blood from the performance space," she "hurr[ies] out so the performers don't catch cold").[45] But a production as storied as Schechner's suffers the flattening out of its mixed reception by dint of its own celebrity. For however much we know that performance is defined by the ephemeral and inimitable relation of event and audience, and that consequently "the interaction between the art object and the spectator" must always be, as Peggy Phelan writes, "resistant to the claims of validity and accuracy endemic to the discourse of reproduction," in the case of a touchstone production, all bets are off.[46] Once it is christened a show that "anyone who wants to know where the modern theatre is going will have to see," *Dionysus in 69* becomes the harbinger of a revolution that has already triumphed: the very necessity of its being seen canonizes the production as the event that we (who want to be in the know) are told to see in it, which is nothing less than the emergence of the modern theatre—or in Nietzschean terms, its rebirth. Even *Dionysus in 69*'s unusually extensive archive, which includes a picture book, two illustrated essays, innumerable reviews, William Shephard's memoirs, Schechner's several *TDR* articles, and Brian De Palma's film of the production, can only memorialize this fait accompli.[47]

There is a maddening paradox to the operation of our disciplinary memory here, insofar as many of the production's remains—particularly the spectacle of De Palma's film—provoke all kinds of questions about the politics of Schechner's "authentic interaction," yet because, as Phelan writes, "performance cannot be saved, recorded or documented," because its value derives from the axiom that it "leave no visible trace" behind, the materials that shore up the show's memorability can never serve the scholar's turn as evidence of theatre's evanescent event.[48] They are merely "a spur to memory":[49] like the *New York Times* review, their function is to remind you that the only way to understand the production's import is to have seen it for yourself.

This conundrum is suppressed (though never quite resolved) in the recourse to orthodoxy: to not know the show is to uphold its acclaim for the reasons critical consensus demands. Because it is increasingly infeasible for everyone "who wants to know where the modern theatre [was] going" to have seen *Dionysus in 69*, that constituency is left to fill in the absence of so obligatory an experience by recovering the memory of the production's claim to fame—namely, that it sets the pattern for the rising avant-garde. And because it is the unforgettable feature of Schechner's now unforgettable version of *The Bacchae* that the synergy of orgiastic sex and mob violence provides the modus operandi of drama's rise and tyranny's consequent fall, in the recessed practices of performance historiography, Schechner's reconstituted rites become indissociable from the progress, and the progressivism, of theatrical modernity. The upshot is this: constrained in our collective memory to signify the immanent triumph of its revolutionary ends—and these are laudable goals, including community enfranchisement, political accountability, and freedom from repression—*Dionysus in 69* effects the canonization of its means—and these are less nice, devolving as they must from a mythic history of sexual humiliation and incestuous cannibalism. From a theatre historian's perspective, one way of accounting for this dubious business is to say that the legacy of Schechner's production turns practitioners and proponents of the stage into Hamlet: we find we have been assigned a revenger's part by a suspect ghost.

Although his defiance of augury comes at a high cost, Hamlet, and particularly the counter-narrative he offers us, is worth a closer look. As is only fitting for a figure so profoundly concerned with the influence of ancient tragedy ("what's Hecuba to him, or he to Hecuba"),[50] Hamlet turns out to model an instructive skepticism before Dionysian tradition. His prolonged hesitation before submitting, finally and fatally, to the ghost's command recalls a recondite passage from *The Birth of Tragedy* in which Nietzsche outlines an unexpectedly strained relation between Euripides and the cult of Dionysus. *The Bacchae*, he writes, is "the work of a poet who has resisted Dionysus with heroic strength throughout a long life—only to end his career with a glorification of his opponent and a suicide, like someone suffering from vertigo who finally throws himself off a tower simply in order to escape the terrible dizziness he can tolerate no longer."[51] According to Nietzsche, Euripides represents an especially illustrious "get" for the Dionysian cause; his capitulation to the power of the theatre's savage god is like Saul's conversion on the road to Damascus: a powerful testament to an insuperable force. It hardly needs to be pointed out that *Dionysus in 69* dramatizes this fable exactly: by accounting his production "a kind of new Mass" or "a revival meeting," Schechner presents *The Bacchae*, and thus the telos of theatre history, as the visitation of "orgiastic-destructive" transcendence upon its benighted audience. To Schechner (as to Nietzsche), the chthonic frenzy that possesses Euripides is tragedy's holy ghost. There is, however, another side to this story. For interestingly enough, Nietzsche reports that what succeeds from *The Bacchae* is the ascendancy of the "Socratic," or rigorously rational, stage. It is not much in the way of extrapolation to then suppose that the poet's leap is less a surrender than a supreme act of protest—one potent enough to inspire a tragic form adverse to the ruthless imperative that Puchner describes. According to this version of theatre history, Euripides' masterwork bequeaths to us an anguished view of tragedy's ritual foundations. Rather like Hamlet's melancholy vacillation before yielding himself up to the demands of his revenge tragedy, *The Bacchae*'s ambivalence before Dionysus's reign of terror ("what has been expected / has not been accomplished") has all the effect of repudiating the theatre's "orgiastic-destructive" drive.

Although this is a history that has gone unchampioned by the likes of Nietzsche or Schechner, we can nonetheless imagine its impact on the discipline: by the exigencies of its persistent ghost, *The Bacchae* would supply us with a theatrical paradigm in which the stage would prove no more pure or free than its civic context, and in which the ecstasies that "cause subjectivity to vanish"[52] in the throes of a righteous revenge would turn out to be the workings of a dishonest ghost—in Hamlet's words, "bestial oblivion" wrought by a "devil" in a "pleasing shape."[53] As Nietzsche has proved, the theatre history that would elaborate this paradigm demands the reclamation of a lost past. Therefore, in what remains of this essay I will turn to two works that are also adaptations of *The Bacchae* but which lack *Dionysus in 69*'s haunting presence in our discipline. It is my ambition to raise their ghosts.

The earliest of these is Philip Massinger's *The Roman Actor* (1626), a play that takes as its subject a troupe of players unlucky enough to serve under Emperor Domitian's rule.[54] Its opening lines declare its relevance to my project: asks one actor, "What do we act today?" Replies the other, "Agave's frenzy, / With Pentheus' bloody end."[55] As this repertorial choice insinuates, the company suffers under a hostile and repressive government: the Senators, rendered as an assembly of Puritan pharisees, persecute the players with antitheatrical prejudice, while the Emperor is a tyrant who indulges his hedonism at any price. Before the end of the first act, the chief tragedian, Paris, is hauled before the Senate to defend the legitimacy of his profession. The timely arrival of Domitian saves the theatre from closure, but Paris soon faces another obstacle to his safety: the Empress Domitia, watching him perform, is roused to such a frenzy of desire that she joins the troupe to play his partner in a love scene. The Emperor, justly suspicious of the verisimilitude of his wife's acting ("Why are you / Transported thus, Domitia? 'Tis a play" [3.2.283–84]), repays his cuckolding by casting himself in a command performance of yet another tragedy to take on the role of Paris's murderer, though the cunning of this retribution is undone somewhat when, delivering the deathblow, the Emperor goes up on his lines:

Domitian: O villain! Thankless villain!—
I should talk now
But I have forgot my part.
But I can do—
Thus, thus and thus. (4.2.281–83)

Like Pentheus, Domitian proves a lousy dissembler of Dionysus's rites, and like Pentheus, he is repaid for his sins against the theatre god in the bloodbath of the last act. But the play's most pointed evocation of *The Bacchae* occurs in its dramatization of the affinity of theatrical and tyrannical discipline—a relation that slips beyond the audience's notice in Schechner's more agitprop production. In *The Roman Actor,* stage and state are caught in the death grip of a mutuality so pronounced that any distinction between actor and political operative, or between acting and political action, is moot; ultimately, statecraft and stagecraft fall together like Holmes and Moriarty at Reichenbach Falls—the one fatal to, yet productive of, the other. Emblematic of this confusion is the fact that Massinger has "Pentheus' bloody end" set the stage for Domitian's tyranny such that *The Bacchae* models the terrorist violence that the state not only baldly appropriates but then visits upon and within the theatre. The confusion of Dionysian slaughter with Domitian's realpolitik makes it clear that for better or (more accurately) for worse, performance and politics are mutually constitutive and play out as all too much the same thing. Indeed, if there is a lesson to be found in Massinger's version of *The Bacchae,* it would seem to be this: any division of the "liberating" force of dramatic performance from the despotic force of imperial power is a misprision that proves deadly to the theatre itself.

In *Callirrhoë*, an 1884 play published under the pseudonym Michael Field, the fallacy of the Manichaean split between Dionysian emancipation and civic stricture is again richly dramatized. This tragedy's eponymous heroine is a figure of spotless virtue who tends her blind father and her gadabout brother somewhere in archaic, pastoral Greece. But the arrival of a throng of Maenads in the local woods imperils her Victorian idyll. For though Callirrhoë mistrusts the "wild and strange" practices of the Bacchants (1.2.15), unseemly as they are to "maiden modesty" (1.3.20), she soon confesses to be weary of her life at the spinning wheel. As she soliloquizes:

> "Can it be meant," I often ask myself,
> "Callirrhoë, that thou shouldst simply spin,
> Be borne of torches to the bridal-bed,
> Still a babe's hunger, and then simply die,
> Or wither at the distaff, who hast felt
> A longing for the hills and ecstasy?" (1.2.154–59)[56]

Callirrhoë offers several stanzas of this kind of pointed self-examination before she seeks the counsel of Coresus, the priest of Dionysus, who fairly slavers for so nubile a novitiate. His pitch is seductive—"ask yourself have you not a deeper need / Than the stale rites of customary gods / Can satisfy?" (1.3.53–55)—but recalling Dionysus's role in Pentheus's murder and her duty to maintain her invalid father, Callirrhoë balks, and disaster ensues. The spurned Coresus calls on

Dionysus to send down a plague upon her village. As the death tally rises, lynch mobs roam the streets, looking for Maenads to blame for their misfortune. In short order, Callirrhoë loses her father and her friends to disease, while her community is a casualty of the local riots. When the curse is finally lifted by the priest's repentant suicide, Callirrhoë chooses to die Coresus's Maenad to escape a society from which she has become profoundly estranged. In a clearing in the woods, she disembowels herself.

What is most remarkable about *Callirrhoë* are the conditions of its authorship; Michael Field was the pen name of Katharine Harris Bradley and Edith Emma Cooper, an aunt and niece who lived together as lovers and artistic collaborators in Victorian England. This extraordinary history cannot help but impact our reception of the work,[57] especially given the unorthodoxy of its heroine, who offers a fierce critique of Ruskin's vision of the "angel at the hearth."[58] Particularly revealing, then, is the tragedy's rejection of the Dionysian for its facile promise of liberation from gender prescripts: the dilemma that Callirrhoë squarely faces is that neither her father's house nor Coresus's sect sanctions her strain of chaste and freethinking femininity. A case study in cultural anomie, *Callirrhoë* demonstrates that the construction of the false divide between cult and dominant culture has fomented a stifling social environment, one that leads conscientious figures to suicide. As a result, the self-sacrifice of its denouement reads much like Euripides' death in *The Birth of Tragedy*: as a searing denunciation of Dionysus's countercultural mystique.

Bradley and Cooper's play was never produced. Although initial reviews of the published work were favorable, once Robert Browning leaked the sex of Michael Field to the press, theatre companies took no interest in a verse drama written by an anonymous bluestocking. To imagine *Callirrhoë* as a work that wields theatrical influence therefore requires our fictionalization of history, along the lines that Bradley pled for in her request that Browning retract his telltale parapraxis: "The report of lady authorship will dwarf and enfeeble our work at every turn.... We must be free to work as dramatists to work out in the open-air of nature—exposed to her vicissitudes, witnessing her terrors: we cannot be stifled in drawing room conventionalities.... Oh with a word you can persuade the critics you have been tricking them: the heart of the mystery is not plucked out."[59] But if we can only speculate as to the ethos of a discipline in which *Callirrhoë* would not have been "stifled," or in which *The Roman Actor* was routinely revived, this is a recovered memory whose time has come. Having long accommodated the spectral creep of a Dionysian orthodoxy that exalts that deity of carnal excess as the sainted foe of all manner of repression, it seems worth conjuring up the "hauntology" of a different kind of theatre god, one whose debauched tyranny leads Euripides to hurl himself, Tosca-like, to a martyr's death.

Under the auspices of this god's ghostly influence, the solicitations of the flesh could never so readily serve the turn as the epistemology of the avant-garde. For one thing, in light of Callirrhoë's blunt rejection of the Maenads' ecdysiastic "liberation," the exhibition of the female body would be difficult to misconstrue as the hallmark of the theatre's ritual purity. For another, in the knowledge that "Pentheus' bloody end" modeled the worst excesses of the Roman Empire to one of its most infamous tyrants, that slaughter would be hard to mistake for a righteous form of political protest. More fundamentally, in the context of a canon of competing adaptations of Euripides' tragedy, the aura of archaeological authenticity around The Performance Group's interpretation would be all but impossible to maintain. The legacy of *The Bacchae* might then have been a rich inquiry into the politics of the play's sacrifice instead of the reconfiguration of performance into "a kind of new Mass," a locus for the transmission of absolute and received truths.

According to this alternative history of Dionysus, taking up *The Bacchae* would no longer mean taking sides in a bloody struggle between theatrical liberation and authoritarian containment. Instead, it would mean recognizing that this struggle is the stage's grandest fiction, a self-sanctifying parable that strains against the play's grisly catastrophe, and one that, as Massinger and "Field" show, neither the theatre nor its patrons can afford to sustain. The terms of their concern find their clearest expression in Nietzsche's philosophy: like Siegfried's dragon and dwarf-slaying crusade, the theatre's revenge against its enemies is a myth that reifies and vindicates a rich set of political convictions. And it is precisely for this reason we had best remember that it remains, nevertheless, a myth.

Notes

This essay won the inaugural Robert A. Schanke Theatre Research award at the Mid-America Theatre Conference in Kansas City, 2005. It began as pre-show lecture for Randy White's excellent production of Colin Teevan's *Bacchai* at Indiana University in February 2005.

1. Martin Puchner argues that *The Bacchae* ought to be Abel's first example of this tragic form. Puchner, "Introduction," in Lionel Abel, *Tragedy and Metatheatre: Essays on Dramatic Form* (New York: Holmes and Meier, 2003), 13.
2. *The Bacchae*, trans. William Arrowsmith, in *The Complete Greek Tragedies: Euripides V*, ed. David Grene and Richard Lattimore (Chicago: University of Chicago Press, 1959), 220.

3. This formulation derives from Colin Teevan's version of the play: "I have come home . . . / . . . / So that I might suspend the disbelief / Of all who dare not believe in me." *Euripides Bacchai: A New Translation by Colin Teevan* (London: Oberon Books, 2002), 17.
4. Puchner, "Introduction," 13.
5. Friedrich Nietzsche, *The Birth of Tragedy and Other Writings*, trans. Ronald Speirs, ed. Raymond Geuss and Ronald Speirs (Cambridge: Cambridge University Press, 1999), 20.
6. Ibid., 17.
7. Ibid., 102.
8. Ibid., 27.
9. Ibid., 22.
10. Ibid., 98.
11. Ibid., 115.
12. Nietzsche's relation to Wagner is famously fraught. See Geuss and Speirs's account of this "love-hate" relationship in their critical introduction to *The Birth of Tragedy* (vii–x).
13. Schechner never mentions Nietzsche. Nonetheless, writes Froma Zeitlin, "Nietzsche's ideas about the Dionysian are clearly an influence" on the production. Zeitlin, "Dionysus in 69," in *Dionysus since '69: Greek Tragedy at the Dawn of the Third Millenium*, ed. Edith Hall, Fiona Macintosh, and Amanda Wrigley (Oxford: Oxford University Press, 2004), 57.
14. Ibid., 51.
15. William Shephard, *The Dionysus Group* (New York: Peter Lang, 1991), 52. Also quoted in Zeitlin, "Dionysus in 69," 59.
16. Dan Sullivan, rev. of *Dionysus in 69* by The Performance Group, *New York Times*, June 7, 1968, 35, col. 3; reproduced in Shephard, *The Dionysus Group*, 138–39.
17. Richard Schechner, *Performance Theory* (New York: Routledge, 1988), 4.
18. Richard Schechner, *Between Theatre and Anthropology* (Philadelphia: University of Pennsylvania Press, 1985); Richard Schechner, "Speculations on Radicalism, Sexuality, and Performance," *Drama Review* 13, no. 4 (1969): 109, 108–9.
19. As Schechner writes in one of his many *TDR* "Comments," "There will always be a commodity theatre, but the real work gets done elsewhere." *Tulane Drama Review* 8, no. 2 (1963): 9.
20. Schechner, *Performance Theory*, 33.
21. Ibid.
22. Zeitlin, "Dionysus in 69," 49. However, concurrent with *Dionysus in 69* was André Gregory's production of *The Bacchae* at Yale Rep in 1969.
23. Richard Schechner, "'The Bacchae': A City Sacrificed to a Jealous God," *Tulane Drama Review* 5, no. 4 (1961): 130.
24. J. L. Styan, *Modern Drama in Theory and Practice 2: Symbolism, Surrealism, and the Absurd* (Cambridge: Cambridge University Press, 1981), 171. Schechner notes that the decision to play the tragedy naked was Jerzy Grotowski's suggestion. Schechner, "Speculations," 94 n. 5.
25. Richard Schechner, *Environmental Theater* (New York: Applause Books, 1994), 43.
26. Styan, *Modern Drama*, 171.
27. Shephard, *The Dionysus Group*, 113.

28. Schechner, "Speculations," 97 n. 9.
29. Ibid.
30. Stephen Bottoms, "The Efficacy/Effeminacy Braid: Unpicking the Performance Studies/Theatre Studies Dichotomy," *Theatre Topics* 13, no. 2 (2003): 177. Bottom's article was the subject of the plenary session of the Performance Studies Conference at the Association for Theatre in Higher Education, July 29, 2004, in Toronto.
31. Schechner, "Speculations," 99.
32. Nietzsche, *The Birth of Tragedy*, 81, 98.
33. Schechner, *Environmental Theatre*, 43.
34. Ruby Cohn, "Old Myths in the New Theatre," *Educational Theatre Journal* 23, no. 4 (1971): 201.
35. Shephard, *The Dionysus Group*, 138.
36. Zeitlin, "Dionysus in 69," 58, 75. Zeitlin takes the phrase from Schechner's essay "The Politics of Ecstasy," in *Public Domain: Essays on the Theater* (Indianapolis: Indiana University Press, 1969).
37. As Leigh Clemons has demonstrated, the sexual politics of *Dionysus in 69* were extensively discussed among the actors in the Group; Clemons, "The Power of Performance: Environmental Theatre and Heterotopia in *Dionysus in 69*," *Theatre Studies* 37 (1992): 72.
38. Marvin Carlson, *The Haunted Stage* (Ann Arbor: University of Michigan Press, 2001).
39. Schechner, *Between Theatre and Anthropology*, 37.
40. Dan Sullivan, quoted in Shephard, *The Dionysus Group*, 139.
41. Nietzsche, *The Birth of Tragedy*, 40.
42. Linda Williams, *Hard Core: Power, Pleasure, and the "Frenzy of the Visible"* (Berkeley: University of California Press, 1989), 5.
43. Schechner, "Speculations," 97 n. 9.
44. Diana Taylor borrows this term from Derrida's *Specters of Marx* to discuss the trace left by performance in cultural memory in her book *The Archive and the Repertoire: Performing Cultural Memory in the Americas* (Durham, N.C.: Duke University Press, 2003), 141–46.
45. Cohn, "Old Myths," 401.
46. Peggy Phelan, *Unmarked: The Politics of Performance* (New York: Routledge, 1993), 147.
47. The picture book is *Dionysus in 69*, written collaboratively by The Performance Group, edited by Richard Schechner, photographs by Frederick Eberstadt, with additional photographs by Raeanne Rubenstein and two folios of photographs by Max Waldman (New York: Farrar, Straus and Giroux, 1970). The essays are Tom Prideaux's in *Life* (March 30, 1969) and Richard Goldstein's in *Vogue* (March 1969). Brian De Palma's film of the production dates from 1970 and was never distributed commercially, though it is now routinely sold online.
48. Phelan, *Unmarked*, 146, 149.
49. Ibid., 146.
50. Shakespeare, *Hamlet*, in *The Norton Shakespeare*, ed. Stephen Greenblatt, Walter Cohen, Jean E. Howard, and Katherin Eisaman Maus (New York: Norton, 1997), 2.2.536.
51. Nietzsche, *The Birth of Tragedy*, 60.
52. Ibid., 17.
53. Shakespeare, *Hamlet*, 4.4.(9.30), 2.2.575, 576.

54. For a brilliant account of the failure of catharsis in *The Roman Actor* see Stephen Orgel, "The Play of Conscience," in *Performativity and Performance,* ed. Andrew Parker and Eve Sedgwick (New York: Routledge, 1993), 133–51.
55. *The Roman Actor,* in *Drama of the English Renaissance II: The Stuart Period,* ed. Russell Fraser and Norman Rabkin (New York: Macmillan, 1976), 1.1.1–2 (717). Future quotations will be followed by act, scene, and line numbers in parentheses.
56. "Michael Field," *Callirrhoë,* Chadwyk-Healey English Verse Drama Full-Text Database, http://bert.lib.indiana.edu:2368/evd/. Future quotations will be followed by act, scene, and line numbers in parentheses.
57. For a biography of "Field" see Emma Donoghue's *We Are Michael Field* (Bath, U.K.: Absolute Press, 1998).
58. This construct is found in Ruskin's *Sesame and Lilies* (Chicago: A. C. McClurg, 1889).
59. Katharine Harris Bradley to Robert Browning, November 23, 1884, British Library, Add.MS.46866, ff. 16–18, excerpted in Rachel Morley, "Constructing the Self, Composing the Other: Auto/Fixation and the Case of Michael Field," *Colloquy: Text, Theory, Critique* 8 (2004): http://www.arts.monash.edu.au/others/colloquy/issue8/index.htm.

The Salvation Lass, Her Harlot-Friend, and Slum Realism in Edward Sheldon's *Salvation Nell* (1908)

—KATIE N. JOHNSON

Doctors, lawyers, butchers and bakers
And some sporty old fellows, as well,
They've been sinners for years
Yet they burst out in tears,
And join the Army, join the Army
Just to be around Salvation Nell.
—FROM THE SONG "SALVATION NELL" (1913)

As the lyrics from the popular 1913 song "Salvation Nell" make clear, Progressive Era culture was preoccupied with stories of salvation. When Edward Sheldon's drama of the same title opened in 1908, the play dazzled audiences with its remarkably realistic portrayal of tenement life, bar culture, and the path to salvation. The opening moments at Sid's bar in Hell's Kitchen showed men swigging real beer, prostitutes soliciting men, and star-actress Minnie Maddern Fiske scrubbing the bar (fig. 1). Long remembered for Fiske's pioneering realistic acting in the title role, *Salvation Nell* significantly influenced the development of modern American drama. Not since *Mrs. Warren's Profession*'s closing in New York in 1905 had a playwright ventured to represent prostitution onstage. Yet, not only did *Salvation Nell* escape Anthony Comstock's censorship clutches; it was widely perceived as groundbreaking during its time. One review called the

Figure 1. Sheet music for "Salvation Nell," by Grant Clarke, Edgar Leslie, and Theodore Morse (New York: Theodore Morse Music Company, 1913).

play "the achievement of the year—the achievement of many years—in our atmospheric and illusive stagecraft."[1] Moreover, during the 1960s theatre scholar John Gassner identified *Salvation Nell* as the best play of 1908.[2] Why have audiences and critics—for almost one hundred years—been riveted by this stark portrayal of New York's underbelly?

While some scholars have paid attention to *Salvation Nell*'s importance for American theatrical realism, little has been written about how the play intersects with Progressive Era reform efforts. This essay's focus is twofold: first, I will draw attention to the significance of *Salvation Nell* in the larger project of constructing what we might call "salvationist" sexuality—self-sacrificing female sexuality that is juxtaposed with the perceived dangers of prostitution; and second, I would like to pressure our understanding of American realism and assess the cultural work of staging what became known as "slum realism."

By all appearances, *Salvation Nell* is about salvation, featuring, as the song goes, a saintly figure with "heavenly grace," a "heavenly face," and "a cute tambourine" (fig. 2).[3] Under the surface, however, the play is also about prostitution; it is the backdrop against which we understand Nell's salvation. Although Nell herself is not a prostitute, she, like Laura Murdock of *The Easiest Way* (1909), seriously considers hooking when circumstances turn dire. In addition, her friend Myrtle (a former chorus girl, now a gold digger) and an entire brothel near the saloon where Nell works keep the plot connected to the sexual underworld. Indeed, more prostitutes appeared onstage in *Salvation Nell* than in any other American social problem play that had yet opened in New York. For a play about salvation, *Salvation Nell* spends almost as much dramaturgical energy portraying the underworld as it does the Salvation Army.

If the prostitute is the metaphor for modernity, as Charles Baudelaire once theorized, then the salvation figure, epitomized by Nell, is modernism's countermetaphor for female sacrifice.[4] While the prostitute is a body of modernist, capitalistic excess—a leaky body that may be purchased, but also one that must be contained—the salvation figure is a body of deprivation, a body so marked by loss that it is worn out by the endless work of reform. Here we see a curious paradox of the salvation figure: precisely because she is a deprived female body, she is free to roam in the public sphere, traversing the same terrain as a prostitute but never succumbing to the underworld or Progressive regulation. Thus, the Salvation Lass is a crucial figure not only in the study of prostitution but also in Progressive Era theatre, precisely because the two figures, Salvation Lass and whore, are inextricably linked.

Salvation Nell's dramaturgical force spins toward a kind of vexed salvation, beginning in the vice-laden underworld. The opening tableau reveals an unforgettable depiction of Sid McGovern's Empire Bar, a dive in New York City's Hell's Kitchen. Within the bar, a collection of "shabby, ill-dressed, poor-looking men of all ages already jovial with liquor" occupy center stage. Four women sit at stage left in the ladies' buffet (the women's section of the bar usually frequented by prostitutes), including two "shabby, painted streetwalkers" named Mabel and Sal, along with two men, presumably clients.[5] Although women are

Figure 2. Minnie Maddern Fiske and Holbrook Blinn in the infamous depiction of Sid's bar in *Salvation Nell* (1908). Photo by Byron, courtesy of the Museum of the City of New York.

present in the bar, it is unmistakably a male space in which men spit in spittoons, grab and sexually harass women (including Nell), pick up prostitutes, and hide from their wives and families. It is, moreover, the first representation of the ladies' buffet onstage, and it was an undeniable inspiration for Eugene O'Neill's 1921 divided barroom scene in *Anna Christie*. Thus, through the opening mise-en-scène—a set that was groundbreaking in realism—*Salvation Nell* frames the action of the play within lower-class bar culture, masculine authority, and the underworld.

The rising action of act 1 is likewise tied to prostitution. Almost immediately after the play opens, a policeman (who is drinking in the bar) announces there is going to be a brothel raid at Madame Cloquette's. It is not a regular arrest, we discover, but rather a public spectacle where the prostitutes are marched through the main street of town for all to see. The anticipation of the raid provides great excitement for the male bar patrons, who, according to the stage directions, are "galvanized to action, gulp down their drinks, and rush toward the door" (567). The crowd treats the brothel parade—or what we might call a (pa)raid—in Bahktinian carnivalesque fashion: "The crowd—hooting, shrieking, yelling—passes along the street in front of the saloon. Such cries as: 'Say girls, ain't he cold,' 'Hooray for Cloquette's,' 'Look at the pink one, she's got the goods all right—all right,' 'Ye would would ye!' 'Now will you be good,' etc., rise above the tumult" (569). This bawdy spectatorship is reminiscent of the rowdy behavior of Bowery B'hoys in mid-nineteenth-century theatre. This theatrical reference is not lost on Myrtle, who escapes the raid: "Nothing' like furnishin' free vaudeville t' all the neighbors!" (567).

We can think of this scene, then, as emblematic of the play itself and indeed of Progressive Era theatre: staging prostitution fulfills a kind of voyeuristic interest of surveying the underworld. More important, theatre participates in the regulation of sexuality; the brothel (pa)raid functions as a public ceremony by which the fallen woman is marked and scorned by dominant culture. Just as the scaffold in eighteenth-century Europe was designated as a public space in which the human subject was disciplined and punished, so the theatre was a regulatory site in which sexual propriety was communicated to audiences.[6] Tellingly, the raid scene demonstrates the paradoxical mimetic space that prostitutes occupy: they take center stage without ever appearing; they captivate the central plot even when they are absent. As in Greek tragedy, certain representations must take place offstage (for the Greeks, murder; for Progressives, brothel interiors). We only *hear* this parade take place, tellingly through the male gaze of customers at Sid's; we do not *see* the prostitutes or the interior of the brothel. This, of course, paralleled the paradoxical position of the prostitute in the culture at large. Ever in the limelight and never far from the Progressive Era gaze, prostitution in American theatre functioned as kind of erotic backdrop for plots ostensibly concerned with social themes. Central yet also peripheral to the main story, the prostitute figure often became realized as the harlot-friend, the necessary counterpart to the Salvation Lass.

The Harlot-Friend

> Against such feeble Action a prostitute stands out as the one bit of virile truth in the Plot. We have been so bored with irrelevant stuff that we welcome the harlot in contrast who is least consistent with herself.
>
> —REVIEW OF *SALVATION NELL* IN *THE DRAMATIST* (1910)

As Peter Bailey points out, Salvation Army lasses who appeared in turn-of-the-century musicals were often juxtaposed with prototypical flirty Gaiety Girls, who often derided the "Goody Goody Girls," proclaiming in one song, "It was silly to be chilly."[7] A crucial component of both salvation and fallen woman stories like *Salvation Nell* is popular audiences' understanding that a character who is a mistress to a wealthy man signifies as a prostitute. Her role is to befriend the female protagonist, only to desert her. We might well wonder, as did reviewer Belle Lindner Israels in 1909, why the harlot-friend is such a central character in *Salvation Nell*: "What is the author's purpose in bringing Myrtle into the play repeatedly and even at times, as in the last act, when the story does not demand it, and showing her entirely as enjoying the fruits of her shame?"[8] Indeed, the harlot character might appear to be excessive to the plot at first glance. Upon closer analysis, however, she is used, as the *Dramatist* put it, "as the one bit of virile truth in the Plot."[9] As a register of truth (or rather, as a construction of Progressive sexual truth) and as a figure who "is at least consistent with herself," the harlot character serves three functions in furthering salvationist ideology in *Salvation Nell*. First, excess and vice—embodied by the harlot—must necessarily be contrasted with the salvation figure, who is defined by extreme material deprivation (compensated, we are told, by the richness of salvation). Second, she is entertaining—the source of comic relief. As with all marginal figures, however, the laughter comes at her expense. Finally, the harlot-friend allies herself ultimately with the men of the drama, demonstrating that there is little space for female bonding in brothel dramas (as in most early American modern plays).

In both *Salvation Nell* and *The Easiest Way*, prostitution is the curse that haunts the female protagonist. While Nell and Laura ultimately take different paths, both have friends who are mistresses/harlots (Myrtle and Elfie, respectively), and each portrays a scene in which the "Goody Goody Girls" are approached by the demimondaines to give up their backbreaking jobs and turn to hooking. The harlot-friend's indulgent, excessive lifestyle is contrasted with the impoverished surroundings of her salvation sister. These scenes reveal the protagonist's dilemma: she must either reject the modern, indulgent lifestyle (which, we are led to believe, can only be supported by prostitution) or submit to the harsh realities of salvation asceticism.

In *Salvation Nell*, Nell's and Myrtle's perspectives on work can be seen as an allegory for how a working girl should live. Each has left grueling work in a sweatshop to find better means of supporting herself, but Myrtle slides into prostitution, whereas Nell works as a scullery maid in Sid's Empire Bar, scrubbing floors and emptying spittoons. In act 1, after Nell's boyfriend, Jim, is hauled into jail for beating a man to death, Nell is left to support herself (and her unborn baby). Because of Jim's violent outburst in the bar, Nell's employer fires her and she becomes homeless. Myrtle offers to help Nell with a place at Cloquette's brothel, where Nell can "get a fair-sized pomp an' some decent duds an' a few drinks" (573). Myrtle's attempts to convince Nell are momentarily successful, but just as Nell is leaving with Myrtle for the brothel, Maggie from the Salvation Army shows up, melodramatically exclaiming, "Yer hain't got her yet!" (574). What follows is what we might call a salvation battle between Maggie and Myrtle as each fights for Nell:

MYRTLE: (*angrily*). Doncher know this is the chance of her life?
MAGGIE: (*glaring at Myrtle over Nell's sunken head*). Yer right! It is the chance of her life—an' the Lord's given it! (574)

In this climactic ending to act 1, Nell chooses salvation, falls into Maggie's arms, "almost sinking to her knees, and bursts into an agony of tears" (574). Unlike Kitty Warren's powerful speech about why she turned to prostitution in *Mrs. Warren's Profession*, this scene in *Salvation Nell* shows that there are never any circumstances under which a woman is justified in turning to prostitution. There is, after all, salvation work. Moreover, it is striking how little dramaturgical space is given to Nell's struggle for salvation. Female salvation—like female bonding—takes a backseat to the plot of this story. Nell is saved relatively quickly and rather without incident in the drama. The remaining two acts focus on her boyfriend Jim's salvation; it is his conversion—not Nell's, and not even that of Myrtle, who is seemingly beyond redemption—that drives the story.

The choice mapped out for Nell at the end of act 1 is telling, for it reveals the rigid, binary opposition between whore and saint that fueled much antiprostitution discourse. As Barbara Meil Hobson has shown in her study of American prostitution, however, this notion of rigid boundaries between prostitutes and salvation women was a construct of the Progressive imagination, as most women who hooked did so as a transitional occupation.[10] Yet, *Salvation Nell* presents only two options, "a life of sordid-harlotry or a life of hard labor and service in the Salvation Army," as one reviewer put it, as if there were no in-between ground (like finding a new job).[11]

The contrast between salvation and whoredom is shown again in act 2, using the prostitute friendship as a conceit to rehearse this morality tale. Eight years have passed since Jim was arrested, and Nell has struggled as a single mother living in a tenement complex. Her work for the Salvation Army is utterly absorbing, manifesting in her own exhaustion as well as her inability to properly see after her son, Jimmy. In the midst of this working-class poverty, "Myrtle enters, handsomely gowned and very distingué in her manner" (578). Nell's hard life is therefore juxtaposed with Myrtle's excessive, if not garish, life of luxury.

If *Salvation Nell* cautions against illegitimate (or, as Judith Butler would have it, unintelligible) sex, it also warns against the pleasures of rising consumer capitalism and women's participation in it.[12] As Lauren Rabinovitz has shown, "women's unregulated appearances in the changing urban topography in the 1880s and 1890s . . . began to challenge this order and to erode the male's exclusive right to the city."[13] The newly moneyed Myrtle embodies, in other words, a troubling conflation of consumption and consumer and, more importantly, does so by upsetting male terrain. The Salvation Lass, by contrast, does not challenge patriarchal order; rather, she upholds it—with an army, no less. Myrtle's very presence in act 2 troubles the rigid boundaries of vice and respectability. No longer working at Cloquette's, Myrtle has accomplished a difficult task: she has moved *upward* from being a cashier at the brothel to the double position of mistress and entrepreneur. Although historical studies show that movement from prostitution was usually downward, Myrtle runs "a real elegant business on Sixth Av'noo, 'bout two blocks south o' Forty-second," where she sells "slightly worn seal-skin garments an' opera cloaks of all kinds. Spangles a specialty." With her newly purchased bourgeois status, Myrtle now claims the subjectivity of respectability: "After all, the position of cashier at even a first-class roulette joint ain't no place fer a lady!" And she asserts that she has risen above the lower-class crowd of Sid's bar: "Naturally, I don' associate no more with people o' his class!" (579).

But the trap of *Salvation Nell*'s plot is that as a harlot-friend, Myrtle can only pretend respectability. Her attempts to transcend her class and sexual deviance are portrayed as humorous, which brings us to the second function of the role of harlot-friend: comic relief. Myrtle's language is overflowing with malapropisms. For example, she says that among her customers at the shop are "a bunch o' these stock-companies actorines" (529). I interpret Myrtle's use of the word "actorine" as a wordplay (or perhaps Freudian slip) that conflates "actress" with "octoroon." The joke not only demonstrates Myrtle's ignorance but also engenders racist-inflected humor. In another instance, Myrtle notes that her shop has outfitted the latest production of *Sapho:*[14]

MYRTLE: I'm on my way to the People's Stock. It's *Sappho* [sic] this week— a swell play! Ever seen it? (*Nell shakes her head.*) Awful sad an' emotional, ye know! Miss De Vere D'Arcy's wearin' some o' my mos' superb gowns! ... I want ye to see the gown Miss D'Arcy wears in the second ac'. Mauve spangles cut princess with a four-foot train, an' a big silver butterfly on the left shoulder! ... I got it from a real prominent lady whose husbend went up the spout last May. By the time she's outer mournin', nobody'll be seen dead in a princess, so she—you'll come, Nell, won't ye? (605)

Myrtle's speech reveals interesting intersections between the theatre and prostitution.[15] Her reference to Olga Nethersole's production of *Sapho*, a play in which the fallen woman is perceived to be a prostitute, is not coincidental. Without realizing it, Myrtle refers to the "sad an' emotional" story, which is in fact her own life story (or soon will be, we are led to believe). This is one of many instances in which the joke is on Myrtle. The other jokes in this speech ("People's Stock" and the widow not being "seen dead" in an outfit) reveal a character who is not aware of her speech; we laugh at her, not with her. As a review in *Everybody's Magazine* made clear, Myrtle's "evil life is glossed over by giving her the best lines in the play, so that one is laughing at her all the time."[16] This comedy undercuts a fully developed character, opting for easy laughs rather than dramaturgical depth, territory reserved for her salvation sister and the man she saves.

Much of the play's comedy comes at the expense of other prostitute characters as well. Myrtle describes the beginning brothel (pa)raid scene as vaudeville for the entire neighborhood. If the raid is lowbrow theatre, as she suggests, it belongs to the genre of comedy. At least this is how the audience interpreted the scene, according to the *New York Times:* "The comedy of the situation, or as such a large part of the audience seemed to regard it, is brought in a scene descriptive of a raid on a disorderly house."[17] Writing in the *Saturday Evening Post* in 1909, John Corbin also noted the use of humor: "Squalid street scenes and various detached episodes of gutter life are shown with the utmost reality and no little humor."[18] Indeed, the playbill describes *Salvation Nell* as "A Divine Comedy of the Slums."[19]

If *Salvation Nell* is a comedy, and a dark comedy at that, then much of the humor it communicates is carnivalesque. The dual disavowal and desire for the lower class is a hangover of nineteenth-century bourgeois identity formation.

As Shannon Bell has shown, the bourgeoisie constructed respectable identities in opposition to the lower-class Others, bodies theorized as both grotesque and desirable: "Desire for the carnivalesque, embodied in the prostitute, was sublimated by the male and female bourgeois subject into the codification, surveillance, and regulation of this body. The repressed desire for the carnivalesque surfaced in the fantasy life of the bourgeoisie."[20] Insofar as theatre participated in the fantasy life of the bourgeoisie, *Salvation Nell* can be seen as a play that participates in the regulation of sexuality in early-twentieth-century American culture.

A third aspect of the harlot-friend character is that her allegiance switches from her female salvationist friend to a man (or men) in the play. Whereas in *The Easiest Way* female friendships are sacrificed to male homosocial desire, in *Salvation Nell* female alliance gives way to compulsory heterosexuality, as Adrienne Rich has termed it.[21] At the beginning of act 2, Myrtle visits Nell to let her know that Nell's lover, Jim, has been released early from jail on good behavior. Her appearance is less as a friend, however, than as a messenger for Jim. Just as Elfie St. Claire of *The Easiest Way* visits Laura at the request of Laura's former lover and sugar daddy, so Myrtle shows up after eight years with a message from Nell's former lover. In both plays, friendship between the women is eclipsed by a heterosexual relationship. Myrtle could have visited Nell at any other point in those eight years, but this would hardly serve the story. Instead, she waits until she bears not only Jim's message but also the playwright's: she is a vessel for the plot, just as she is for male sexual desires. It is as if both Sheldon and Walter could not imagine a scene in which two women might otherwise meet.

Given this dramaturgical framing, *Salvation Nell* prevents satisfying female bonding between women, especially between harlots and their salvation sisters. Myrtle herself articulates the improbability—or, as the script puts it, "futility"—of their friendship in act 2:

MYRTLE: ... But how ye could demean yourself by livin' in a Rescue House, I don't understand!
NELL: (*simply*). I was alone—I didn't have no one to go to.
MYRTLE: (*in surprised reproach*). Why, ye had me!
NELL: I—(*Stops, realizing the futility*). But what's it matter now?
MYRTLE: (*impressively*). Well, anyway, I called there to see if I couldn't do somethin' to get ye out, fer yer own sake, Nell. "Rescue Home" sounds like it might be fer stray cats! An' if yer'll believe it, the female that ran the joint wouldn't let me inside the door. "Madam," I says to her, "I'm glad ye consider yer establishment no place fer a *lady*!" (580)

Invoking again the trope of respectability (by calling herself a "lady") and playfully using the pun "Madam" (an underworld tag) to refer to Hallelujah Maggie, Myrtle tries to narrow the social gap between herself and Nell. But this is a story about the disparity between the two lifestyles, not the similarities; it is a play concerned with polarities, not subtleties. Nell rejects Myrtle's friendship because she doesn't want to turn to prostitution, but that decision only makes sense within a dualistic mind-set. There are other scenarios to be imagined here. Myrtle could have, for instance, helped Nell lead a decent life; she is a businesswoman, after all ("Spangles a specialty"!). But as Sheldon conceives it, the two women may not occupy dramaturgical intimacy. Tellingly, in the array of production photographs that appeared in the popular press, there are none of Myrtle and Nell together, nor of Maggie and Nell. Textually and visually, *Salvation Nell* makes clear that the harlot-friend must remain polarized to her salvation sister.

Slum Realism

We might well ask, as did John Corbin when writing about *Salvation Nell* in 1909, "What is the purpose of this elaborate exploitation of the slums? Or is there any purpose in it?"[22] While much has been written about David Belasco's contributions to realism, little has been in print about Edward Sheldon's importance in the development of American dramatic realism.[23] Although he is often eclipsed in these discussions, Sheldon is, I believe, a more important figure in the rise of realism onstage than critics have acknowledged, albeit not a figure to be regarded uncritically. If *Salvation Nell* was "a milestone in theatre realism,"[24] as Allen Churchill recalled in his memoir of Broadway, then it has been "an overlooked milestone in American theatre" history, as Albert Cohn has argued.[25] Perhaps Eugene O'Neill said it best himself when he expressed his gratitude to Sheldon for inspiring his own playwriting: "Your *Salvation Nell*, along with the work of the Irish Players on their first trip over here, was what first opened my eyes to the existence of a real theatre as opposed to the unreal—and to me then, hateful—theatre of my father. . . . So, you see, I owed you this additional debt of long standing."[26] While most critics credit O'Neill as the first American dramatist to break away from Continental and British drama and establish great American theatre, the shift came much earlier. American theatre scholar Brenda Murphy concurs: "It was Edward Sheldon, in *Salvation Nell* (1908), who took the greatest step toward integrating setting with character and action to create the forceful sense of character-determining milieu that realist critics demanded."[27] One need only look at the extensive stage directions for the opening scene—

what Murphy calls "an extensive but central document in the development of realistic setting"—to see Sheldon's elaborate vision for the realistic stage.[28] Of course, this elaborate exactitude in set design and acting recalls the work of Belasco, whom many critics credit as a leading executor of staging realism.[29] And while in many ways Belasco has eclipsed Sheldon in the pantheon of American theatre history, *Salvation Nell* influenced Belasco's work more than we have thus far realized. In many ways, as Ethan Mordden notes, *Salvation Nell* stole Belasco's thunder: "Just before Eugene Walter looked in on the System that oppresses independent women, Edward Sheldon wrote on slum life—the whole life—gave his script to Mrs. Fiske, and turned a corner for American drama, using the framework of melodrama to demonstrate what Belasco's 'realism' should have been all along; not the look of a place but the *sense* of it."[30] As the *Philadelphia Star*'s headline put it in 1909, "Belasco Out Done [*sic*] in *Salvation Nell*."[31]

If Belasco had been bested, he was in the audience on opening night to witness it himself. Eric Wollencott Barnes, in his biography of Sheldon, noted this evening as follows: "What thrilled him [Sheldon] most, a young man hoping to make his mark in the theatre, was a glimpse of the white mane and clerical collar of David Belasco in the shadows of a proscenium box."[32] No doubt Belasco was making notes for his upcoming production of *The Easiest Way*. It may not be coincidental, therefore, that *Salvation Nell*'s designer, Ernest M. Gros, would be Belasco's set designer on *The Easiest Way* just weeks later. Although it is difficult to verify Belasco's intentions, it seems likely that he intended *The Easiest Way* to rival *Salvation Nell*'s realism.

Salvation Nell's realism therefore influenced not only the shaping of *The Easiest Way* but also the emergence of American realist theatre and what became known as "slum realism." Although New Yorkers had gotten a taste of the bawdy underworld with *Zaza* in 1899, nothing had prepared Broadway for *Salvation Nell*'s "forty grimy characters, its bums, its loafers, its barroom hangers-on, its lost women, its gruesome children, its noise of drunken revelry, and its sinister suggestions of—worse," as critic Alan Dale of the *New York American* put it.[33] As the *Milwaukee News* reported, the precision with which the barroom was assembled revealed relentless attention to documentary detail:

The barroom of the act is more than a faithful reproduction of a saloon in New York's Hell Kitchen. Every article in the dive came from a saloon of that section of New York.... He [Mr. Fiske] bought the bar (a massive mahogany affair), the mirrors, the swinging doors, the tables, the bottles, the chairs, the glasses, the cash register, the electric fixtures, and a multitude of other accessories. In addition, he photographed the interior of the saloon before the purchase was moved.[34]

Fiske's acquisition of artifacts from Hell's Kitchen recalls the work of an ethnographer, a technique later copied by Belasco.

A similar triumph of realistic scenery was achieved in *Salvation Nell*'s third act, set in the Cherry Street tenement project. Desiring to "make a faithful copy of actual conditions," Mr. Fiske and a photographer arrived at the Cherry Street district.[35] Both men were chased off, however, by residents who resented having their photos taken without their permission. With hat in hand, Mr. Fiske reportedly returned to Cherry Street the next day and told them what he was up to and asked for their help. They agreed. The following description of act 3 shows the exactitude with which the scenic artists constructed the set:

> The rise of the curtain on this act discovers five-story tenement exteriors, with real fire-escapes, from which wash and rags dangle; fruit stands and saloons, and a row of small stores; the well-known Salvation Army headquarters; sidewalks and street lamps, and fire plugs. The ensemble weighs some ten tons and the back scene covers just twenty-five hundred square feet. The little item of rags and wash fills four trunks. And twenty-four hours are required to set the entire act.[36]

The elaborate depiction of Cherry Street is surely impressive; still, it is important to ask whose laundry—four trunks full—was being aired.

In addition to much of the set being composed of "authentic" materials from the slums, many of the supporting actors were not actors at all but residents of Cherry Hill. According to Archie Binns in his book *Mrs. Fiske and the American Theatre,* the Fiskes achieved realism by having residents of the slums portray themselves. Mrs. Fiske related the detailed process of selecting and training the cast to Alexander Woollcott:

> I cannot *begin* to tell you how many times Mr. Fiske and I virtually dismissed an entire company; how over and over again members of the cast were weeded out and others engaged; how over and over again we would start with an almost entirely new company, until every part, from Holbrook Blinn's down to the very tiniest, was perfectly realized; how much there was of private rehearsal; of the virtual opening of a dramatic conservatory; how much of the most exquisite care before *Salvation Nell* was ready.[37]

Paradoxically, the incorporation of ethnographic research and Hell's Kitchen residents blurred the line between reality and representation at the same time it mediated those representations.

In spite of that paradox, audience members and critics applauded *Salvation Nell*'s pioneering realism in stagecraft. Several reviews likened the representation onstage to photography, one calling it "a photographic reproduction of squalor."[38] Another reviewer suggested that *Salvation Nell*'s realistic artistry surpassed photography: "It is more true to life than a photograph, because it is not photographic but artistic, and because the picture is not made by the mechanical means of a lens but is sketched in and fully painted with vigorous, vivid and virile strokes by a hand which ought to become that of a master."[39] And *Theatre Magazine* called it "uncommon realism" and "a triumph of stage management and acting."[40]

Other critics disapproved of the play precisely because it was all too real. Alan Dale claimed that the play's modest run (seventy-one performances) was due to its realistic portrayal of slum life: "I could not see a lasting success for *Salvation Nell*. . . . Psychological plays and pathological novels come and go, are praised or censured. But they never last, because they are all real."[41] Hector Fuller of the *Washington Herald* argued fiercely against these "realistic pictures of phases of life that ordinary healthy-minded people deem best to ignore," noting that this "modern tendency toward realism in literature and the stage seems to be to out-Zola Zola at his worst."[42] *Hampton's Magazine* faulted this "ludicrous and inconsequential play" for "wallow[ing] around in the slums to a Zola's taste."[43] The *New York Times* reported that the details overwhelmed the plot: "The main incidents lose their actual proportions in the haze of the unnecessary surrounding details," making it more of a "theatrical report" than a true drama.[44] *Metropolitan Magazine* agreed: "The story is frequently sacrificed to the creation of the atmosphere of the lower world."[45] Acknowledging that "no such artistically realized pictures of actual life have ever been presented on the American stage," John Corbin wrote that *Salvation Nell* was finally "little more than a moving picture of the slums."[46]

Virtually all of the reviews, therefore, whether positive or negative, demonstrated *Salvation Nell*'s profound investment in the real, which was produced with such verisimilitude that the distinctions between signifier and signified appeared to collapse. The review in the *Milwaukee News,* for instance, did not regard the bar onstage as a representation of Sid McGovern's bar but rather as the bar itself: "Act one is, therefore, Sid McGovern's Tenth avenue bar."[47] And to an interpreter of early-twentieth-century realism, it certainly appeared to be the case. Fiske and set designers Ernest Gros and D. Frank Dodge literally reassembled Sid's Empire Bar onstage (Belasco would mimic this process in purchasing an authentic flophouse and reassembling it onstage for the set of *The Easiest Way*). It was a working bar that served real beer to real Hell's Kitchen residents—some of whom allegedly got drunk onstage.

At the very same time that *Salvation Nell* was a kind of ur-theatrical anthropology, it also sought to portray with empathy the lives of "the other half," as reformer Jacob Riis termed the poor of New York.[48] One repeated message in the press was that *Salvation Nell* created a sense of "oneness with mankind." When it opened in Washington, D.C., for instance, one reviewer wrote that the play united the bourgeoisie with their counterparts in the slums: "It caught the sensibilities of a highly cultured Capital audience in a grip of iron and sent the members of that audience out into the street with a new sense of the oneness of mankind and a new realization of the beauty that lies in the regeneration of the human soul."[49] Another review credited the play's representational strategy as universally human and not at all invasive: "Neither playwright nor players have sought an obtrusive or spectacular veracity. These are the people, they seem to be saying to their audiences, whose story for the instant we would tell."[50] It urges audiences, the review continued, to view the slums "sympathetically and understandingly."[51]

This theme is underscored in a scene between Nell and a fellow Salvation Army worker, Major Williams, who, like playwright Sheldon, came from a wealthy family:

MAJOR (*a little bitterly*): Why, there's just as much misery on Fifth Avenue as there is on Tenth! But I thank God for it—it led me to salvation!
NELL (*timidly*): Then we're sort of alike, you an' me—ain't we? Even though we started from diff'rent places.
MAJOR (*tenderly*): The only difference was that I had every chance and you had none! (584)

Major Williams and Nell are therefore "sort of alike," he contends, despite class difference. This perceived universality was echoed in some reviews, which noted that *Salvation Nell* had a general appeal across class lines. As the *Brooklyn Citizen* reported, "No play has aroused such discussion from Lyuon's in the Bowery to the tea room at the Plaza as *Salvation Nell*."[52] According to *New York North Side News*,

It is rare indeed that a play in the first three nights of its run becomes such a general topic of the barrooms. They are talking about it almost as much on Tenth Avenue as they are on Fifth Ave.; there isn't a barroom in town where the wonderful realistic picture of the Hell's Kitchen dive shown in the first act has not aroused intense interest, and there isn't a club, a café, nor any place where men and women gather that you don't hear of Mrs. Fiske and Salvation Nell.[53]

But was *Salvation Nell* actually seen by the people living in tenements? If people were discussing the play in barrooms, did it mean they saw it? And, were those from Tenth Avenue discussing the play the same way as those from Fifth? It seems unlikely. In spite of the play's efforts to unite people across class barriers, *Salvation Nell* created an illusory sense of unification at the cost of collapsing class differentiation. Class disparity became effaced, that is, in the very act of asserting universality. The most obvious gap between that which was represented onstage and real life was the divide between the bourgeois audience and the slum characters portrayed. *Metropolitan Magazine* observed, "This may be called a social study, but we see only one side of the picture. It starts in the slums, it ends in the slums, and none but slum types appear."[54] The representation of tenement inhabitants, played by a colossal cast composed of more than forty residents of the slums, offered a scopophilic view of working-class life. Such a portrayal fueled Progressive Era notions that the poor were in need of salvation. "The poor and working classes," George Chauncey has remarked, "were characterized in [bourgeois] ideology by their lack of such control; the apparent licentiousness of the poor, as well as their poverty, was taken as a sign of the degeneracy of the class as a whole."[55] The nightly appearances of Hell's Kitchen residents in these roles—comparable, perhaps, to current reality television shows that focus voyeuristically on the lower class—sparked bourgeois interest. Problematically, these characters were portrayed two-dimensionally, serving as the "background against which the figure of the little, cowed, helpless scrubwoman stands out in mordant contrast," as the *New York Times* put it.[56] "There is no depth to the portraits" of these shallowly written characters, who were introduced "for the sole purpose of emphasizing the soddenness of life," this same review stated.[57] As Brenda Murphy points out, Sheldon's attempts to mark class distinction through dialogue were not always believable, as he succumbed often to platitudes.[58]

In stark contrast to the "slum types" onstage, "a highly cultured Capital audience" filled the house in Washington, D.C., where "society was well represented."[59] The playbill suggests much about the upper-class and bourgeois clientele of the New York Hackett Theatre, in which there are advertisements for "the remarkable 1904 Vintage" of Mumm's champagne, Lindt chocolate, furs, gowns, "strictly first-class pianos," and garages (a new possession of the business class).[60] *Everybody's Magazine* noted the ease with which upper-class audiences embarked upon what they called "a slumming excursion": "The audience can wear their best clothes, occupy comfortable seats, and, from their vantage ground of respectability and prosperity, see and hear the life of the slum, knowing they are safe from any unpleasant personal experience."⁶¹ Just as audiences were filling the seats at upscale venues like the Hackett Theatre, so working-class audiences attended other kinds of amusements, as Kathy Peiss and Richard Butsch have shown.⁶² Theatregoers from the slum, in other words, likely never ventured uptown to the Hackett. The juxtaposition of the champagne crowd with slum denizens onstage reveals an upper-class fascination with a low Other, an intricate repulsion-fascination that is crucial, as Peter Stallybrass and Allon White have argued, to the formation of the identity of those in power.⁶³

While *Salvation Nell* portrays Hell's Kitchen, the underbelly of New York, it does not dwell on the working class's supposed degeneracy. Casting Mrs. Fiske, an esteemed actress, in the role of a lower-class charwoman let the production have it both ways: *Salvation Nell* offered both slumming and class salvation. More than this, Fiske's class privilege reassured the audience that the production had not lost touch with hegemony (not unlike the practice of having a straight actor play gay roles). While Sheldon dispensed "with the star entrance for Mrs. Fiske," as Mordden notes, Mrs. Fiske's celebrity performance, to use Michael Quinn's term, as well as her middle-class status, ghosted the role.⁶⁴ Previously, audiences had seen Mrs. Fiske portray middle-class or bourgeois strong women (e.g., the title character in *Hedda Gabler*). In contrast to these roles, according to Walter Eaton, in *Salvation Nell* "it was almost painful to see and feel her in such an uncouth, unmoral, gutter-bred female, slopping up a barroom."⁶⁵ As Alan Dale wrote, "in the first act the mawkishness seemed beneath her."⁶⁶ Mrs. Fiske's acting triumph, like Mrs. Carter's in *Zaza*, was her ability to perform a lower class. It is precisely her middle-class privilege that afforded Fiske a performative class mobility, thereby allowing her to salvage this character from the clutches of the slum. As one review noted, "Then she soared above slumland into the realms of drama we understand."⁶⁷ Clearly, the "we" in the article assumes a bourgeois spectator. *Salvation Nell* therefore asserted both sexual and class redemption. It seems quite clear, then, that it catered to, as the *New York Times* put it, "a sensation-hunting populace" who had "a morbid, vulgar curiosity" of slum life.⁶⁸ The audience members who could afford a ticket at the Hackett were not the denizens of Tenth Avenue, who were likely more inclined to attend vaudeville or other popular entertainments. As *Everybody's Magazine* put it succinctly, "The chief reason for its popularity, apart from the acting, lies probably in the almost universal passion of the well-to-do to 'go slumming.'"⁶⁹

If the well-to-do went slumming when they attended *Salvation Nell*, they would have another opportunity a few weeks later when Belasco premiered one more story of prostitution (and failed salvation): *The Easiest Way*. Both slumming and slum realism were popular pursuits during the Progressive Era. While all of these issues intersect with the sexual underworld—indeed *require* harlot characters for contrast—the story of salvation in this play subsumes the story of prostitution. Once used in the service of slum realist dramaturgy, prostitute characters are readily dispensed with. *Salvation Nell* is therefore not a story about Nell's salvation, or Myrtle's salvation, or any other woman's salvation, but rather about Nell's work to save her man. The Salvation Lass is, disappointingly, a character who eschews her desires and her harlot-friend. In the framework of salvation, Goody Goody Girls might have "heavenly grace" and a "heavenly face," but only if they leave the underworld, and capitalistic pursuits, behind them.

Notes

The epigraph for this essay is taken from Grant Clarke, Edgar Leslie, and Theodore Morse, "Salvation Nell" (New York: Theodore Morse Music Co., 1913), 2–3.

1. H. T. Parker, "Mrs. Fiske and Mr. Sheldon in 'Salvation Nell,'" *Boston Evening Transcript*, April 16, 1909, 12.
2. John Gassner, ed., *Best Plays of the Early American Theatre: From the Beginning to 1916* (New York: Crown, 1967), 557–616.
3. Clarke, Leslie, and Morse, "Salvation Nell," 2.
4. Charles Baudelaire, "Allegory," *Les fleurs du mal*, trans. Richard Howard (Boston: Godine, 1982), 155.
5. Edward Sheldon, *Salvation Nell*, in Gassner, *Best Plays of the Early American Theatre*, 558; subsequent citations of the play will appear parenthetically.
6. Michel Foucault, *Discipline and Punish: The Birth of the Prison*, trans. Alan Sheridan (New York: Vintage Books, 1977).
7. Peter Bailey, "'Naughty but Nice': Music Comedy and the Rhetoric of the Girl, 1892–1914," in *The Edwardian Theatre: Essays on Performance and the Stage*, ed. Michael R. Booth and Joel H. Kaplan (Cambridge: Cambridge University Press, 1996), 46.
8. Belle Lindner Israels, "'Salvation Nell'—A Lost Opportunity," *Charities and the Commons: A Weekly Journal of Philanthropy and Social Advance*, January 23, 1909, 705–6.
9. "*Salvation Nell*: A Hopeless String of Dissociated Episodes," *Dramatist* 1, no. 3 (1910): 52.
10. Barbara Meil Hobson, *Uneasy Virtue: The Politics of Prostitution and the American Reform Tradition* (New York: Basic Books, 1987), 109.
11. Parker, "Mrs. Fiske and Mr. Sheldon," 12.
12. Judith Butler, *Bodies That Matter: On the Discursive Limits of "Sex"* (New York: Routledge, 1993).
13. Lauren Rabinovitz, *For the Love of Pleasure: Women, Movies, and Culture in the Turn-of-the-Century Chicago* (New Brunswick, N.J.: Rutgers University Press, 1998), 7.
14. During the run of *Salvation Nell*, Olga Nethersole twice revived the part she originated in 1900.

15. Myrtle's shop is at the heart of the theatre district, only a few blocks away from the Hackett Theatre itself, where *Salvation Nell* was running (on Forty-second Street and Eighth Avenue).
16. Review of *Salvation Nell, Everybody's Magazine* 20 (1909): 420.
17. "Acting Redeems Play of Sordid Life," *New York Times,* November 18, 1918, 15.
18. John Corbin, "The Drama of the Slums," *Saturday Evening Post,* March 20, 1909, 15.
19. Program of *Salvation Nell* from the Hackett Theatre, dated December 7, 1908, *Salvation Nell* clipping file, Shubert Archive, New York City.
20. Shannon Bell, *Reading, Writing, and Rewriting the Prostitute Body* (Bloomington: Indiana University Press, 1994), 43.
21. Adrienne Rich, "Compulsory Heterosexuality and Lesbian Existence," in *Feminist Frontiers II,* ed. Laurel Richardson and Verta Taylor (1979; reprint, New York: McGraw Hill, 1989), 120–41.
22. Corbin, "The Drama of the Slums," 15.
23. See Ethan Mordden, *The American Theatre* (New York: Oxford University Press, 1981), 50; and Brenda Murphy, *American Realism and American Drama, 1880–1940* (Cambridge: Cambridge University Press, 1987).
24. Allen Churchill, *The Great White Way: A Re-Creation of Broadway's Golden Era of Theatrical Entertainment* (New York: Dutton, 1962), 141.
25. Albert Cohn, "*Salvation Nell:* An Overlooked Milestone in American Theatre," *Educational Theatre Journal* 9 (1957): 11–22.
26. O'Neill quoted in Eric Wollencott Barnes, *The High Room: A Biography of Edward Sheldon* (London: W. H. Allen, 1957), 49. O'Neill was referring to his father, the famous actor James O'Neill.
27. Murphy, *American Realism,* 88.
28. Ibid.
29. See Don B. Wilmeth, *American Theatre History, 1865–1915,* vol. 1 of *Theatre in the United States: A Documentary History,* ed. Barry Witham (Cambridge: Cambridge University Press, 1996), 285.
30. Mordden, *The American Theatre,* 50.
31. "Belasco Out Done in *Salvation Nell,*" *Philadelphia Star,* March 23, 1909.
32. Barnes, *The High Room,* 47.
33. Alan Dale, "Mrs. Fiske at Her Best—Play Held Audience Amazed," *New York American,* December 5, 1908, in Minnie Maddern Fiske Scrapbooks 1908–09, Container 60, Library of Congress, Washington, D.C.
34. "Real Tenement Scenes in Mrs. Fiske's Play," *Milwaukee News,* March 6, otherwise unidentified clipping in Minnie Maddern Fiske Scrapbooks 1908–09, Library of Congress.
35. Ibid.
36. Ibid.
37. Alexander Woollcott, *Mrs. Fiske, Her Views on Actors, Acting, and the Problems of Production* (1917; reprint, New York: B. Bloom, 1968), 21–22.
38. Allen D. Albert Jr., "'Salvation Nell' Study of Squalor," unidentified clipping, *Salvation Nell* clipping file, the Museum of the City of New York.
39. "Belasco Out Done in *Salvation Nell.*"
40. "Salvation Nell," *Theatre Magazine* 9 (January 1909): 2–3.

41. Alan Dale, "A Chronicle of New Plays," *Cosmopolitan*, April 1909, 569–72.
42. Hector Fuller, *Washington Herald*, February 2, 1909, *Salvation Nell* clipping file, Museum of the City of New York.
43. "Mrs. Fiske Goes to the Slums for a Plot," *Hampton's Magazine* 22 (February 1909): 245.
44. "'Salvation Nell' a Theatrical Report on Life in the Slums," *New York Times*, November 22, 1908, VI:7.
45. "The Drama of the Month," *Metropolitan Magazine*, January 1909, 452.
46. Corbin, "The Drama of the Slums," 15.
47. "Real Tenement Scenes in Mrs. Fiske's Play."
48. Jacob Riis, *How the Other Half Lives: Studies among the Tenements of New York* (1890; reprint, New York: Dover, 1971).
49. Albert, "'Salvation Nell' Study of Squalor."
50. Parker, "Mrs. Fiske and Mr. Sheldon," 12.
51. Ibid.
52. Unidentified article, *Brooklyn Citizen*, January 8, 1909.
53. "Clergy Are Impressed with Play's Moving Power," *New York North Side News*, December 6, 1908.
54. "The Drama of the Month," 450.
55. George Chauncey, *Gay New York: The Making of the Gay Male World, 1890–1940* (London: Flamingo Original, 1994), 36.
56. "'Salvation Nell' a Theatrical Report on Life in the Slums," 7.
57. Ibid.
58. Murphy, *American Realism*, 94.
59. See Albert, "'Salvation Nell' Study of Squalor"; and "Mrs. Fiske in 'Salvation Nell' at the Belasco," *Washington Post*, February 2, 1909.
60. Playbill, *Salvation Nell*, December 7, 1908. *Salvation Nell* clipping file, Shubert Archive.
61. Review of *Salvation Nell*, *Everybody's Magazine*, 424.
62. See Kathy Peiss, *Cheap Amusements: Working Women and Working Class Leisure in Turn-of-the-Century New York* (Philadelphia: Temple University Press, 1986); and Richard Butsch, *The Making of American Audiences: From Stage to Television, 1750–1990* (Cambridge: Cambridge University Press, 2000).
63. Peter Stallybrass and Allon White, *The Politics and Poetics of Transgression* (Ithaca: Cornell University Press, 1986).
64. Mordden, *The American Theatre*, 51. See also Michael Quinn, "Celebrity and the Semiotics of Acting," *New Theatre Quarterly* 4 (1990): 154–61.
65. Walter P. Eaton, *New York Dramatic Mirror*, November 28, 1908, 3.
66. Dale, "Mrs. Fiske at Her Best."
67. Ibid.
68. "'Salvation Nell' a Theatrical Report on Life in the Slums," 7.
69. Review of *Salvation Nell*, *Everybody's Magazine*, 420.

Irony Lost

Bret Harte's Heathen Chinee and the Popularization of the Comic Coolie as Trickster in Frontier Melodrama

—JACQUELINE ROMEO

"Plain Language from Truthful James" was by its author's own account "the worst poem I ever wrote, possibly the worst poem anyone ever wrote."[1] Bret Harte readily admitted that the poem's publication in the September 1870 issue of *Overland Monthly* was mere happenstance.[2] He needed to fill the pages of the already slim edition. Regardless of his intentions, the poem "was as nearly an overnight sensation as was possible in the days when San Francisco was four or five days distance from New York via transcontinental railroad," forever fixing in every Euro-American's mind the character of Ah Sin.[3] The Heathen Chinee (as he was later nicknamed) was ready to join the family of ethnic and racial types born in nineteenth-century America and raised on its popular stage.[4]

The narrative poem is about two miners, Bill Nye and "Truthful" James, and a "naive" Chinaman, Ah Sin, who are playing a game of euchre. Nye and James intend to cheat Ah Sin out of all his money. Although Ah Sin had previously feigned ignorance of the game, he suddenly begins winning every hand. He is better at cheating than either Nye or James, literally beating the American masters at their own "game" (cheating). The hypocrisy is revealed through the irony of the poem's closing stanzas, in which Nye and James catch Ah Sin and run the "clever" Chinaman out of the game. It is perfectly acceptable for the miners to cheat, but not the Heathen Chinee. Here is the poem in its entirety:

> Which I wish to remark,
>   And my language is plain,

That for ways that are dark
    And tricks that are vain,
The heathen Chinee is peculiar,
    Which the same I would rise to explain.

Ah Sin was his name;
    And I shall not deny,
In regard to the same,
    What the name might imply;
But his smile it was pensive and childlike,
    As I frequent remarked to Bill Nye.

It was August the third,
    And quite soft was the skies;
Which it might be inferred
    That Ah Sin was likewise;
Yet he played it that day upon William
    And me in a way I despise.

Which we had a small game,
    And Ah Sin took a hand:
It was Euchre. The same
    He did not understand;
But he smiled as he sat by the table,
    With the smile that was childlike and bland.

Yet the cards they were stocked
    In a way that I grieve,
And my feelings were shocked
    At the state of Nye's sleeve,
Which was stuffed full of aces and bowers,
    And the same with intent to deceive.

But the hands that were played
    By that heathen Chinee,
And the points that he made,
    Were quite frightful to see,—
Till at last he put down a right bower,
    Which the same Nye had dealt unto me.

Then I looked up at Nye,
    And he gazed upon me;
And he rose with a sigh,
    And said, "Can this be?"
We are ruined by Chinese cheap labor,"—
    And he went for that heathen Chinee.

> In the scene that ensued,
>   I did not take hand,
> But the floor it was strewed
>   Like the leaves on the strand
> With the cards that Ah Sin had been hiding,
>   In the game "he did not understand."
>
> In his sleeves, which were long,
>   He had twenty-four jacks,—
> Which was coming it strong,
>   Yet I state but the facts;
> And we found on his nails, which were taper,
>   What is frequent in tapers,—that's wax.
>
> Which is why I remark,
>   And my language is plain,
> That for ways that are dark
>   And for tricks that are vain,
> The heathen Chinee is peculiar,—
>   Which the same I am free to maintain.[5]

Margaret Duckett explains in "Plain Language from Bret Harte" that in the context of his life work the poem can only have "one interpretation: it is a satiric attack on race prejudice."[6] Before and after the poem, Harte had been a critic of anti-Chinese prejudice. Among his *Bohemian Papers* was "John Chinaman," in which Harte, despite the dehumanizing title, attempted to portray a "real" Chinaman for his audience. He admitted to only knowing his subject professionally rather than personally—"John" was the family's laundryman—but Harte's great affection and regard is obvious. His acquaintance with John led Harte to conclude that he is "generally honest, faithful, simple, and painstaking."[7] Although this was not the most enlightened response, anything less than hostility toward the Chinese was considered quite liberal at the time.

In San Francisco in 1860, Harte found a post as staff writer at *The Golden Era*. Two years later he married Anna Griswold—who sang contralto in a Unitarian choir—and began to produce a series of satiric articles known as the *Bohemian Papers*, whose subjects ranged from "Melons" to "A Rail at the Rail." By 1864 he had moved from *The Golden Era* to the prestigious paper *The Californian* and won a literary cause célèbre as editor of *Outcroppings, Being a Selection of California Verse* (1865). Finally, in 1868 he was named editor in chief of *Overland Monthly*, a new literary magazine he helped to found. It was in this magazine that "Plain Language from Truthful James" first appeared, securing for Harte fame (and infamy) for the rest of his life.

To recoup the irony lost on the readers of "Plain Language," Harte wrote a more direct and poignant poem entitled "The Latest Chinese Outrage."[8] This time, Ah Sin reappears as the leader of a group of Chinese laundrymen who confront several miners for refusing to pay their laundry bill. Although the miners are greatly outnumbered, one, Joe Johnson, charges headlong into the mob of Chinese while screaming: "A White Man is here!" The laundrymen gather around him and retreat back to their camp. The other miners, following after, arrive at a tree surrounded by several Chinese men. From the tree hangs a bamboo cage with a sign in Chinese that Harte translates for the reader: "A White Man is here!" Inside the cage is Joe Johnson dazed with opium, the pipe still dangling from his mouth. His eyebrows have been shaved, a queue is attached to his head, a "coppery hue" is painted on his face, and he wears "a heathenish suit."[9]

This poem, although also ironic, is far less ambiguous than "Plain Language." By the poem's end it is clear that Harte is a critic of California politicians who run only on the strength of their anti-Chinese platform. Whether Harte was a racist, ultimately, is not the question, since the complexity of the issue defies such a simplistic judgment. What *is* worthy of pursuit is an understanding of his earlier poem's popularity and the subsequent image it produced of the Chinese comic type, or Comic Coolie, in frontier melodrama.[10]

One version of the poem's origins claims that "Harte sent the poem as a light parody of the topical 'Chinese Question' to Ambrose Bierce, then editor of the *San Francisco News-letter*. Bierce promptly returned the piece, urging Harte to publish such a fine poem in the *Overland*." Another suggests that "Harte wrote off the piece simply as an exercise in low humor, a mockery which imitated the famous chorus of Swinburne's romantic 'Atalanta in Cylon.'"[11] The etymology of the word *irony* includes a meaning from classical Greek comedy: it derives from the *eiron,* or the underdog, weak but clever, who regularly triumphed over the stupid and boastful *alazôn*. In "Plain Language," Harte made his Chinese character the *eiron* with a twist.

Francis Cornford, in *The Origin of Attic Comedy,* deferred to Aristotle's *Ethics* when he classified the three original comic types as the Buffoon (*bomolchos*), the Ironical type (*eiron*), and the Imposter (*alazôn*).[12] According to Cornford, the Imposter "claims to possess higher qualities than he has, the Ironical man [*eiron*] is given to making himself out worse than he is. . . . In comedy a special kind of Irony practiced by the Imposter's opponent is feigned stupidity. . . . The word *eiron* itself in the fifth century appears to mean 'cunning' or (more exactly) 'sly.' . . . The *eiron* who victimizes the Imposters masks his cleverness under a show of clownish dullness."[13] However, Harte's poem mixes popular parody with social criticism, because unlike his Greek counterpart, the *eiron*, the "sly" Ah Sin is discovered and the comic inversion turns violent. The fact remained: despite Ah Sin's "cunning" he was still Chinese and would never be fully accepted by his Euro-American brethren. I will elaborate on this point in the latter part of this essay, as the *eiron*'s other name is "trickster."

Unfortunately, the subtlety of the poem's irony was beyond the comprehension of most of its readers. Instead, its audience embraced it as an anti-Chinese tract.[14] Much animosity was shown to the Chinese in the years preceding the poem. The Irish, in particular, were threatened by the Chinese laborers who appeared to be supplanting them. As early as March 1867, Harte had written in a piece published in the *Springfield Republican* that the "quickwitted, patient, obedient, and faithful" Chinese were "gradually deposing the Irish from their old, recognized positions in the ranks of labor."[15] And, unfortunately, the timing of Harte's poem coincided with some of the worst anti-Chinese violence ever witnessed up to that time.

By the 1860s "yellow peril" began to seize the Euro-American psyche, especially on the West Coast, as other immigrant groups vied for the same jobs as the Chinese. In 1869 this intolerance was exacerbated by a commercial depression that coincided with the completion of the transcontinental railroad. By 1870, the year Harte's poem was published, an anti-Chinese convention held in California unified the state's labor movement and passed a resolution to halt Chinese immigration. The tensions culminated in riots in Los Angeles in which more than twenty Chinese were killed.[16]

Since copyright laws were difficult to enforce, the Western News Company of Chicago, attempting to capitalize on the popularity of Harte's poem, issued a pirated illustrated edition that sold phenomenally well (fig. 1).[17] It featured nine loose pages that were sold in an engraved envelope, perhaps suitable for framing. The cartoonlike figures are naively drawn with exaggerated features that heighten the comic effect (figs. 2–10). The first three panels introduce our characters: Truthful James, Ah Sin, and Bill Nye. The artist is apparently unfamiliar with the surroundings of a California mining town, for the landscape is left empty. James (fig. 2), looking more like Bowery B'hoy than miner in top hat and tattered tails, rises from his chair as if to begin his story. Ah Sin (fig. 3) wears the garments of an urban Chinese immigrant rather than those of the coolie. Bill Nye (fig. 4) looks the most like a miner with his suspenders, knee patches, pipe, and pickax.

The facial characteristics are the most distorted. Both Nye and James have very large hooked noses, and Nye's chin curves so that it almost touches the tip of his nose, like the Punch character in a Punch and Judy Show (all three are

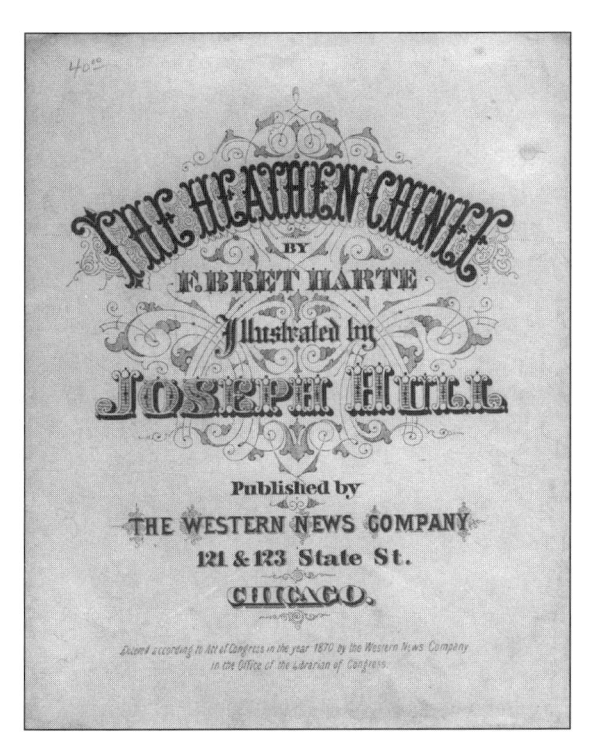

Figure 1.

Illustrations from "The Heathen Chinee" by Bret Harte, illustrated by Joseph Hull (Chicago: Western News Company, 1870). Courtesy of the Clifton Waller Barrett Library of American Literature, Special Collections, University of Virginia Library (credit for Figures 1–10).

Figure 2. (bottom left); Figure 3. (bottom right).

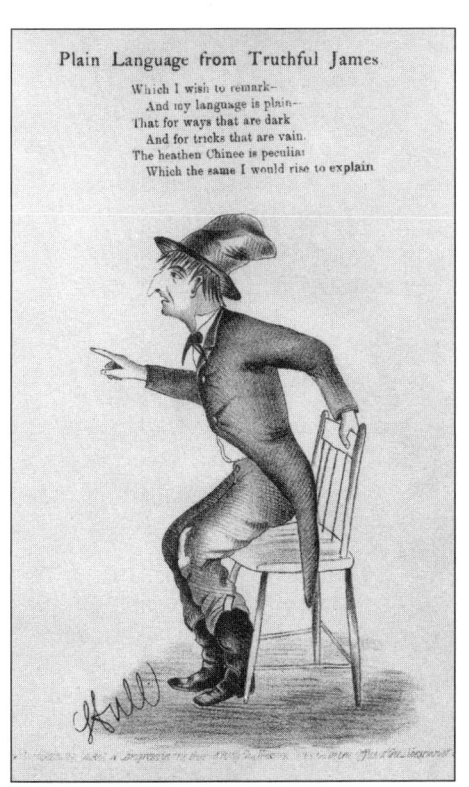

Figure 4. (top left);
Figure 5. (bottom left);
Figure 6. (top right);
Figure 7. (bottom right).

Bill Nye.
It was August the third
And quite soft was the skies
Which it might be inferred
That Ah Sin was likewise:
Yet he played it that day upon William
And me in a way I despise.

Which we had a small game,
And Ah Sin took a hand
It was Euchre. The same
He did not understand;
But he smiled as he sat by the table,
With the smile that was child-like and bland

Yet the cards they were stocked
In a way that I grieve,
And my feelings were shocked
At the state of Nye's sleeve;
Which was stuffed full of aces and bowers,
And the same with intent to deceive

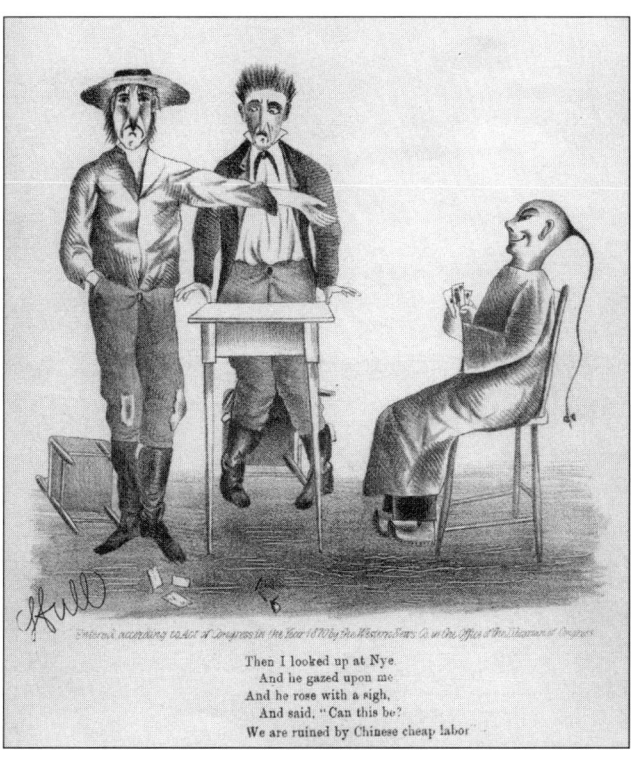

But the hands that were played
By that heathen Chinee,
And the points that he made,
Were quite frightful to see—
Till at last he put down a right bower,
Which the same Nye had dealt unto me.

Then I looked up at Nye
And he gazed upon me
And he rose with a sigh,
And said, "Can this be?
We are ruined by Chinese cheap labor."

And he went for that heathen Chinee

In the scene that ensued
 I did not take a hand,
But the floor it was strewed
 Like the leaves on the strand
With the cards that Ah Sin had been hiding,
 In the game "he did not understand."

In his sleeves, which were long
 He had twenty-four packs—
Which was coming it strong,
 Yet I state but the facts.
And we found on his nails, which were taper,
 What is frequent in tapers—that's wax.

Figure 8. (top left); Figure 9. (bottom left); Figure 10. (top right).

drawn to resemble puppets). Nye's cheeks, nose, and chin are shaded as if flushed from too much drink. Neither Nye nor James is smiling—in fact, they frown throughout the entire narrative. Upon Ah Sin's long, melon-shaped face are set two slanted eyes that look slightly crossed, as if his hair is pulled back too tight, and his queue is as long and thin as a rat's tail. A profile of Ah Sin (fig. 5) depicts a rodentlike nose and face as he sits grinning ear to ear in the midst of the game.

As the drama unfolds, we see by panel 5 (fig. 6) that Ah Sin is holding a winning hand. Nye points to Ah Sin accusingly (fig. 7), but he faces the viewer with his nose and chin protruding forward like the beak of a pelican. Panel 7 (fig. 8) graphically depicts the violence implied by line 42 of the poem: "And he went for that heathen Chinee." Nye in a rage lifts the table up over his head while kicking Ah Sin in the stomach with his left foot. Ah Sin's playing cards (which he had so carefully hidden up his sleeve) fly about the room, giving visual credence to the lines: "But the floor it was strewed / Like the leaves on the strand / With the cards that Ah Sin had been hiding / In the game 'he did not understand.'" Nye's face is drawn in the most grotesque, clownlike manner with round, rosy cheeks, flushed chin and nose that are pointed and cruel, and hair that sticks up on end, while Ah Sin no longer wears his silly grin.

Nowhere in Harte's verse is there any indication that a riot ensued or that anyone other than the three men is part of the narrative. Yet panel 8 (fig. 9), the most overtly racist and the most obvious example of how Harte's poem could be misinterpreted, depicts a barroom brawl where Ah Sin is tossed up into the air by a gang of drunken hooligans wielding liquor bottles (and somebody's boot) and shooting off a gun.

The last panel (fig. 10) returns the viewer to the narrator, as Truthful James repeats his opening stanza. With cigarillo in mouth, one hand in his pocket, and the other outstretched, he delivers his last lines as if they were a gentle warning:

> Which is why I remark,
>   And my language is plain,
> That for ways that are dark
>   And for tricks that are vain,
> The heathen Chinee is peculiar,—
>   Which the same I am free to maintain.

The irony of the poem was so lost on the artist and publishers of this bootlegged version that they supplied their own solution to the "Chinese Problem": mob violence against Ah Sin.

A second unauthorized version of the poem appeared in the *Supplement to Frank Leslie's Illustrated Newspaper* on January 21, 1871. It was subsequently issued in 1872 as a pocket-sized, blue paperback pamphlet advertising the Rock Island Line and Pacific Railroad: "The Only First Class Road in the West" (fig. 11).[18] Artistically more refined, the depiction of the two miners is more sympathetic than in the Hull version. Their clothes and demeanor more accurately reflect the poem's setting. Ah Sin, on the other hand, is portrayed as a sinister creature with feline features and a ratlike queue, as in the other edition. The illustrator of this rendition does not go so far as to depict gang brutality, yet a panel is added in which Nye, holding a curved dagger, is poised to cut off Ah Sin's braid (fig. 12).

Despite Harte's disavowal of the poem, he attempted to ride the tide of popularity it produced. After receiving a prize of ten thousand dollars for most exciting young writer in America from the Boston publishing house of Fields, Osgood & Co. in 1871, Harte and his family headed east. On his way he stopped in Chicago to visit the offices of the Western News Company, the publishers of the first pirated copy of his poem. While there "he skulked around the counters, made inquiries of the cash-boys, and took notes of what he saw," reported the *Chicago Republican*.[19]

In a letter to James R. Osgood, his new publisher, dated March 6, 1871, Harte agreed to have his poem illustrated by Sol Eytinge Jr., the staff illustrator at James R. Osgood & Co. He wrote: "I had some talk with Eytinge this morning, and think I gave him several ideas about the 'Heathen Chinee' and his pagan

Illustrations from "The Heathen Chinee" by Bret Harte ([Chicago]: Rock Island Line and Pacific Railroad, 1872), based on the 1871 version in the *Supplement to Frank Leslie's Illustrated Newspaper*. Courtesy of the Clifton Waller Barrett Library of American Literature, Special Collections, University of Virginia Library (credit for Figures 11–12).

Figure 11.

Figure 12.

brother—the California miner."[20] Harte's interest in republishing the poem with illustrations was twofold: first, his attempts to interdict the further sale of the Western News Company version were unsuccessful; and second, he wanted to benefit from its popularity himself. On April 29, 1871, "Plain Language from Truthful James" with Eytinge's illustrations was printed in *Every Saturday*. Just as Harte had hoped, it was an immediate success.[21]

The artwork in this edition (fig. 13) is much more sophisticated than that of its predecessors. As in the Hull and Rock Island versions, Truthful James opens the eight-panel story with mouth parted as if in midsentence (fig. 14).[22] He has a miner's ruggedness, with a scraggly beard and mustache, high cheekbones covered by leathered skin, a bandanna around his neck, a flannel shirt, and high boots.

Panel 2 (fig. 15) offers a striking contrast to the earlier versions. In the Eytinge rendition, Ah Sin stands slightly pigeon-toed in the middle of an open log-cabin door with the California landscape in the distance under "quite soft skies." His cheeks are plumped by an impish grin, and he nibbles playfully on his queue like a child. He wears the outfit of the coolie Harte later described in his play *Two Men of Sandy Bar* (1876): "dark-blue blouse, and dark-blue drawers gathered at the ankles [in this case, knees]; straw conical hat, and wooden sabots."

By the third panel, Bill Nye is introduced (fig. 16). All three men sit at a table engaged in a game of euchre. Nye is as scruffy-looking and weather-beaten as his partner. In profile Ah Sin is made to look more clownish and sinister, and his smile is far too broad to be natural. The violence in line 42 is portrayed graphically in much the same way as in its two antecedents (fig. 17), but the escalation to a riot is abandoned, and the fight appears to be a fairer, one-on-one contest (fig. 18). While Nye sits on Ah Sin's limp body in panel 7 (fig. 19—reminiscent of the Rock Island version), James pulls the twenty-four packs of cards from Ah Sin's sleeve. There is a sense that Ah Sin might be unconscious for a while, but no real harm has come to him. The final panel (fig. 20) reveals the true irony of the poem. Truthful James, with his eyes cast to the right and his index finger pressed to the side of his nose, ponders thoughtfully, as if he doesn't really understand what had happened.

Gary Scharnhorst, in his "'Ways That Are Dark': Appropriations of Bret Harte's 'Plain Language from Truthful James,'" claims that the text of the poem omits any overt violence and hence that the Harte-Eytinge collaboration interprets the poem in the same way as the previous, pirated ones.[23] The violence of the poem, however, is not literal but implied, just like the irony, so to ignore it would do an injustice to the ironic tone.[24] Harte had spent some years around

Illustrations from "The Heathen Chinee" by Bret Harte, illustrated by Sol Eytinge Jr. (Boston: James R. Osgood & Co., 1871). Courtesy of the Clifton Waller Barrett Library of American Literature, Special Collections, University of Virginia Library (credit for Figures 13–20). Figures 13 and 14 (top); Figures 15 and 16 (bottom).

AND HE WENT FOR THAT HEATHEN CHINEE.

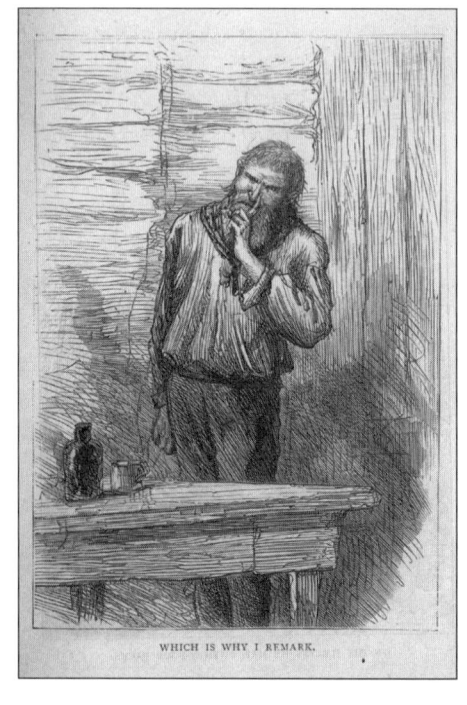

THE SCENE THAT ENSUED.

IN HIS SLEEVES HE HAD TWENTY-FOUR PACKS.

WHICH IS WHY I REMARK.

Figures 17 and 18 (top); Figures 19 and 20 (bottom).

the mining camps and understood their inhabitants, whose hypocrisy often led them to violence. Scharnhorst insists that "the sketches do not dispute the anti-Chinese reading," but he fails to acknowledge that irony creates ambiguity.[25] The poem would be read any way the public wanted. In the end the Chinaman, Ah Sin, could only be perceived by Euro-Americans as his name implied, "I sin."

The cultural impact the poem exerted throughout the rest of the nineteenth century cannot be underestimated. William Purvience Fenn discusses in *Ah Sin and His Brethren in American Literature* the poem's influence on immigration policy—it was regularly quoted from in Congress—and its popularity abroad, especially in England.[26] Scharnhorst explains in detail the various appropriations of the text beyond the two examples given in this essay. The poem was set to music several times, including the compilations known as *The Heathen Chinee Songster*[27] and *The Heathen Chinee Musical Album*.[28] Scharnhorst also has located at least fourteen parodies of the poem written during the 1870s.[29]

Eventually, the poem's notoriety even extended to the New York stage. Although the Heathen Chinee appeared in frontier melodramas before Harte's poem, the character's presence was limited to only two extant dramas of note: Alonzo Delano's *A Live Woman in the Mines; or, Pike County Ahead* (1857) and Joseph A. Nunes's *Fast Folks; or, The Early Days of California* (1858). (There is no known record of performance of the former and only two known performances of the latter, in San Francisco and Philadelphia.)[30] Throughout the 1860s the Comic Coolie—a more precise term for the role this character played in frontier melodramas—seemed to disappear from the stage, most likely because the nation was at war and the Chinese question was too closely related to the one about African slavery. After the war, the character's reappearance is assured and sustained by the introduction of Harte's poem. With its subsequent illustrations and appropriations, the foundations were laid for the establishment of the Chinese comic type on the American stage.

One of the first producers to exploit the Chinaman's comic possibilities was Augustin Daly, who literally transported the Heathen Chinee of Harte's poem from the page to the stage. *Horizon* (1871), Daly's first attempt at a frontier melodrama, was an "original drama of contemporaneous society and of American frontier perils. In five acts and seven tableaux."[31] Instead of premiering at Daly's Fifth Avenue Theatre in New York, the play was produced down the street at the Olympic Theatre under the management of Daly's father-in-law, John Duff (Daly gave the play to Duff in order to assist him during an economic setback). On March 21, 1871 (seven months after the publication of "Plain Language from Truthful James"), the play opened with George L. Fox playing the role of "a distinguished member of the Third House at Washington," that is, a crooked politician, and Miss Agnes Ethel as the heroine, or the "White Flower of the Plains."[32]

Daly knew little about the "real" West. He was born in North Carolina and spent most of his life in New York City. As the consummate producer, however, he knew that the old melodrama could be made new again by adding a bit of local color known as "frontier life." In this way he borrowed liberally from the western writers who knew the scene better than he. Marvin Felheim observes in *The Theatre of Augustin Daly* not only that *Horizon*'s heroine (Med) is placed in a similar situation to that of Lotta Crabtree's character in *Heartease,* produced only the year before, but that the opening of act 2 bears a striking resemblance to the opening of Harte's short story "The Outcasts of Poker Flat" and that the character of John Loder is the same as Harte's gambler, John Oakhurst.[33]

What Felheim does not mention is that the beginning of act 3 of *Horizon* re-creates the scene of Harte's most famous poem. The act opens on Big Run River where the stage is meant to represent the head of a flatboat. Soldiers are loading the boat with "bags, barrels and bundles from the shed" while Cephas and other "darkies" are stacking wood (the scene is a strange hybrid of riverboat and frontier culture). Cephas is described as "A Fifteenth Amendment" in the dramatis personae, and his character—like that of the Chinaman—functions purely as comic relief. On the ground nearby are the Heathen Chinee (described as he "who does not understand"), "Uncle Billy" Blakely (a drunkard),[34] and Wahcotah (the "friendly" Indian who turns out not to be so friendly) playing a game of euchre:

Ceph. comes down and leans on his stick of wood, looking over the group of card players.
CEPH: Hi! dars de way dem trash has of musin' dereselves. [*To Chinee.*] Hi! you, play de ace, you cussed fool.
BLAK: Play the ace? Why, not him! He's tried five aces on us already.
CHINEE: Me no understand!
BLAK: Don't understand, eh? Well, what you *don't* understand would furnish brains for a mosquito.
CEPH: Hi! golly! Chinee wipe nigger out, eh?
BLAK: Well, for "Ways that are dark and for tricks that are vain." Why he's won all my terbacker already! Ain't you Chinee?
CHINEE: Me poor chap! No understand Melican. [*Sudden grab at trick Blak. is about to take.*] Mine, Melican!
WAHCOTAH: Throwing down cards. Ugh! Cheatee!
BLAK: [*Drawing a dirk.*] That's the sixth ace in his hand; let me go for that heathen. [*Chinee starts up, runs toward shed. Blak. after him, stopped by Ser.*][35]

Instead of two miners, there is only "Uncle Billy" and an "Injin." In this game it is clear that neither Blakely nor Wahcotah is attempting to cheat the "Chinee." The Chinaman's subterfuge is discovered by the introduction of a fourth character, Cephas. As in the poem, the Heathen Chinee feigns ignorance, but to no avail. Blakely recites one of the most famous lines from the poem—"for ways that are dark and for tricks that are vain"—just before the Chinaman manages to escape his wrath.

Although *Horizon* ran for nearly eight weeks, by nineteenth-century standards—and compared to Daly's more successful enterprises, such as *Under the Gaslight* (1867)—it was a dismal failure. The play deviates from the romanticized frontier melodramas of the 1830s, when the West was still Kentucky and the literary model was James Fenimore Cooper's Leatherstocking series.[36] By 1871, the year of Daly's production, the West extended to California and Cooper's "noble savages" were reimagined as "murdering heathens."[37] (The "heathen" epithet was something they would have in common with the Chinese.) On the eastern seaboard, a vogue for western characters and costumes was vitalized by Harte's writings about western mining camps, especially his "Plain Language from Truthful James."

The following year, *California; or, The Heathen Chinee* (1872) opened at the Bowery Theatre. It ran for two weeks and does not seem to have had any revivals in subsequent years, at least not in New York. It is difficult to ascertain exactly what the play is about, since no extant script exists. However, a notice in the *New York Herald* on May 27, 1872, described it as "The Grand California Equestrian Drama, in three acts, written expressly for the theatre by J. H. Warwick. . . . This magnificent spectacle drama has been produced at enormous cost. . . . First appearance of Mr. O. B. Collins and his famed trained Steed, San Juan. . . . Mr. C. Warwick especially engaged for the great character part of Ah Sin." Ah Sin is described as "a Chinaman, who can't play poker."[38]

A playbill from June 7 of that year includes a list of other lively characters, including Bill Nye, "a gambler"; Patsey Cogen, "from the Jim of the Say"; Dandy Jack, "a Cockney Thief"; Pickles, "an Amateur Prig"; Wong Lee, "a Chinese Washman"; Black Sheep, "of Genuine Nature"; and various other "Miners, Hunters, Chinese, Ladies and Gentleman, for the Great Sensation Scenes of this Piece, by an extra Auxiliary [sic] Force, engaged expressly for this occasion." A synopsis of the three acts given below the cast of players indicates that there was at least one gambling scene with Ah Sin, "who learns the mysteries of poker" from Bill Nye. The play was clearly not imagined as a frontier melodrama, however, since act 2 digresses into a minstrel olio when "De Minstrel's return from de war" and Ah Sin plays his "wonderful chopstick solo."[39] The play is worth mentioning here in that, judging from this brief description, it can be assumed that the playwright borrowed something from Harte's poem.[40]

Oddly, it took another four years (if one includes the play above) before another frontier melodrama—complete with Comic Coolie—arrived on the New York stage. And coincidentally, it was Harte himself who brought the character back to life. Determined to cash in on the substantial profits a Broadway hit could provide, he wrote *Two Men of Sandy Bar* (1876).[41] Unfortunately, "the scenario is so convoluted as to defy brief synopsis," explained one critic.[42] Nevertheless, Roger Hall succeeds in doing so in his *Performing the American Frontier, 1870–1906*:

> The plot involves Sandy, a generous young drunk living on the Southern California ranch of Don Jose Castro. Sandy helps Don Jose's fiery daughter, Jovita, hide her clandestine meetings with a secret lover, but Don Jose, thinking the lover is Sandy, fires him. About that time, Alexander Morton arrives at the ranch seeking his wayfaring son and accompanied by his loquacious legal adviser, Colonel Starbottle. Morton believes that Jovita's secret lover, John Oakhurst, is his lost son and invites him to San Francisco. The scene switches to Sandy Bar, a little town in the mountains, where Mary Merritt teaches school. Sandy and Mary are close friends [I would say would-be lovers], but their relationship is shattered when Mary comes to believe—incorrectly—that Sandy is married. Disillusioned, Mary leaves for San Francisco, where Oakhurst is now ensconced as the scion of the Morton mansion. Eventually a ranch hand and Hop Sing,[43] a Chinese Laundryman, bring the real son—Sandy—to the house. At the curtain Oakhurst and Sandy, whose once strong friendship had been carelessly destroyed, reconcile, Morton accepts Sandy as his son, Sandy is reunited with Mary, and Oakhurst marries Jovita.[44]

The play was a flop.[45] A critic from the *New York Telegram* declared that "Mr. Harte enjoys this day the single anomaly of having written a very bad play," except for the character of the Chinese laundrymen, Hop Sing.[46] The role was quite small, nine lines in all, but the character actor Charles T. Parsloe Jr. made the most of them. The *Boston Daily Globe* from November 7, 1876, panned the play but praised Parsloe's Hop Sing: "He manages to make it one of the funniest characters in the play."

Harte had not intended to exploit, yet again, the Chinese identity he helped to create. By his own admission, the character was only meant as a brief comic interlude between the overly dramatic elements of the play. However, he found himself once more at the center of attention. Certainly Parsloe's performance had a great deal to do with the character's success, but the model of the "Heathen Chinee" was Harte's.

The *New York Telegram* reviewer had also suggested that in "the hands of a skillful dramatist, Mr. Hop Sing would have been a prominent character."[47] A year later, his wish was partially fulfilled. Again Harte, desperate for money, decided to capitalize on his new creation. With Mark Twain, he wrote *Ah Sin* (1877), a play that featured Parsloe as the main character.[48] Again Parsloe's performance was exemplary, but because of a combination of hot weather and poor dramatic writing—exacerbated by Harte and Twain's petty bickering—this play, too, was short-lived. The *Dramatic News* on August 4, 1877, reported: "Of *Ah Sin* which is a harrowingly thoughtless aggravation of our present hot weather, we forbear to speak of as a drama—principally because it isn't one, and our conscience is yet tender."[49]

Regardless of *Ah Sin's* demise, it is important to recognize how Harte transformed the Ah Sin of the poem into the Ah Sin of the play, since this transformation informed forever the Chinese comic type in theatre. From a few lines in *Two Men of Sandy Bar* to a starring role in *Ah Sin*, the Heathen Chinee is finally given a voice (albeit a theatricalized one), and the nineteenth-century stage was ripe for it. Holger Kersten has observed that nineteenth-century American drama and popular entertainment seemed to delight in language in a way that "looked like the growing nation was surveying its linguistic diversity."[50]

One of the most striking characteristics of performing the Comic Coolie was the verbal rendering of what was thought to be the Chinese-American dialect, or "pidgin." A few Euro-American authors, such as Harte and Twain, attempted to portray this dialect accurately, while others were amateurish and careless. One author even went so far as to provide the following caveat to his play: "The Chinese dialect as written here (and elsewhere in America) is at best but a poor imitation, but good enough to be funny, which is the only object in view."[51] Nonetheless, *all* of them fail when it comes to the use of the Chinese language itself. A common stage direction reads: *talking Chinese all the time.* Invariably this meant Chinese gibberish.

To most critics, Parsloe excelled in the mastery of this "gibberish." The *Boston Daily Globe* on November 7, 1876, confirms that Parsloe's "imitation of the pigeon [sic] English of the pagan" in Harte's *Two Men of Sandy Bar* makes him one of the funniest characters in the play. Parsloe's obituary from the *New York Dramatic Mirror* on January 29, 1898, states that it "was universally acknowledged that he copied with singular accuracy . . . the pigeon [sic] English of the 'Heathen Chinee' of the Pacific Slope."[52] Robert G. Lee asserts in his book *Orientals: Asian Americans in Popular Culture* that this "conjoining of pidgin with nonsense simultaneously diminished the status of Canton English as an important commercial language and infantilized its speakers."[53]

However, an alternative interpretation might consider Ah Sin—as represented by Harte and Parsloe—as the Euro-American immigrant's *eiron* rather than as a child. The nation-building of the nineteenth century depended on immigration, which in turn required socialization to sustain its plurality. Socialization attempts to move us farther away from our instinctual behaviors. These behaviors can never be completely repressed, but they can be channeled in a more "appropriate" direction. Frontier melodrama provided such a channel, acting as surrogate "primitive" to a society that was rapidly moving toward the "pluralistic," the "modern," and the "civilized." One example of a way to channel unsocialized aggressions was evident in the Euro-American's theatrical response to the Chinese immigrants who appeared in cities all over the United States after the completion of the transcontinental railroad.

Finally, Harte's ironic character as expressed in his poem is realized through Parsloe's performance of him. As the first successful delineator of Harte's character, Parsloe was trained in the circus and pantomime and informed his representation of the Chinaman with the elements of the clown.[54] The pidgin gibberish spoken by Parsloe had less to do with the Chinese language and more to do with the verbal anarchy that the clown brings to the stage. Although no definitive image of Parsloe was found in his role as Hop Sing, a review of *Ah Sin* (1877) indicates that the "character of Ah Sin is essentially the same as the Chinaman of 'The Two Men of Sandy Bar,' with the exception that we see him more."[55] Harry Murdoch's caricature of Parsloe (fig. 21) has been identified both with Parsloe's role as Hop Sing and as Ah Sin, and a photo at the Harvard Theatre Collection identifying him as Wing Lee in a later play, *My Partner* (fig. 22), confirms that Parsloe cultivated a similar (if not identical) look in all three of his best-known portrayals of the Comic Coolie.[56]

From the caricature and photo, Parsloe's interpretation of the role can be understood as one that did not completely adhere to Eytinge's illustration of Harte's poem. Wearing light-colored short pants that are rolled up midcalf, and a western-style cap rather than the conical straw one of the coolie, it is apparent that Parsloe allowed himself some artistic license. The cap is slightly too small to fit around the head properly, maximizing the comic effect, and his large paunch and "peculiar gait" (as described by many reviewers) are reminiscent of the techniques of a circus clown. His carrying of a carpetbag and umbrella completes the comic picture.

The Comic Coolie as "clown" has archetypal roots in the *eiron*, and the *eiron*'s other name, as mentioned earlier, is "trickster."[57] (Of course, this trickster was for a Euro-American audience, since no real Chinese would see himself in such a portrayal.) Since Parsloe's performance is nearly impossible to

Figure 21. Harry Murdoch's caricature of Charles T. Parsloe as Hop Sing in *Two Men of Sandy Bar* by Bret Harte. Courtesy Harvard Theatre Collection, Houghton Library, © Harvard University.

Figure 22. Photo of Charles T. Parsloe as Wing Lee in *My Partner* by Bartley Campbell. Courtesy Harvard Theatre Collection, Houghton Library, © Harvard University.

re-create, the poem and the play *Ah Sin* will have to serve as a visual and aural score of how Harte's trickster—through Parsloe's clowning—was brought to life.

Cultural critic Lewis Hyde, in his book *Trickster Makes This World: Mischief, Myth, and Art,* explains the trickster's role in society: "When he lies and steals, it isn't so much to get away with something or get rich as to disturb the established categories of truth and property and, by so doing, open the road to possible new worlds."[58] The Comic Coolie, Ah Sin, both in the poem and in the play, had a similar function. He did not appear merely for comic relief. He steals and lies, but only in order to reveal the truth. The character was the immigrants' trickster, because their survival depended on it. He taught them how to negotiate the hostile and confusing world they now found themselves in.

Unlike the poem's character, the play's Ah Sin does not engage in an actual card game, he only observes one. The villain, Broderick, has challenged Plunkett—a character driven to exaggeration, but a harmless, kind soul—to a game of draw. Ah Sin is fond of Plunkett, and he knows that Broderick is out to swindle him. Ah Sin, gun in hand, slips behind a clearing and fires a shot in the air to distract the two men. When they stop their game and investigate, Ah Sin sneaks up to the unguarded cards and stacks them so that Plunkett comes out the winner, hence revealing another "category of truth" that undermines the unspoken law of the West: "good guys always come in last."

Another instance of the trickster's cunning is revealed in act 2. When the gold digger Miss Plunkett drops her handkerchief, Ah Sin picks it up and places it up his sleeve without her noticing. A few lines later Miss Plunkett finally becomes aware of Ah Sin's presence and asks him a question. Ah Sin answers, "Good day, John." Miss Plunkett indignantly replies, "My name is not John." After a few more lines she realizes she has lost her handkerchief and asks him if he has seen it. Ah Sin, after a short interrogation—he wants to make sure that the handkerchief truly belongs to her and not some gentleman—pulls out a rolled-up stocking, hands it to her, and walks away.

Ah Sin's stealing of the handkerchief has less to do with getting rich than it does with subverting a "category of property." What real use could he have for a woman's handkerchief in a mining town inhabited by rough-and-tumble men? Nor does his cheeky address to her as "John" have anything to do with an ignorance of American women's names; rather, it is a subtle way of disrupting another "category of truth." Most Euro-Americans addressed male Chinese as John (Chinaman) without any regard to their real name. By calling Miss Plunkett "John," Ah Sin pointedly makes reference to this habit.

Later in the play, Ah Sin has the evidence necessary to indict the murderer, Brockett, but because of the 1854 landmark decision that "classed the Chinese with Indians, officially depriving them of their rights," he could not testify in court.[59] A blood-stained coat is the crucial evidence needed, and of course the Chinese laundryman has hold of it. In order for justice to be served, he must devise a way in which the truth can be told. Because of his status, however, unconventional and (to the puritan mind) devious methods must be employed. Thus the Heathen Chinee, like the trickster, behaves subversively. By lying and stealing, he disrupts the status quo.

Ah Sin also has a tendency "to imitate." One of the trickster's names is "imitator."[60] In trickster mythology every animal has a way of looking at the world; each has its own nature, except trickster. Trickster has no way. He can only imitate others. Often the Heathen Chinee is represented as imitating those around him, because he is ignorant of the ways of his new land. For instance, the Ah Sin of the poem imitates the unscrupulous miners' game of cheating, and the Ah Sin of the play, in act 3, "imitates" setting a table with equally disruptive results. The urbane Mrs. Tempest, in an attempt to stay "civilized" amid the coarse mining-camp environment, tries to teach Ah Sin how to set a table. Unfortunately, she makes several mistakes in her lesson: slamming the table leaf, allowing the tablecloth to fly away, and setting the dishes too near the table's edge so that they fall off. Ah Sin, in perfect imitation, repeats every one of her mistakes, for this kind of activity is hardly part of his "nature."

At first glance this imitative quality might seem rather inane: the trickster or Heathen Chinee has the ability to copy others but no ability of his own.[61] Nevertheless, there is an advantage to this, says Hyde in reference to the trickster, for "whoever has no way but is a successful imitator will have, in the end, a repertoire of ways."[62] To the newly arrived immigrant, this concept is invaluable. Having no "way" can facilitate adaptation to unfamiliar surroundings. Hyde continues: "Having no way, he is dependent on others whose manner he exploits, but he is not confined to their manner and therefore in another sense he is more independent. Having no way, he is free of the trap of instinct, both 'stupider than the other animals' and more versatile than any."[63]

There are cases, too, in which Ah Sin is able to incite laughter at another character's expense. In act 1 of *Ah Sin*, Broderick, the villain, who has just slain Plunkett, a fellow miner, is afraid that Ah Sin has witnessed his evil deed, and so attempts to take him out with a pickax.[64] Ah Sin, in a typical act of subversion, pretends to be searching through his carpetbag of tricks. The rest of the stage directions read:

Broderick retreats downstage until he reaches the stump of a tree . . . and secures in his hand a pick, which he holds behind him as he cautiously approaches Ah Sin. Ah Sin, watchful of him, yet seemingly preoccupied, continues to draw articles from a carpet bag, a few silver spoons, a chicken, a pair of stockings, a tablecloth, and finally, as Broderick approaches him closely and raises pick, a revolver which he cocks and accidentally as it were (chord) covers Broderick with it—Broderick halts and drops his pick noisily.[65]

When the poem "Plain Language from Truthful James" is read with the same irony, Nye and James are the butt of the joke; they have been "duped" by "the dupe." After Ah Sin, in the final scenes of the play, has negotiated with Broderick to receive half his rich mines and "$10,000 to boot" for aid in preventing Broderick's hanging, he immediately produces the man, Plunkett, whom Broderick had been accused of murdering. Ah Sin had known all along that Plunkett was still alive.

Ah Sin might be a bungler, in either the poem or the play, but he is far from an idiot. Social psychologist William McDougall lists "stupidity which can turn out to be cleverness" as one of the primary components of trickster as clown.[66] The humor may derive from a linguistic misunderstanding (e.g., mistaking the word "John" for a woman's name) or from ignorance of American customs (setting a table by breaking all the dishes), but what he lacks in "intelligence" he makes up for in cleverness. Despite all, Ah Sin is able to play his tricks with relative impunity, survive any situation with relative ease, and even assist others along the way.

After the failure of *Ah Sin*, Harte moved his family to Europe, never to return. Fame had ruined his career. Meanwhile, Parsloe went on to co-star with Louis Aldrich in Bartley Campbell's *My Partner* (1879), building upon the success he had achieved as the premier interpreter of Harte's stage Chinaman. The play went on to become one of the most profitable shows of its day, yet Parsloe died in penury,[67] perhaps proving that irony works in real life as well as fiction.

Condemnation is an easy tool to use against Harte and Parsloe and their representation of the Heathen Chinee, but the Comic Coolie may also be interpreted in a more ironic way. The character was not just a frivolous anomaly. He was the Euro-American immigrant's trickster. He represented their plurality and provided an outlet for the stresses of assimilating into the New World—stresses that only the trickster could overcome. Whether conscious or not, Harte's and Parsloe's portrayal of the Comic Coolie was illustrative of the both/and conundrum of the trickster, the strange paradox that asks us to live in a morally ambiguous universe, yet an infinitely more interesting one.

Notes

Special thanks to Claire Conceison, David Mayer, and Gary Scharnhorst for their kind support in the writing of this article.
1. Quoted in Patrick Morrow, *Bret Harte* (Boise, Idaho: Boise State College, 1972), 26.
2. The *Overland Monthly* was a San Francisco literary magazine of which Harte was a founding member, 1868–70.
3. Gary Scharnhorst, "'Ways That Are Dark': Appropriations of Bret Harte's 'Plain Language from Truthful James,'" *Nineteenth-Century Literature* 51, no. 3 (1996): 378.
4. I use "type" as a synonym for "stereotype" throughout this article in order to maintain a certain "neutrality" toward the latter's typically negative connotation.
5. Poem taken from Bret Harte, *Poems and Two Men of Sandy Bar, a Drama* (Boston: Houghton Mifflin, 1896), 129–31.
6. Margaret Duckett, "Plain Language from Bret Harte," *Nineteenth-Century Fiction* 11 (March 1957): 242.
7. "John Chinaman," in Bret Harte's *Gabriel Conroy, Bohemian Papers, Stories of and for the Young*, vol. 2 (Boston: Houghton, Mifflin, 1896), 222.
8. "The Latest Chinese Outrage" first appeared in *New York Spirit of the Times*, February 2, 1878, 705.
9. "The Latest Chinese Outrage," in Harte, *Poems and Two Men of Sandy Bar*, 142–45.
10. Derived from the Tamil or Gujarati term meaning "laborer," the Chinese name "coolie" refers to a system of indentured servitude that was, ironically, never instituted in the United States. Throughout this article I will refer to this particular Chinese comic type as the Comic Coolie, also known as the Heathen Chinee.
11. Morrow, *Bret Harte,* 25.
12. Francis Cornford, *The Origin of Attic Comedy* (Ann Arbor: University of Michigan Press, 1961). These comic types are further pursued in Northrop Fryes's "The Mythos of Spring" in his *Anatomy of Criticism: Four Essays* (Princeton, N.J.: Princeton University Press, 1957).
13. Cornford, *Origin of Attic Comedy,* 119–20.
14. Scharnhorst, "'Ways That Are Dark,'" 377–99. His excellent study of the poem details its misappropriations in the debate over immigration policy and the Chinese.
15. Quoted in Scharnhorst, "'Ways That Are Dark,'" 379. Original editorial reprinted in *Bret Harte's California: Letters to the "Springfield Republican" and "Christian Register," 1866–1867*, ed. Gary Scharnhorst (Albuquerque: University of New Mexico Press, 1990), 114.
16. Also known as the Los Angeles Massacre, the riots occurred in October 1871.
17. F. Bret Harte, *The Heathen Chinee* (Chicago: Western News Company, 1870). Nine loose leaves with lithographed illustrations by Joseph Hull, title from envelope. Clifton Waller Barrett Library of American Literature, Special Collections, University of Virginia Library, Charlottesville [hereafter cited as CWB].
18. Bret Harte, "Heathen Chinee" (Chicago: Chicago, Rock Island Route, 1872), CWB.
19. *Chicago Republican,* March 15, 1871, quoted in Scharnhorst, "'Ways That Are Dark,'" 387.
20. Gary Scharnhorst, ed., *Selected Letters of Bret Harte* (Norman: University of Oklahoma Press, 1997), 48.

21. Scharnhorst, "'Ways That Are Dark,'" 388.
22. The chapbook version begins with the portrait of Ah Sin (fig. 15). He also appears on the cover, his popularity surpassing even that of the storyteller, Truthful James.
23. Scharnhorst, "'Ways That Are Dark,'" 379.
24. A facsimile of the original manuscript of the poem reveals that two lines were omitted from the published version. In stanza eight, after the final line, "In the game he did not understand," is written, "These smacks upon Chinese free / labor, I swiftly would make to explain." This would confirm that Harte had intended a violent interaction between Ah Sin and Nye.
25. Scharnhorst, "'Ways That Are Dark,'" 388.
26. William Purvience Fenn, *Ah Sin and His Brethren in American Literature: Delivered before the Convocation of the College of Chinese Studies, June 1933* (Peking: College of Chinese Studies Cooperating with California College in China, 1933).
27. *The Heathen Chinee Songster: A Choice Collection of the Latest Copyright Songs, Minstrel Melodies, and Popular Ballads of the Day* (New York: Beadle, 1871).
28. *The Heathen Chinee Musical Album* (New York: DeWitt, 1871). The first musical setting of the poem was "The Heathen Chinee," song and chorus, words by "Bret Harte," music by Charles Towner (Chicago: Root & Cady, 1870). The second was by F. Boot (Boston: Oliver Ditson & Co., 1870). See also Krystyn R. Moon's *Yellowface: Creating the Chinese in American Popular Music and Performance, 1850s–1920s* (New Brunswick, N.J.: Rutgers University Press, 2005).
29. Scharnhorst, "'Ways That Are Dark,'" 382 n. 20. I even located an image of the minstrel performer, Ben Cotton, as the "Heathen Chinee" in blackface. The image is essentially the same as the Harte/Eytinge version except Ah Sin's face is darkened.
30. American Theatre, San Francisco, July 1, 1858, and Arch St. Theatre, Philadelphia, January 20, 1859.
31. Augustin Daly, *Horizon* (New York: Printed, as manuscript only, for the author, 1885), cover. James McCloskey's *Across the Continent* (1870) is often cited erroneously as one of the first frontier melodramas of the 1870s to contain a Chinese character. A survey of period playbills, however, indicates that the Chinese character (eventually named "Ah Veree Tart") was not introduced in *Across the Continent* until after Charles T. Parsloe played the Comic Coolie (Hop Sing)—to great acclaim—in *Two Men of Sandy Bar* (1876). See playbill for New Park Theatre (Brooklyn), November 12, 1877, in New York Playbills (Brooklyn, 1876–1908), Harvard Theatre Collection, The Houghton Library, Harvard College Library, Cambridge, Massachusetts [hereafter cited as HTC].
32. Daly, *Horizon*, Dramatis Personae.
33. Marvin Felheim, *The Theatre of Augustin Daly* (Cambridge: Harvard University Press, 1956), 67–74, quoted in *Plays by Augustin Daly*, ed. Don. B. Wilmeth and Rosemary Cullen (Cambridge: Cambridge University Press, 1984), 32. The similarities between Med and Lotta and *Heartease* and *Horizon* were first noted in Constance Rourke's *Troupers of the Gold Coast; or, the Rise of Lotta Crabtree* (New York: Harcourt, Brace, and Co., 1928).
34. Another character borrowed from Harte's "The Outcasts of Poker Flat."
35. Daly, *Horizon*, 34–35.
36. Wilmeth and Cullen, *Plays*, 32. This outmoded version of the "noble savage" is paro-

died in *Horizon*, as two sophisticates from the East (Columbia Rowse and Mr. Smith) continually make reference to Cooper's romanticized "savages" until the villains of the drama prove to be the very Indians they had idolized.

37. Roger Hall, in *Performing the American Frontier, 1870–1906* (Cambridge: Cambridge University Press, 2001), explains that "sensational action" dominated melodrama in the 1870s. However, *Horizon*, by "combining a central love story with sensational attacks," managed to locate "a midpoint between action and sentiment" (41).
38. Quoted in Stuart W. Hyde, "The Chinese Stereotype in American Melodrama," *California Historical Society Quarterly* 34 (December 1955): 360–61.
39. New York Playbills, Bowery Theatre, HTC.
40. Another drama, *Gold*, appeared at Jean Burnside's theatre (The Broadway) on April 8, 1872. The dramatis personae may have included a character named Ah Sin, but my research has not yet yielded any definitive results.
41. The play is based on Harte's prose tales "Mr. Thompson's Prodigal" and "An Episode of Fiddletown." The pre-Broadway run was in Chicago, July 17–22, 1876; it premiered in New York from August 28 to September 23 and then toured the East and Midwest until January 1877. In September 1878 it played in San Francisco.
42. Gary Scharnhorst, *Bret Harte* (New York: Twayne, 1992), 54.
43. The Chinese name was taken from Harte's short story "Wan Lee, the Pagan" (1874).
44. Hall, *Performing the American Frontier*, 89.
45. Ibid., 90.
46. Undated clipping, 1876, *Two Men of Sandy Bar* clippings file, HTC.
47. Ibid. A letter dated September 21, 1876, from Bret Harte to Robert Roosevelt confirms Harte's apprehension in making the "Heathen Chinee" a main character: "As to the Chinaman, don't you think he would become tiresome and monotonous as the central figure in a three act play?" G. A. Cevasco and Richard Harmond, "Bret Harte to Robert Roosevelt on the Two Men of Sandy Bar: A Newly Discovered Letter," *American Literary Realism, 1870–1910* 21, no. 1 (1988): 61.
48. Pre-Broadway run in Washington, D.C., May 7–12, 1877, and in Baltimore, May 14–19, 1877; it premiered in New York at Daly's Fifth Avenue Theatre on July 31, 1877, and closed on August 26, 1877.
49. Although *Ah Sin* was a dismal failure, it did manage to tour for three months. The success of Parsloe's Chinaman prompted him to commission his own play, Bartley Campbell's *My Partner* (1879), and to revise his role as the Comic Coolie (now called Wing Lee rather than Ah Sin, but the characters were identical). *My Partner* proved so wildly popular that it toured for years afterward.
50. Holger Kersten, "Using the Immigrant's Voice: Humor and Pathos in Nineteenth-Century 'Dutch' Dialect Texts," *Melus* 21, no. 4 (1996): 3. Robert G. Lee, in *Orientals: Asian Americans in Popular Culture* (Philadelphia: Temple University Press, 1999), mentions that John Dillard—in his *Black English: Its History and Usage in the United States* (New York: Random House, 1972)—explains how a variety of pidgins and creoles were in widespread use in the nineteenth-century American West (36).
51. T. S. Denison, *Pasty O'Wang* (1895), in *The Chinese Other 1850–1925: An Anthology of Plays*, ed. Dave Williams (Lanham, Md.: University Press of America, 1997), 127.
52. Parsloe's rendition of the Comic Coolie in Twain and Harte's *Ah Sin* was so successful that a "Chinee-Song" was written expressly for him by Harry R. Williams (Detroit:

R. Stephens, 1877). The lyrics highlight the fear of miscegenation that extended beyond black and white, as Ah Sin's Irish wife leaves him for an "American" man.
53. Lee, *Orientals*, 37.
54. Parsloe's Ah Sin was more accurately described by one reviewer as "a Bowery Boy in a short gown, grinning, and mixing the dialect of Washington Market with the business of Tony Pastor's." *New York Spirit of the Times*, August 4, 1877.
55. Unknown newspaper, n.d., *Ah Sin* clippings file, HTC.
56. Gary Scharnhorst identifies the photo as Parsloe in *Ah Sin* in *Bret Harte: Opening the American Literary West* (Norman: University of Oklahoma Press, 2000), 126. George C. D. Odell labels the photo "Charles T. Parsloe as Hop Sing" in *Annals of the New York Stage*, vol. 10 (New York: Columbia University Press, 1938), 192.
57. Martin Banham, ed., *The Cambridge Guide to Theatre* (Cambridge: Cambridge University Press, 1995), s.v. "clowns."
58. Lewis Hyde, *Trickster Makes This World: Mischief, Myth, and Art* (New York: North Point Press, 1998), 13.
59. Dave Williams, *Misreading the Chinese Character: Images of the Chinese in Euroamerican Drama to 1925* (New York: Peter Lang, 2000), 79.
60. Hyde, *Trickster Makes This World*, 42.
61. Ibid., 43. The Chinese are often reviled (or revered) for their ability to copy or imitate well.
62. Ibid.
63. Ibid., 45.
64. At the end of the play we discover that Plunkett has survived the massacre.
65. Bret Harte and Mark Twain, *Ah Sin*, in Williams, *The Chinese Other*, 55.
66. Banham, *Cambridge Guide*, s.v. "clowns."
67. Hall, *Performing the American Frontier*, 125.

BOOK REVIEWS

Labanotation: The System of Analyzing and Recording Movement. By Ann Hutchinson Guest. 4th ed. New York and London: Routledge, 2005. 487 pp. $35.00 paper.

John Hodgson asks in the preface of his 1996 biography, *Mastering Movement: The Life and Work of Rudolf Laban,* "Why is Rudolf Laban's work not better known?" This dance theorist was one of the most influential thinkers in a long line of analyzers and practitioners of dance and movement. Laban was directly influenced by Françoise Delsarte's work on mime and gesture, and he knew many of the leading performers, teachers, and designers of the early twentieth century, including Emil-Jacques Dalcroze, Isadora Duncan, and Adolphe Appia. He came under the influence of the dadaists as part of a circle of artists who frequented the Cabaret Voltaire in Zurich. He influenced dancers and choreographers for generations to come, including Mary Wigman, Kurt Jooss, and Pina Bausch. His most significant contribution to dance was his 1928 publication of *Kinetographie Laban,* a dance notation system that came to be called "Labanotation" and is still used as one of the primary movement notation systems in dance. Laban also published a book on bodily movement in industrial settings (*Effort: Economy in Body Movement*), and he continued to teach and do research in England until his death in 1958. His theories of choreography and movement continue to serve as one of the central foundations of modern European dance.

Labanotation, or Kinetography Laban (as it is known in some parts of Europe), is a system of movement notation that is also used for dance notation. Its function is to preserve dance movements, just as music notation preserves the order of the notes and other musical elements. Over the last fifty years, Laban's ideas for defining bodily movement have been applied in the areas of dance, therapy, education, industry, and theatre. Ann Hutchinson Guest, who first wrote about Labanotation in 1954, has now produced a fourth edition of her book, which is more detailed than any of the previous publications.

The major difficulty in comprehending the Laban system is the intricate way it is recorded. It is quite detailed and requires close reading to familiarize the reader with the variety of notations. Fortunately, Guest has provided introductory chapters to explain the basic terminology, including motif, effort-shape, and structure descriptions. The motif description provides a general statement about the most dynamic feature of the movement, whereas the effort-shape description examines the energy transfer based on space, time, weight, and flow. The structure description examines body, space, and time. Most acting students are familiar with Laban's analyses of effort based on space (direct or indirect), time (sudden or sustained), weight (strength or lightness), and flow (free or restricted). When studying Laban movement, students are often required to use these levels of effort to create a character. For example, a surreal character may suggest a "gliding" movement (indirect, sustained, light, and free).

Guest divides the remainder of her book into twenty-two short chapters that concentrate on specific parts of the body. Each chapter begins by explaining a variety of movements of the particular area, offers illustrations of the movement, and records the movements on a notation scale. For example, one chapter examines the "touch and slide" of the foot, which measures a specific part of the foot touching the floor and the extent to which its weight and direction are applied to the movement. "Tilting," "turning," "gestures," and "rotating" are topics of other movements examined in separate chapters. The chapter on "systems of reference" is probably the most useful guide to understanding Labanotation; here Guest clearly explains the "axes" of the body and how Laban saw the body moving in space via a series of interconnected planes. She concludes the book with several appendices of different variations of the notations as well as glossaries of symbols and explanations of terms.

This text might be of great value to stage directors, who could record more detailed movements for characters rather than relying on traditional blocking notes. A director could show the "effort" of the character to do a series of actions not only in terms of dance steps but also in terms of psychological or symbolic displays. A Greek tragedy, a musical, or a play with intricate movement would benefit from a recorded notation system like this one. Because of the system's obvious application to dramatic staging, however, I wish Guest had applied these ideas more liberally to dramatic work. One chapter that might have been more developed in this regard, entitled "Relationship," examines relationships based on bodily movements. Guest uses terms such as "awareness," "addressing," "closeness," and "support" to define movements that generate a relationship between two people onstage. She uses the time component to explore the duration of the relationship and gives examples of canceling, facing, and retaining an encounter. Guest might have shown how some of these options can produce theatrical gesture (e.g., Brecht) or symbol (e.g., Kabuki theatre).

Nevertheless, Guest's purpose was not to produce a new notation for blocking dramatic scenes but rather to show the reader detailed methods for documenting movement. Because of her persistent efforts in recording movement notation, Rudolf Laban's efforts in explaining and analyzing movement are no longer unknown. This edition may spur others to produce further applications of the theories of this erudite dancer/choreographer.

—CHRISTOPHER OLSEN
Virginia State University

Women, Modernism, and Performance. By Penny Farfan. Cambridge: Cambridge University Press, 2004. xi + 173 pp. £45.00 cloth.

In *Women, Modernism, and Performance,* Penny Farfan argues that women's performance and writing about performance significantly helped to shape modernist writing and twentieth-century theatre. She examines the work, theory, and reception of several women linked by chains of influence and acquaintance: primarily, Elizabeth Robins, Ellen Terry, and Virginia Woolf.

Woolf's two reviews of Chekhov and Shakespeare productions present performance as a means to challenge "accepted readings of familiar texts and to bring alternative readings into the mainstream" (91). Seeing a play is "a disturbing confrontation" between personal interpretation of the script and public performance (91). This observation perfectly describes the experiences of Farfan's other subjects. In her 1905 essay "Woman's Secret," Robins declares that "Schliemann may uncover one Troy after another . . . and never come the nearer to what Helen thought," because "all that is not silence is the voice of man." Robins, a Kentucky-born playwright and actress-manager, built Ibsen's fame in London and appeared in eight of his plays, mostly self-produced. Despite this, she ultimately decided that Ibsen had revolutionized drama only in its aesthetics. By 1928 she "distinguished between his [Ibsen's] contribution to the cause of actresses and his non-contribution . . . to the cause of women's emancipation" (12). She was painfully aware that Ibsen's Hedda Gabler is a stymied artist: Hedda's destruction of her ex-lover Eilert Lovborg's literary masterpiece fails to compensate for her own lack of creative agency. Detecting Nietzschean "glorification" of the implicitly masculine "individual will" throughout the Ibsen canon, Robins attempted, in her own play *Votes for Women,* to give voice to the feminist concerns that eluded her flawed idol (24). The name of this play's heroine, Vida Levering, or "Life-Lifting," emphasizes her difference from the abject fury Hedda.

Robins embraced Ibsenian realism's capacity to create female characters more psychologically complex than those, as Sheila Stowell has noted in *A Stage of Their Own: Feminist Playwrights of the Suffrage Era* (1992), whom Robins called the "chocolate-box type." In comparison, her contemporary Ellen Terry's stylized performances of Shakespeare might seem conservative. For Farfan, however, Terry's interpretations pursue feminist aims. Rejecting the assumption that Lady Macbeth is "unsexed," despite the soliloquy, Terry found her seemingly aberrant actions determined by patriarchal principles. In Terry's words, Lady Macbeth is "a mistaken woman . . . first of all a wife" whose "'ambition is all for her husband,' whom she discovers to be both weaker and more evil than she knew" (23). In her (re)interpretation of Lady Macbeth, Terry applied her theory that "to act" is to "make the thing written your own" (47). Perhaps the crown held aloft by the reptilian fatale in Sargent's iconic painting of Terry symbolizes, not abstract and autonomous power, but the image of her lord.

Farfan considers the fictional resurrection of a young Terry in Woolf's play *Freshwater,* begun by 1919 and performed privately in 1935. As *Freshwater* developed, "Terry" took it over from its original protagonist, photographer Julia Margaret Cameron. In it, Woolf makes Terry reject the role of the wife-muse to her painter-husband George Frederic Watts. *Freshwater* critiques "self-abnegating femininity," using images of fish and swimming to signify the uncontrolled woman and her escape (54). Watts wants to freeze Terry, but she becomes the one who got away. *Freshwater* suggests "liberating notions of the self" that, in her novels, Woolf depicts using more fragmented, modernist narrative forms (63). Although *Freshwater*'s Terry is able to leave Watts for an artist's life, Woolf's many studies of women as performers determine that the actress achieved only a partial self-liberation, due to the dearth of good roles for women onstage and off (63).

In a chapter on Isadora Duncan, Farfan contends that Duncan's widespread posthumous characterization as a "tragic" heroine, doomed to misery and premature destruction, in some accounts by her own actions, has eclipsed her accomplishments as a choreographer. Just as Robins untangled the ideologies in which the Ibsenian "new woman" was canonized, Farfan identifies those that inform the revisionist tragedy of Duncan. Another fascinating case study in the volume concerns the "Dreadnought Hoax" of 1910, in which Virginia Stephen (later, Woolf), her brother, and some male friends used dress-up, blackface, and improvisation to convince naval officers that they were on a royal diplomatic mission from Abyssinia. Farfan finds acting in this impromptu integral to Woolf's writing career, as the act and its unpleasant consequences for her brother influenced her understanding of patriarchy as performance. I found it intriguing that, in a photograph of the "Abyssinians" helpfully reproduced by Farfan, Virginia Stephen appears to have participated in this largely male-devised performance without fully cooperating with the intended illusion. She is dressed as a man, but her body language signifies conventional femininity. Her eyes stare at the floor instead of the camera, and her arms are close to her body (90). Is this a deliberate intervention, a refusal to act on cue, a decision of the photographer's, or an accident?

Farfan identifies several of her subjects as lesbian artists and discusses their attempts to counteract the usual silencing of the lesbian subject, but she excludes Robins from this discourse. I wondered why, given Robins's long-term domestic partnership with the physician Octavia Wilberforce, and Robins's pronouncement, which Farfan notes, that if Duncan had "been a feminist, she'd have been less unhappy because she 'allowed' heterosexual relationships 'to devastate her'" (4). Robins's Vida Levering works "to eradicate the helplessness of women," while the heroines of the post-suffragist novels *Nightwood* (Djuna Barnes, 1937) and *The Well of Loneliness* (Radclyffe Hall, 1928) identify more with a gender-diverse lesbian and gay community. However, Robins's insistence, in *Votes* and the earlier play *Alan's Wife* (written with Florence Bell), that women should not be convinced that they need to live with or depend upon men arguably places her in a tradition of lesbian feminism at least as securely as Barnes or Hall.

Women, Modernism, and Performance vividly shows how Robins and other women writers and artists challenged patriarchal interpretations of women's experience, envisioning a truly universal mainstream literary and theatre culture and influencing early-twentieth-century culture. Both theatre scholars and practitioners should find it illuminating and vital.

—REBECCA NESVET
University of Gloucestershire

BOOK REVIEWS

Making Americans: Jews and the Broadway Musical. By Andrea Most. Cambridge: Harvard University Press, 2004. 253 pp. $29.95 cloth.

The burgeoning field of musical theatre academic writing has a welcome new addition in Andrea Most's *Making Americans: Jews and the Broadway Musical*. Most joins an emerging group of scholars who investigate musicals for more than anecdotal meaning by contextualizing the works within their historical period or interrogating them for encoded thematic concerns. She takes a fresh and insightful look at some of the classics of the American musical stage through the lens of the Jewishness of their creators, exploring their resulting tensions and ideologies.

Most posits that the celebratory theatricality of the musical comedy genre was particularly suited to illustrate the Jewish people's long-honed ability to redefine themselves. As Most argues, "The mid-century musical expressed both anxiety about difference and delight in the apparently limitless opportunities America afforded for self-invention" (1). According to the author, Jews imagined an idealized America and "wrote themselves into that scenario as accepted members of the mainstream American community" (1–2). As she argues, the musicals of the 1920s contained overtly Jewish characters who celebrated their ability to invent themselves in highly theatrical ways. Later, as the integrated musical attained dominance, specifically Jewish characters disappeared and were replaced by encoded versions of the Other. Through a chronological set of musical case studies, Most examines not only the changing definitions of what it means to be Jewish but also how those definitions interact and overlap with the fluid definition of "American." Each musical she examines contains thematic concerns of identity, difference, and community; each includes a "vision of a utopian liberal society" (3) that grows more "tolerant or egalitarian" (3) during the play; and each uses a central love story to test the openness of that society and to circumscribe its values.

In chapter 1, "Acting American: Jews, Theatricality, and Modernity," Most points out the frequently remarked but rarely interrogated fact that the overwhelming majority of musical theatre creators have been Jewish. She ventures to explain the trend through a necessarily brief historical analysis of Jewish self-invention strategies. She poses that a Jewish need to create a "split consciousness" (14) began as early as the sixteenth century and survived the centuries to act as a central engine in forming the mid-twentieth-century musical. Chapter 2, titled "Cantors' Sons, Jazz Singers, and Indian Chiefs: The Invention of

Ethnicity on the Musical Comedy Stage," first offers a brief analysis of *The Jazz Singer*. Most then opposes the play's implied set of values with the celebratory theatricality of Jewish comedians Eddie Cantor in *Whoopee* and Willie Howard in *Girl Crazy*. Whereas *The Jazz Singer* implies that Jewish identity is an immutable *racial* consideration, Cantor and Howard inhabit a dizzying series of characters in order to demonstrate theatrical self-invention's power to move beyond racial definitions. In this chapter Most provides particularly rich analyses of the conventions of Jewish comedians performing in blackface as females or as Native Americans.

Briefly noting the rest of the topics addressed in Most's book will serve to underline its range and variety. Her chapter "Babes in Arms: The Politics of Theatricality during the Great Depression" examines the 1937 *Babes in Arms* script in relation to the American Jewish liberalism of the New Deal era. Chapter 4, "'We Know We Belong to the Land': The Theatricality of Assimilation in *Oklahoma!*" provides a cogent analysis of the pivotal musical's varying definitions of difference. Most opposes Jud Fry's unassimilable racial "blackness" with Ali Hakim's ethnic Otherness. Only the latter can be integrated into the all-important Rodgers and Hammerstein community. Most's next chapter, "The Apprenticeship of Annie Oakley: Or, 'Doin' What Comes Natur'lly,'" opposes *Oklahoma!* with the self-conscious theatricality of Irving Berlin and Dorothy Fields's *Annie Get Your Gun*. The author provocatively argues that Berlin and Fields's work celebrates the self-invention that the integrated and thus essentialist leanings of *Oklahoma!* begin to negate. In her final chapter, "'You've Got to Be Carefully Taught': The Politics of Race in *South Pacific*," Most deconstructs Rodgers and Hammerstein's "liberal" racial ideologies. In this chapter and throughout the book, she carefully separates authorial intentions from results. While she points out the manner in which *South Pacific* backfires and reinscribes the very racism it purports to detest, she does not shortsightedly accuse the creators of an anachronistic lack of political correctness. Instead, she acknowledges the celebratory and utopian ideals behind their idea of community. In a coda, "'I Whistle a Happy Tune,'" Most provides a brief analysis of *The King and I* in terms of its McCarthy-era orientalism, again placing the show in its historical context: the prevailing political and social concerns of the Jewish community.

Throughout the text, Most provides rigorous and thought-provoking analysis. She writes most strongly when using history to contextualize the musicals, often in new and enlightening ways. One of only a few concerns with the book is that at times her analyses read very deeply into matters that seem more tangentially connected to her central thesis, such as when she performs a detailed reading of gender politics in *Annie Get Your Gun*. Most takes a wide view of her subject, one not mired in particularity, but occasionally the view seems a bit too wide and we briefly lose sight of her central thesis. In addition, given Most's almost flawless research, I was surprised by her assertion that the Siamese children in *The King and I* act as the dancers in the "Uncle Tom's Cabin" ballet. As this detail is central to her analysis of the work, it seems critical to note that this statement is incorrect: the Royal dancers, a separate adult ensemble, perform this piece, not the children.

This book builds on Most's dissertation, and several chapters have been published previously in scholarly journals. Clearly, Most has been germinating these ideas for some time, and her depth of thought is evident. *Making Americans* proves a thought-provoking, compellingly written, and incisive work, one I highly recommend to all scholars in the field, and indeed to all interested in the compelling subject matter.

—JESSICA HILLMAN
University of Colorado at Boulder

The Cambridge History of British Theatre. 3 vols. Edited by Peter Thomson. Cambridge, U.K.: Cambridge University Press, 2004.
Vol. 1: *Origins to 1660*. Edited by Jane Milling and Peter Thomson. xxix + 540 pp. $175 cloth.
Vol. 2: *1660 to 1895*. Edited by Joseph Donohue. xci + 481 pp. $175 cloth.
Vol. 3: *Since 1895*. Edited by Baz Kershaw. xxxiv + 562 pp. $175 cloth.

All three volumes of *The Cambridge History of British Theatre* were released in December 2004 under the general editorship of Peter Thomson, with each volume having its own independent editor. The volumes follow the same format, with front matter that includes notes on the contributors, a general preface, an introduction by the volume editor, and a chronology that lists events in British theatrical history in parallel with important political and social happenings. These chronologies range from a modest twelve pages in volume 1 (which oddly starts with 1540, though the volume covers British theatre from its beginning) to the massive seventy-three pages in volume 2. A rationale for what is included in these chronologies, especially when events outside Britain are mentioned, is not provided, and the logic of the choices made is not obvious. The front matter is followed by a selection of individually authored essays.

Volume 1, which covers British theatre from Roman times to 1660, has nineteen essays by seventeen contributors plus the two editors. These, along with the forty illustrations, take up 476 of the volume's 569 pages (counting front matter). Volume 2, which covers the period from 1660 to 1895, has twenty essays by sixteen contributors plus the general editor, Thomson, and the volume editor, Joseph Donohue (who contributed three essays). These, along with thirty-five illustrations, take up 439 of the volume's 572 pages. Volume 3, which covers British theatre from 1895 to 2002, has twenty-three essays by twenty-one contributors and the volume editor, Baz Kershaw. Along with the forty-five illustrations of this volume, the essays take up 512 of its 596 pages. So the essays average twenty to twenty-five pages. In each volume the essays are followed by an extensive list of works cited, which includes a large number of citations to essays by the contributors. Each volume is also fully indexed, but there is no comprehensive index to all three volumes. The editors and Cambridge University Press are to be especially praised for their use of footnotes in these volumes. The footnotes are sparse, and sometimes they seem to be used when they are not necessary and omitted when they would be most helpful, but it is very rare to find citations at all in this kind of general history, and the use of footnotes saves the reader enormous amounts of time in not having to search out endnotes, which in volumes of this size and complexity would have been worse than useless. In his general preface to this history, Thomson notes that a general "'history' is not the place for scholars to talk in secret to other scholars" (xvii), and that is perhaps the greatest strength of this work. The essays take on many of the theoretical issues that have become important to modern historians without demanding that the reader have a strong background in modern historiographic theory. The writing is clear, accessible, and with very few exceptions, remarkably accurate in the content it conveys. Only in a few essays does there seem to be an assumption of a level of knowledge about theatre history that may exceed the grasp of the average reader.

In the general preface, Thomson lays out the organization of the essays: "Each of the volumes includes some essays which are broad surveys, some which treat specific themes or episodes, some which are socio-theatrical snapshots of single years and some which offer case studies of particular performance events" (xvii). Across the three volumes, the broad surveys he mentions include the first essay in volume 1, by John C. Coldewey, covering British theatre from Roman times to the Renaissance; two essays in volume 2 covering theatre from 1660 to 1895 by Donohue; and a volume 3 essay on British theatre from 1895 to 1946 by Dennis Kennedy with an overlapping essay on theatre from 1940 to 2002 by Baz Kershaw. All are remarkable in the amount of information they pack into a very condensed form. The Coldewey essay covers the longest span of time and suffers most from the need to be so abbreviated. It does provide some much-needed insight into the Roman occupation of Britain, but it leaves the impression that we know a lot less about Roman mime performances in the provinces than we actually do. Coldewey also accepts the Lowther reconstruction of our only fully excavated Roman theatre, the theatre at Verulanium (St. Albans), without noting how out of character with the rest of the Roman theatres it is or how it might fit in with the multipurpose theatres of Gaul. There was little time for that, however, because this essay is also the only one of the nineteen essays in volume 1 that deals with the Middle Ages. Coldewey manages to cover the topic reasonably well by paying little attention to the performance aspects of the great cycle plays, which are generally such a large part of histories of the medieval period in England, and focusing on the less-well-known plays performed elsewhere. This leaves the coverage of the Middle Ages rather slim, though the next three essays do pick up on aspects of medieval drama as they were manifest in the sixteenth century. The remaining surveys work better because they have less time to condense.

The theatrical snapshots of single years covered across all three volumes are 1553, 1599, 1642, 1776, 1895, and 1926. All are important years, but 1553 and 1926 seem arbitrarily selected as key years in the history of British theatre, and readers will have their own suggestions for years they would like to have seen included. The year 1895 was selected for the break between volume 2 and volume 3, and the essay dealing with that year argues that the key event of significance, among several others of importance, was George Bernard Shaw's appointment as drama critic for the *Saturday Review*. But that event is not even noted under 1895 in the chronology section of volume 3, and Kennedy, in his survey essay at the beginning of that volume, refers to 1895 as "not historiographically remarkable" (3), but it is at least one of several possible candidates for marking the transition into modern theatre.

The case studies in these three volumes are Ben Jonson's *Every Man in His Humour* (1601, revised 1612), Thomas Middleton's *A Game at Chess* (1624), John Gay's *The Beggar's Opera* (1728), Leopold Lewis's translation of *The Bells* (1871), Cicely Hamilton's *Diana of Dobson's* (1908), Ena Lamont Stewart's *Men Should Weep* (1947), and the Theatre Workshop's *Oh What a Lovely War* (1963). Except for *Men Should Weep,* all seem to have been selected for their commercial success and not for their influence on dramatic literature, but beyond that it is hard to see a logic to the selection of these particular plays.

The essays treating "specific themes or episodes" are too numerous to list here, but along with the expected topics, such as "Working Playwrights, 1580–1642" by Roslyn L. Knutson, "Stage Design from De Loutherbourg to Poel" by Christopher Baugh, or "The Establishment of Mainstream Theatre, 1946–1979" by John Bull, they include such topics as "The Bible as Play in Reformation England" by Paul Whitfield White, "Theatre and the Female Presence" by Joanne Lafler, and "Towards National Identities: Welsh Theatres" by Ioan Williams. Given the inclusion of Welsh theatre in volume 3, it is hard to understand why it was not given more attention in volume 1, where Scottish theatre is discussed only to 1603. The Welsh theatre to 1603 was far more significant, and technically Scotland was not British until the eighteenth century. The real puzzle, however, is why Ireland is not given far more attention in this history.

A real strength of volume 1 is the way so many of the essays incorporate findings from the *Records of Early English Drama* (REED), some of which have not even been published by REED yet. The editors of all three volumes have done an excellent job selecting contributors of outstanding scholarly credentials, but it is not always clear that they have used these scholars to their best advantage. Jane Milling, the coeditor of volume 1, for example, writes on "The Development of a Professional Theatre, 1540–1660," when her real strength is in Restoration theatre and modern theory. Few people in the world know more about the topic she wrote on than Andrew Gurr, but he was assigned to do the snapshot of 1599, a task a far less knowledgeable scholar could have done. This is undoubtedly a reflection of the complexity of getting so many authors together for such a massive undertaking. The editors note that they have followed chronology but not been dominated by it. The care for chronology given to volume 2 is one of its great strengths, while the lack of care for chronology in volume 3 makes it seem less coherent as a volume.

The cost of these volumes will ensure that the audience they are aimed at will be able to read them only in libraries. It is encouraging, however, that the three-volume *Cambridge History of American Theatre*, which came out between 1998 and 2000, was published in paperback at the end of 2005 at a much-reduced cost. We can only hope that these three volumes on British theatre go to paperback more quickly so that they can be put in the hands of the audience they were intended for. These are exceptionally fine works that merit a wide readership.

—FRANKLIN J. HILDY
University of Maryland, College Park

BOOK REVIEWS

Dancing Identity: Metaphysics in Motion. By Sondra Fraleigh. Pittsburgh: University of Pittsburgh Press, 2004. 285 pp. $32.50 cloth.

Dancing Identity: Metaphysics in Motion is a collection of nine essays written over a fifteen-year period by dancer, choreographer, and philosopher Sondra Fraleigh. Part memoir, part manifesto, the essays chart her intellectual journey into dance and articulate her vision for dance as a transformative force. Throughout the book she engages with and draws together a wide array of discourses, including phenomenology, poststructuralism, feminism, somatics, physics, ecology, and autobiography. However, in the midst of this intellectual range the essays consistently return to a single source—the body. *Dancing Identity* is at its best when Fraleigh offers her sustained and detailed reflections on how the body manifests philosophy, and how philosophy structures itself as a dance.

The center of Fraleigh's arguments for dance as a transformative force comes from phenomenological, body-centered "thick" descriptions of dance from the dancer's perspective. Fraleigh reconstructs her own dances in poetry and prose from the inside out, using the kinesthetic feeling of these experiences as a guide. She also peppers her essays with quotes from other dancers on what it feels like to dance, thereby granting the too-often-muted performer a voice on the scholarly page. In *Dancing Identity*, Fraleigh attempts to counter the enlightenment model of the rational, fully commanding self: listening to the body intently demonstrates that the body is always in a process of "becoming." The self that is constituted from its first-of-all-physical encounter with the world exists interrelationally in its ever-changing-ness. Being embodied in this way also implies a different mode of intersubjectivity. Chapter 1, "Embodying Metaphysics," offers a helpful overview of Western theories of embodiment (with a cross-cultural, contemporary Japanese component), into which Fraleigh asserts her own definition: "I like 'embodiment' as a nondualistic process descriptive. It contains material intelligence (body) and the transformative prefix 'em-,' which give it motion. 'To be embodied' is quite different from 'to have a body,' which splits subject from object and indicates 'possession' as the outcome—hence, possessive materialism: self-mastery, mastery of others, owning bodies" (21). In chapter 5, "A Dance of Time Beings," Fraleigh critiques Heidegger's phenomenology for precisely this emphasis on "mastery." For Heidegger, the desired state of "authentic being" is reached when the subject, in a moment of vision, gains mastery over the everyday. Fraleigh suggests that instead of mastery, the somatic strategy of "matching" be applied—"matching" is "opening present time, being alive to it," or giving full attention to any given task without controlling or dominating the outcome. For Fraleigh, this intense bodily and environmental listening forms the basis for personal, social, and even ecological transformation.

Dancing Identity thus personalizes philosophy and channels "theory" toward therapeutic ends. Dance analysis serves as an illustration. In chapter 2, "First Sounds," Fraleigh explains how, from a feminist perspective, philosophy needs to "darken" and "descend" from "the presumed enlightenment of the rational self and escalating positions of authority" (19). For Fraleigh, dances that explore female expressions of hysteria, the subconscious, and the irrational register a feminist protest and, for their performers, facilitate an internal revaluing. Mary Wigman's *Witch Dance* (1926) and butoh dancer Natsu Nakajima's ghost figure in *Niwa* (1982) serve as examples. The terms "darken" and "descend" also imply that Fraleigh privileges certain forms of dance as more therapeutically effective: in particular, she cites the downward spirals of modern dance technique; the nonhierarchical choreographic methods of the 1960s Judson Church choreographers; and Japanese butoh's interest in the surrealist macabre. Chapter 7, "Messy Beauty and Butoh Invalids," opposes the upward strivings of ballet aesthetics and Cunningham technique to butoh's introspective, "descendent beauty," proposing that an aesthetic revaluing of darkness rescues the spiritual feminine. At times this alignment seems too strictly drawn; butoh, for example, in its inception in the 1960s, participated in a long tradition in Japan, beginning with Noh theatre in the thirteenth century, in which the primordial "feminine"—the first performers in Japan were female shamans—was appropriated by male performers as the nostalgic, now irrecoverable "essence" of Japan. Overall, though, this chapter offers a helpful, succinct introduction to butoh with a comparative east-west aesthetic perspective.

Another recurring theme in *Dancing Identity* is the attempt to reconcile somatic therapy with postmodern theory. Somatics posits a "natural" body and strives toward holism; postmodernists declare that the body is socially constructed and expose the subject in a state of disintegration. While her embodied reflections on the self-as-process square with the postmodern dislodgment of the unified subject, Fraleigh argues that our bodies are both natural and social phenomena and that we experience holism within the integrity of a sensory experience patterned on nature. In chapter 8, "Existential Haircut," Fraleigh argues, against Foucault, that agency is possible for a body in tune with natural forces: "Freedom is not a battleground for waging wars of mastery and intervention, but a synergy of natural energy and structures (practiced and performed) in life, art, and everyday actions" (209). She concludes this chapter with "Somadance Untangling," how-to instructions for a somatic dance exercise, to offer readers the opportunity to experience their own bodily agency. By illustrating how phenomenology might repoliticize postmodernism for its critics, Fraleigh offers a major contribution.

Dancing Identity is not a conventional dance studies work. It might not find an obvious place on the syllabi of introductory courses in dance or theatre history, for example. At times I wanted more connective prose between Fraleigh's dance analysis sections (particularly of Fraleigh's *Miss America* dance biography of 1975 and of Twyla Tharpe's 1986 ballet *In the Upper Room*) and the philosophical examinations that preceded them. However, in addition to drawing together an eclectic and fruitful mix of disciplines, *Dancing Identity* especially succeeds as a demonstration of how to represent verbally what dance *does*. Chapter 4, "Anti-Essentialist Trio," frames a philosophical conversation between Simone de Beauvoir, Judith Butler, and Maurice Merleau-Ponty as an improvisational choreography. Putting these three theorists in a "dance" together, she explains in terms of movement how their conceptual moves condition the interactions of their bodies. This is an ideal of dance writing that Fraleigh beautifully realizes in *Dancing Identity*.

—CARRIE GAISER
University of California–Berkeley

Doing Shakespeare. By Simon Palfrey. London: Arden Shakespeare, Thomson Learning, 2005. ix + 300 pp. $15.99 paper.

In a world that produces a new article on *Hamlet* every day, *Doing Shakespeare* is an original and long-overdue resource for theatre scholar-artists. Too often wavering between adaptation and slavish adherence to the text, university theatre department productions rarely attempt the kind of analysis that Palfrey suggests here. Yet it is exactly this kind of analysis that can result in extraordinary productions and high-level critical thinking from student actors. Even more exciting is the possibility of using the principles Palfrey suggests Shakespeare employs in new work. What prevents new playwrights from employing imagery and metaphor, rhetoric and character, as Shakespeare did? If the obstacle is only a lack of awareness of Shakespeare's process, of how his language worked, that obstacle is now all but smashed by *Doing Shakespeare*.

The book is broken into two parts: part 1 is concerned with words, part 2 with characters. Each chapter heading is a question, which is briefly answered in the abstract given at the beginning of the chapter and explored more fully within the chapter itself. The questions themselves are easily accessible (e.g., chapter 5, "Why rhyme?" or the even more immediate chapter 11, "Did they do it? Sex and heroines") and enable each chapter to stand alone. Additionally, each chapter abstract cites the plays that will be used to illustrate the language featured in that chapter, thus enabling a director or actor to skip directly to those examples originating in a specific play.

The thread running through all of part 1 is Palfrey's contention that "a drama committed to original metaphor as a primary means of making its worlds means . . . that language . . . is itself finding out what might be present; it is its own barometer of possibility" (38). For Shakespeare, language is the fusion of style and content into a coherent whole. When this whole is approached by actors and directors through close analysis, a microcosm of imagery, relationships, connotations, and emotionally charged rhetoric appears as a nearly inexhaustible ecosystem, a world of specific, organically linked acting and directing possibilities.

As for part 1, so for part 2. From an emphasis on language as its own creation we move to an emphasis on character creation, and more specifically, the negotiated spaces between audience, actor, and text as the ground or arena for character construction. Beginning with the concept that the terminology of "character," "role," or any other denotation of a speaking part has a value implied by its use, Palfrey considers the implications of a number of such differing denotations as a prelude to the concept of shifting or negotiated reality of character. Once again, the discrete chapters enable a reader to examine closely the specific contested areas where character creation occurs. Where are these areas? They lie within the interstitial tensions and juxtapositions created by Shakespeare—between form and content in the soliloquy; between identities that mirror and double character, in a kind of embodied antithesis; between the audience's "illicit curiosity" and the text. The actor and director, whether using or generalizing from the examples provided here, are again rewarded with a wealth of possibilities for their work.

Doing Shakespeare provides a thorough, accessible grounding in Shakespeare's most vibrant skills as a playwright, namely his talent for language and characterization. Close analysis of the "negative space" within Shakespeare's language, rhetoric, and characterization creates a field of opportunity for actors and directors in their creative work, but it is even more enticing for the playwright. Rather than relying on the recent-model naturalistic language and

Euclidean character, the new playwright under the influence of *Doing Shakespeare* can perhaps attempt the creation of character—and world—in suspension, resident in the tension between form and content, between connotation and figurative vehicle. By using the analyses presented here as models, the new playwright may find indeed that imagination bodies forth the forms of things unknown.

—ADRIANNE ADDERLEY
University of Missouri, Columbia

The Case for Shakespeare: The End of the Authorship Question. By Scott McCrea. Westport, Conn.: Praeger, 2005. xiv + 280 pp. $42.95 cloth.

Is it possible that the greatest playwright the world has ever known was actually an impostor? Many scholars have put forth such a theory, claiming that William Shakespeare is undeserving of his prominent place in literary history since he was little more than an actor passing off the work of another as his own. In response to those accusations, many others have worked to defend William Shakespeare and to establish him as the rightful author of those works that have been attributed to him. Considering the significance of the Shakespearean canon, it is easy to see why this topic has received so much attention and why it seems to incite such passionate arguments both for and against. The title of Scott McCrea's new work *The Case for Shakespeare: The End of the Authorship Question* gives a clear indication as to which side McCrea has chosen to fight for in this scholastic battle. This book offers a clear, straightforward argument: given the substantial amount of evidence that supports William Shakespeare as the Author, and given the lack of any concrete evidence that disproves him as the Author, only one conclusion may be drawn: Master William Shakespeare from Stratford was in fact the true Author. Well versed in the many facets of this debate, McCrea offers a wealth of research couched in a most conversational style. This rather academic book is easily accessible, and by the book's end there are few who would still question the legitimacy of the great William Shakespeare.

The book is divided into two sections: part 1, "The Man Who Wrote the Plays," focuses on William Shakespeare, and part 2, "The Men Who Didn't," focuses on other possible writers who have been proposed over the years. In the first half of the book, McCrea not only offers evidence that supports William

Shakespeare as the Author but also addresses the more prominent of those theories which claim that Shakespeare was an impostor. In doing so he highlights the fallibility and the false assumptions embedded within such theories. With the first two chapters, McCrea analyzes posthumous evidence to establish the fact that William Shakespeare the actor, William Shakespeare the writer, and William Shakespeare of Stratford were the same person. After making logical inferences based on Shakespeare's life (chapter 3), after proving that the Author need not have been a soldier, a scholar, or a renowned traveler (chapter 4), or a lawyer (chapter 5), or a member of the nobility (chapters 6 and 7), McCrea humbly asks, "Does any of this mean William Shakespeare wrote the plays? Yes and no. It means he didn't *not* write them. What we know about Shakespeare is consistent with the Author" (124). McCrea leaves the reader to combine this double-negative endorsement with the earlier posthumous testimony to draw the only logical conclusion: Shakespeare, and no other, wrote the plays.

In the latter half of the book, McCrea systematically dismantles the more plausible among the theories of alternate authorship. In chapter 9 he is able to quickly discount Sir Francis Bacon, William Stanley (the sixth Earl of Derby), and Christopher Marlowe. The remaining chapters in this section are dedicated to the most popular alternate candidate, the Earl of Oxford, Edward de Vere. Chapters 10 and 11 focus on the autobiographical discrepancies and the social inconsistencies between the Earl of Oxford and the Author of the plays. McCrea then uses chapters 12 and 13 to tackle the oddity of the Earl of Oxford's death (since it seems to have preceded the death of the Author as well as the creation of several other "Shakespearean" plays). In chapter 14, McCrea analyzes works by both the Earl of Oxford and the Author, arguing that the differences between the two in terms of spelling and rhyming style clearly indicate that those writings were not penned by the same person.

One of the more appealing aspects of this book is McCrea's relaxed style. This book moves with a quick pace as McCrea pieces together evidence in order to compile an irrefutable case. Using chapter titles such as "The Third Man," "The Suspects," "The Accused," and "Motive and Means," he has consciously written a book that reads like a case file waiting to be closed. This investigative framing device allows the book to move forward with a kind of suspenseful momentum, all the while asking the reader to render a judgment in favor of Shakespeare.

McCrea's unorthodox—at times even acerbic—tone proves to be another advantage he has in making his case for Shakespeare. A twenty-six-page chapter that lists the details of Shakespeare's life bears an ironic title "The Vacuum." When concluding his discussion of all of the evidence that points to Shakespeare as the Author, McCrea sarcastically notes that "The man and the Author were almost certainly one. (Almost? Well, yes. We can't be *absolutely* certain, but then we can't be absolutely certain about the Earth revolving around the sun either: only the evidence tells us that it's so.)" (126).

McCrea outwardly acknowledges that his subtitle, "The End of the Authorship Question," is one of hubris. According to McCrea, there will never be an end to the authorship debate, because it has turned into an argument of faith, and "no appeal to evidence can ever convince true believers, because nothing can disprove their fixed idea" (217). While accepting that, in the final pages he rather eloquently makes one last argument for the man from Stratford. For McCrea, disbelief in Shakespeare as the Author always stems from the same poor syllogism: "If Shakespeare was unlearned, but the man who wrote the plays had learning, then Shakespeare was not the man who wrote the plays" (13). This is why it is of great artistic importance that anti-Stratfordians acknowledge Shakespeare as the true Author. In accepting his authorship, they are letting go of prejudiced beliefs that lead to erroneous conclusions. To doubt the ability of a man to write such great works simply because he lacked formal education perpetuates a rather cynical viewpoint. To doubt Shakespeare as the Author is to doubt the very possibilities of the imagination. In this heartfelt defense of Shakespeare, Scott McCrea seems to take on the persona of a modern-day Hamlet urging skeptics to understand that there are more things in heaven and earth than are dreamt of in their philosophy.

—JULIA SCHMITT
Stetson University

Susan Glaspell: Her Life and Times. By Linda Ben-Zvi. New York: Oxford University Press, 2005. 476 pp. $45.00 cloth.
Midnight Assassin: A Murder in America's Heartland. By Patricia L. Bryan and Thomas Wolf. Chapel Hill: Algonquin Books, 2005. 278 pp. $23.95 cloth.

Two new contributions to Glaspell scholarship make compelling reading and provide much new information for scholars of theatre, American literature, and women's studies. In her new life of Susan Glaspell, Linda Ben-Zvi gives us an accurate, exceptionally well-researched, and skillfully written account of the Pulitzer Prize–winning playwright's life and works. The most thoroughgoing Glaspell biography published to date, Ben-Zvi's book, twenty years in the making, draws on interviews with an impressive number of Glaspell's colleagues, friends, and family members as well as on holdings in the major manuscript repositories previously consulted by other Glaspell biographers. Moreover, Ben-Zvi's access to privately held documents has resulted in much new material about many aspects of Glaspell's life about which we previously had little information, such as her pioneer ancestry, relationship with her mother, college activities, pre-Provincetown years in Chicago, and, most importantly, her relationships with Norman Matson, a novelist with whom she lived for eight years, and Langston Moffett, a frequent companion during her final decade. Of the previously unexamined documents that Ben-Zvi worked with are Norman Matson's unpublished autobiographical novel, in which Glaspell appears as "Ruth," and the first-person "Notes for American Biography" by Glaspell, which is held by the Shain Library at Connecticut College. Because Glaspell kept few diaries or journals, this essay is a significant discovery.

Ben-Zvi sets out to examine the life of the Pulitzer Prize–winning playwright within a number of different contexts, and consequently her book actually tells three stories: Glaspell's story; the story of George Cram Cook, her husband; and the story of the Provincetown Players, the little-theatre company they founded in 1915. This tripartite emphasis makes an important contribution to scholarship in American theatre history. By including detailed discussions of Glaspell's and Cook's work with the Provincetown Players, Ben-Zvi gives us a fuller, more complex understanding of how this group actually operated and, in so doing, dispels the widespread impression that modern American drama began with Eugene O'Neill and that he was mainly responsible for the Provincetown Players' success. Although it contains a few errors of fact, none very important, Ben-Zvi's book adds much to our knowledge of all three subjects without losing its focus on Glaspell. One way that Ben-Zvi achieves unity and focus despite dealing with a wealth of information on many topics is to emphasize throughout the theme of the pioneer that runs through Glaspell's life and works; not only did Glaspell draw upon her own pioneer background in much of her work, but she took a pioneering role in creating a new kind of American drama, in focusing cultural attention on women's lives and issues, and in continually breaking new ground and working against outmoded or too-confining structures, be they social, literary, or theatrical.

Another welcome addition to Glaspell scholarship is Patricia Bryan and Thomas Wolf's *Midnight Assassin,* a study of the 1901 murder trial of Margaret Hossack, which Glaspell covered as a young journalist and on which she based her most famous play (*Trifles*) and short story ("A Jury of Her Peers"). An essential addition to the libraries of Glaspell scholars, this book builds on the research that Linda Ben-Zvi conducted in the early 1990s, originally published in *Theatre Journal* as "Murder, She Wrote: The Genesis of Susan Glaspell's *Trifles*," and expands on research Bryan published in 1997 in the *Stanford Law Review* ("Stories in Fiction and in Fact: Susan Glaspell's 'A Jury of Her Peers' and the 1901 Murder Trial of Margaret Hossack").

Written in lively, nonfiction novel style, *Midnight Assassin* provides a full account of the murder of Iowa farmer John Hossack and the subsequent trial of his wife, Margaret, which ended in her first-degree murder conviction. Although Glaspell's play and story suggest that Margaret did, in fact, murder her husband, Bryan and Wolf provide much information—taken from interviews, court transcripts, newspaper accounts, and other documents—that suggests several other possibilities. Three case studies of nineteenth-century American women in troubled family relationships, two of whom were tried for the murders of their relatives, are embedded within the narrative and deepen our understanding of Margaret Hossack's situation.

Bryan and Wolf are not able to tell us who killed John Hossack and why; however, their book is valuable for the social context it establishes, a social context that illumines why Margaret Hossack was so easily convicted in a case based on compromised, questionable, incomplete, and circumstantial evidence. Thus, in its treatment of topics such as late-nineteenth-century gender roles, legal and judicial practices, and cultural norms governing rural Midwestern community and family life, *Midnight Assassin* offers anyone who is planning to teach or stage *Trifles* much valuable information that will enhance his or her understanding of one of America's most famous one-act plays.

Perhaps the book's greatest strength lies in its historicized and regionalized discussion of gender, a primary theme in both *Trifles* and "A Jury of Her Peers." As the authors point out, "It was a time when notions about justice, law, and the roles of men and women in society were in transition" (xiv). Specifically, the book expands our understanding of how gender-based values and expectations drove the Hossack trial and shaped its conclusion. Although several years earlier, Lizzie Borden had been acquitted of the murder of her parents, the tall, sturdily built, unattractive Margaret Hossack, in her mid-fifties at the time of her husband's death, could not project to the jury the same aura of femininity, in those days inextricably linked to notions of innocence and goodness, that worked so well for the young Massachusetts woman. Moreover, evidence that Mr. Hossack had repeatedly threatened, hit, and thrown objects at his wife, which a defense attorney today might find useful in creating sympathy among the jurors for his client, was downplayed by Mrs. Hossack's lawyer, keenly aware that his jury of conservative Iowa farmers would construe any neighbor's testimony about domestic violence in the Hossack household as private familial business that should not be shared with outsiders and as stronger evidence of Mrs. Hossack's motive for murder than of Mr. Hossack's reprehensible behavior. Further, along with its detailed examination of the stories that witnesses, largely male, told on the stand in the Hossack trial, the book also focuses on the stories of Margaret Hossack's female neighbors that the jury did not hear, suggesting that Glaspell may have found these untold but compelling stories, as well as the reason for their exclusion, to be the major source of inspiration for her play as well as of its spine and through-line.

Ben-Zvi and Bryan and Wolf have made lasting contributions to Glaspell scholarship; their books are highly recommended reading.

—MARCIA NOE
The University of Tennessee at Chattanooga

Paul Green: Playwright of the Real South. By John Herbert Roper. Athens: University of Georgia Press, 2003. xiii + 320 pp. $34.95 cloth.

A major study of Paul Green's life and work was too long overdue. Green—a Pulitzer Prize winner, leading figure in the vaunted Southern Literary Renaissance, pioneer in creating serious dramatic roles for African-American actors, collaborator with numerous influential artists (Kurt Weill, Jasper Deeter, and Orson Welles among them), and inventor of the popular form of outdoor historical pageant-play he called "symphonic drama"—left a sizable footprint on the midcentury American theatrical landscape. Yet no volume of criticism on Green's plays has been published since the early 1970s, and no biography since 1951—three decades before his death. Thus John Herbert Roper's *Paul Green: Playwright of the Real South* is of vital importance, despite some limitations and blind spots, for filling a vacuum too long ignored by scholars.

Despite the prominence of "Playwright" in its title, this biography examines Paul Green more as a man of ideas than as a man of the stage. At every important juncture of Green's life, Roper positions his subject between ideological poles planted in young Paul's mind by two University of North Carolina professors. Playwriting mentor Frederick Henry Koch urged his star pupil to observe the world as a realist, to write as folklorist. "Write about the folk you know," Koch instructed, "and even better, write about the folk you are" (45). Conversely, as a student of philosophy, Green also absorbed the urgings of Professor Horace Williams to "Hegelize yourself. That is, find the truth in the opposite side ... absorb the moment of negation" through which might be achieved "more reality, more God, more of spirit ... moving up through spheres" of consciousness (68). As Roper tells it, Green's artistic career and entire life history represent a decades-long working out of this profound intellectual struggle forged at Chapel Hill—of Koch versus Williams, the social recorder versus the moral visionary, a realistic poet of the here and now versus a neo-Hegelian idealist ruminating on the next phase of human spiritual progress.

This struggle translated into Green's pursuit of a "literature of the Real South [focused] on the denizens of the deep woods of eastern Carolina as the subjects of both art and politics. Such a focus sharpened the view of race and color and caste. Blackness. Whiteness. Brownness. High Yellow. Passing. The mixing of these peoples" (80). Koch's protégé celebrated this rich Carolinian ethnography throughout his writings, especially in his most celebrated folk dramas such as the comic one-act *The No 'Count Boy* and tragedies *In Abraham's Bosom* and *The House of Connelly*. But Williams's disciple treated these same rural Carolinians not only as subjects for sociological study but also as "people who lived in a spiritual no-man's land ... [who] struggle to make moral sense of their lives" (81) amid the changing modern world. Roper's fascination with Green's intellectual life, his tunneling through layers of thought and theory, provides a valuable new perspective on Green's oeuvre. Those curious how a white land-owning southerner became one of the (white) American stage's most racially sensitive playwrights of the 1930s will find much to ponder. Roper's focus on philosophy yields an incisive interpretation of Green's most enduring work, *The Lost Colony*—the apotheosis of "symphonic drama," still performed regularly in the open air on Roanoke Island, Virginia—as a "spiral of Hegelian synthesis" (181) embracing the variegated hues of American society, and the American landscape itself, in a national march toward justice and civic empowerment.

Less evident in this biography is a sense of the theatre as an art that lives and breathes in a world more concrete and problematic than that of a priori thought. Amid much admiration for Green's lifelong belief in "Hegelian integrationism and radical idealism" comes a brief, unexamined admission that Green was "by no means at peace with 'the race question,' and was himself a morass of contradictions about blacks" (84). What precisely were those contradictions, and how should they color our admiration for his radicalism? How did this playwright's work mirror and sometimes exacerbate the American theatre's racial pathology, even while offering a step of progress beyond it? Why did some African-American artists and critics view Green's dramaturgy with skepticism and resentment, while others praised it and staged it? What were the limitations of the white Broadway liberalism practiced by Green and others (Ridgely Torrence, Eugene O'Neill, Marc Connelly), and how did this man's experiences and writings sit within that wider context? Critical interrogation of Green's "progressive" racial politics is crucial to evaluating his position within American theatre history. The slippage between ideal and real goes largely unexamined.

Still, certain sections of the book will prove of interest to theatre historians. There are accounts of Green's work with the Group Theatre, including his collaboration with Weill on the groundbreaking antiwar musical *Johnny Johnson*. Roper details Green's historic partnership with Richard Wright on the stage adaptation of *Native Son*—conducted in full view of the UNC campus, in eager defiance of its Jim Crow restrictions—as well as the subsequent losing battles Green waged with Welles and John Houseman for creative control over the script.

Unfortunately, the author's critical voice becomes most forceful when discussing matters of minor consequence to Green's living art: troubling moments of anti-Semitism in his private letters and conversations, uneasy relationships with Marxist theories and Communist groups, backtracking on opposition to American involvement in World War II, and a curious friendship late in life with longtime political foe Senator Jesse Helms. For those interested primarily in Green's theatrical activities, such discussions are detours away from a central path not thoroughly charted.

Too, Roper's prose shows some distracting idiosyncrasies: addiction to pet phrases like "damnable Jim Crow," for instance, and a tendency to start sentences and paragraphs with "Too . . . " Were the Paul Green shelf in the library more crowded, this biography would be easier to bypass. Empty as that section stands, *Paul Green: Playwright of the Real South* proves an informative but imperfect examination of an under-studied American dramatist and thinker.

—JONATHAN SHANDELL
New York University

Arthur Miller: A Critical Study. By Christopher Bigsby. Cambridge and New York: Cambridge University Press, 2005. 514 pp. $29.99 paper.

Any serious scholar of American drama will recognize the name of Christopher Bigsby. Author of the excellent three-volume *Critical Introduction to Twentieth-Century American Drama* (1982–85) and the editor of *Arthur Miller and Com-*

pany (1990) and the *Cambridge Companion to Arthur Miller* (1997), among various other important works, Bigsby is Professor of American Studies and Director of the Arthur Miller Centre at the University of East Anglia. Perhaps more importantly, he has been personally acquainted with Miller for some twenty years, often interviewing him and gaining access to rare rehearsal materials and archival resources. The result is a text of extraordinary thoroughness and insight. *Arthur Miller: A Critical Study* is likely to remain the most sustained and penetrating examination of Miller's work for a long time to come.

Bigsby's study profits not only from his intimate knowledge of Miller and his work but from his broad awareness of twentieth-century American culture and the major writers who depict it. He threads his discussions of the various works with telling references to the major political and social events that shaped Miller's view and the American writers who influenced him. For the most part he follows the chronology of Miller's works, incorporating biography and cultural history with analysis as he moves from text to text.

It would be difficult to single out particular chapters, given both the range of the coverage and the depth of Bigsby's discussions. Each exploration of a text is enriched by the way Bigsby arches backward and forward across the canon, noting, for example, how journeyman plays Miller wrote as an undergraduate at the University of Michigan introduce themes and even characters reflected in much later works, how *Death of a Salesman* echoes in *Mr. Peters' Connections*, how *Incident at Vichy* anticipates *After the Fall*, or how *Resurrection Blues* mirrors *The Man Who Had All the Luck*. Throughout he draws surprising and insightful links as he also finds meaningful similarities among other Miller texts and works by other authors. Not only does he observe revealing similarities between Miller and socially conscious writers like Odets, Wright, Fitzgerald, Hemingway, and a host of others, but he presents sometimes surprising comparisons, as when he shows how closely Miller employed the absurd in his plays even while he openly rejected it, or how much as a Jewish writer he mirrored in his dramas the fiction of Saul Bellow.

Bigsby's readings of the "later" plays are especially noteworthy. He reclaims the significance of *After the Fall*, for example, observing that too many critics who first reviewed it were (and one might argue still are) "obsessed with the image of Marilyn Monroe. Few chose to concern themselves with the wider concerns of the play which attempted to explore the nature of innocence and guilt, of betrayal and denial, of a history seemingly too implacable to absorb or too recent to understand" (232). Bigsby offers discriminating analyses of *The Ride Down Mount Morgan, Broken Glass, Mr. Peters' Connections* (which he shows is a "theater in the head" like *Death of a Salesman* and *After the Fall*), and Miller's last two dramas, the bitingly satiric *Resurrection Blues* and *Finishing the Picture* (for which Bigsby used a 2003 typescript provided by the author). Interestingly, in reference to the last play Bigsby barely mentions Marilyn Monroe, concentrating on the richness of the text itself even though the autobiographical reference to the filming of *The Misfits* is a given. He notes that Miller first began the play in 1977–78 and observes that he returned to it in part as a response to the invasion of Iraq, which he thought illegitimate.

As he summarizes and simultaneously analyzes the plays (including the early radio plays), short stories, and longer fiction, Bigsby provides a full and exhaustive narrative of Miller's remarkable career. He writes perceptively not only about the plays but also about Miller's seldom-discussed fiction, including illuminating explorations of the novel *Focus* and several of the major short stories, including "The Prophecy," "Homely Girl," and "The Turpentine Still." Although the chapters follow chronological order, Bigsby includes separate chapters that address important topics. After a chapter on *A View from the Bridge*, Bigsby devotes a chapter to Miller's "Hegelian sense of the tragic" (198), which, in Bigsby's view, Miller largely abandoned with *After the Fall*. Another chapter addresses Miller's concept of time, concluding that throughout the plays, in Miller's sense, history "makes authentic demands and provides a spine to mere events" (125). Two chapters are concerned with Miller as Jew. In an eloquent chapter entitled "The Shearing Point," Bigsby contends that for Miller the concentration camp "was the shearing point, the place where civilization began to crack and the abyss appeared, the place where we were reminded that death has dominion over us" (334). And he ends his book with a provocative discussion of "Arthur Miller as a Jewish Writer," in which he incorporates a number of telling references to other prominent Jewish authors and challenges the criticism of some scholars who accuse Miller of not being Jewish enough. He contests the claim of Martin Gottfried that Miller did not engage Jewish themes or characters until the early 1960s. Bigsby offers ample evidence of Miller's Jewish consciousness from the beginning of his career, and especially after his visit to Mauthausen in 1962. He rightly concludes that Miller "is of the Book, aware of the mythic potency of its archetypes" (481), and that he "addressed the Holocaust to an extent that no other American dramatist would do" (484).

To be sure, this is an original study. Bigsby makes sparse use of secondary criticism and, with few exceptions, makes little attempt to incorporate the studies of other Miller critics. Rather, he draws upon his own deep awareness of Miller and the full spectrum of the primary texts, as well as differing versions of seminal works, although he alludes throughout to a vast range of contemporary and some earlier writers to draw important critical discriminations. Simply put, *Arthur Miller: A Critical Study* is a major contribution to our understanding and appreciation of one the true giants of twentieth-century drama.

—TERRY OTTEN
Professor Emeritus, Wittenberg University

BOOKS RECEIVED

Assael, Brenda. *The Circus and Victorian Society.* Charlottesville: University of Virginia Press, 2005.

Badenhausen, Richard. *T. S. Eliot and the Art of Collaboration.* Cambridge: Cambridge University Press, 2005.

Canning, Charlotte M. *The Most American Thing in America: Circuit Chautauqua as Performance.* Iowa City: University of Iowa Press, 2005.

Cefalau, Paul. *Revisionist Shakespeare: Transitional Ideologies in Texts and Contexts.* New York: Palgrave Macmillan, 2004.

Glazer, Peter. *Radical Nostalgia: Spanish Civil War Commemoration in America.* Rochester, N.Y.: University of Rochester Press, 2005.

Goring, Paul. *The Rhetoric of Sensibility in Eighteenth Century Culture.* Cambridge: Cambridge University Press, 2004.

Hoenselaars, Ton, ed. *Shakespeare's History Plays: Performance, Translation, and Adaptation in Britain and Abroad.* Cambridge: Cambridge University Press, 2004.

Hoskins, Jim. *The Dances of Shakespeare.* New York: Routledge, 2005.

Hughes, Derek, and Janet Todd, eds. *The Cambridge Companion to Aphra Behn.* Cambridge: Cambridge University Press, 2004.

Griffiths, Huw, ed. *Shakespeare: Hamlet, a Reader's Guide to Essential Criticism.* New York: Palgrave Macmillan, 2005.

Lane, Jill. *Blackface Cuba, 1840–1895.* Philadelphia: University of Pennsylvania Press, 2005.

Leggatt, Alexander. *Shakespeare's Tragedies: Violation and Identity.* Cambridge: Cambridge University Press, 2005.

Lesser, Zachary. *Renaissance Drama and the Politics of Publication: Readings in the English Book Trade.* Cambridge: Cambridge University Press, 2005.

Maley, Willy, and Andrew Murphy. *Shakespeare and Scotland*. New York: Manchester University Press, 2004.

Marrapotti, Michele. *Shakespeare, Italy, and Intertextuality*. New York: Manchester University Press, 2004.

Moe, Christian H., Scott Parker, and George McCalmon. *Creative Historical Drama: A Guide for Communities, Theatre Groups, and Playwrights*. Carbondale: Southern University Press, 2005.

O'Leary, Catherine. *The Theatre of Antonio Buero Vallejo: Ideology, Politics, and Censorship*. Rochester, N.Y.: Tamesis Books, 2005.

Panek, Jennifer. *Widows and Suitors in Early Modern English Comedy*. Cambridge: Cambridge University Press, 2004.

Patterson, Michael. *The Oxford Dictionary of Plays*. New York: Oxford University Press, 2005.

Pemble, John. *Shakespeare Goes to Paris: How the Bard Conquered France*. London: Hambledon and London, 2005.

Plotkins, Marilyn J. *The American Repertory Theatre Reference Book: The Brustein Years*. Westport, Conn.: Praeger, 2005.

Rothwell, Kenneth S. *A History of Shakespeare on Screen: A Century of Film and Television*. 2nd ed. Cambridge: Cambridge University Press, 2005.

Rush, David. *A Student Guide to Play Analysis*. Carbondale: Southern Illinois University Press, 2005.

Stone, Wendell C. *Caffe Cino: The Birthplace of Off-Off Broadway*. Carbondale: Southern Illinois University Press, 2005.

Trevor, Douglas. *The Poetics of Melancholy in Early Modern England*. Cambridge: Cambridge University Press, 2004.

Vaughan, Virginia Mason. *Performing Blackness on English Stages, 1500–1800*. Cambridge: Cambridge University Press, 2005.

Walker, Julia A. *Expressionism and Modernism in the American Theatre: Bodies, Voices, Words*. Cambridge: Cambridge University Press, 2005.

Wells, Judith. *Service and Dependency in Shakespeare's Plays*. Cambridge: Cambridge University Press, 2005.

CONTRIBUTORS

MILLY S. BARRANGER is Alumni Distinguished Professor Emerita at the University of North Carolina at Chapel Hill. She is the author of *Margaret Webster: A Life in the Theatre* (University of Michigan Press, 2004), *Understanding Plays* (Allyn & Bacon, 2004), and *Theatre: A Way of Seeing* (Wadsworth, 2006). She is presently at work on a biography of Broadway producer Cheryl Crawford.

DAVID A. CRESPY is Associate Professor of Playwriting at the University of Missouri. He is the author of *Off-Off-Broadway Explosion* (Back Stage Books, 2003).

CHARLES R. HELM is Director of Performing Arts at the Wexner Center for the Arts. Since joining the Wexner Center in 1991 as the Director, he presented Spalding Gray regularly in the Wexner's performance seasons.

KATIE N. JOHNSON is an Associate Professor in the English Department of Miami University of Ohio. Her first book, *Sisters in Sin: Brothel Drama in America*, is forthcoming by Cambridge University Press in 2006.

ELLEN MACKAY is Assistant Professor of Renaissance Drama in the English Department of Indiana University. She is completing a manuscript on tragedy and the anti-history of theatre in early modern England.

JACQUELINE ROMEO is a doctoral candidate at Tufts University. She is currently finishing her dissertation, titled "The Making of an American Stereotype; Or, the 'Comic Coolie' in Nineteenth-Century Frontier Melodrama."

CONTRIBUTORS

DEANNA M. TOTEN BEARD is Associate Professor of Theater at Baylor University. Her recent work includes a chapter titled "American Experimentalism, American Expressionism, and Early O'Neill" in Blackwell's *A Companion to Twentieth-Century American Drama* (2005).